Left Parties and Social Policy in Postcommunist Europe

Left Parties and Social Policy in Postcommunist Europe

EDITED BY

Linda J. Cook, Mitchell A. Orenstein,
and Marilyn Rueschemeyer

Westview Press
A Member of the Perseus Books Group

Copyright © 1999 by Westview Press, A Division of HarperCollins Publishers, Inc.
Published in 1999 in the United States of America by Westview Press, 5500 Central Avenue, Boulder, Colorado 80301–2877, and in the United Kingdom by Westview Press, 12 Hid's Copse Road, Cumnor Hill, Oxford OX2 9JJ

Find us on the World Wide Web at www.westviewpress.com

A CIP catalog record for this book is available from the Library of Congress.
ISBN 0-8133-3568-X (hc)   0-8133-3569-8 (pbk)

The paper used in this publication meets the requirements of the American National Standard for Permanence of Paper for Printed Library Materials Z39.48-1984.

10   9   8   7   6   5   4   3   2   1

Table of Contents

Acknowledgments   vii

1   Left Parties and Policies in Eastern Europe
    after Communism: An Introduction   1
    Dietrich Rueschemeyer

2   Social Policy in Postcommunist Europe:
    Legacies and Transition   11
    Dena Ringold

3   The Return of the Left and Its Impact on the Welfare State
    in Russia, Poland, and Hungary   47
    Linda J. Cook and Mitchell Orenstein

4   The Return of Left-Oriented Parties in Eastern Germany
    and the Czech Republic and their Social Policies   109
    Marilyn Rueschemeyer and Sharon L. Wolchik

5   Transitional Politics or Public Choice?
    Evaluating Stalled Pension Reforms in Poland   145
    Michael J. G. Cain and Aleksander Surdej

6   The Role of the Hungarian Nonprofit Sector in
    Postcommunist Social Policy   175
    Robert M. Jenkins

7   The Political Economy of Social Policy Reform in Russia:
    Ideas, Institutions, and Interests   207
    Michael McFaul

8   Conclusions   235
    Linda J. Cook, Mitchell A. Orenstein, and
    Marilyn Rueschemeyer

About the Editors and Authors   249
Index   253

Acknowledgments

The editors would like to express our gratitude to the Thomas J. Watson Institute for International Studies at Brown University and its director, Tom Biersteker, for multifaceted sponsorship of this research. The papers in this book grew out of a conference organized by the editors at the Watson Institute in October 1997.

We would like to thank all the conference participants, including those who did not contribute a paper but contributed so much to our discussions, and Leslie Walaska Baxter, who provided able organizational assistance. Since then, this project has been in the capable hands of Fred Fullerton of the Watson Institute's publications group, and we thank him for his timely assistance in preparing this manuscript for publication. Thanks also to Martine Haas for her assistance with the graphics.

We would also like to thank Rob Williams of Westview Press for seeing this book through and the Department of Political Science of The Maxwell School of Citizenship and Public Affairs at Syracuse University for a course reduction that allowed Mitchell Orenstein to complete work on this project.

—*The Editors*

Left Parties and Social Policy in Postcommunist Europe

1

Left Parties and Policies in Eastern Europe after Communism: An Introduction

DIETRICH RUESCHEMEYER

If the collapse of European Communism in 1989–1990 came as a great surprise, it was nearly as much a surprise that four or five years later parties of the left made substantial electoral gains across Eastern Europe. True, some observers had considered social democracy all along as the best alternative to communism or, perhaps better, to authoritarian state socialism. They therefore expected moves toward social democratic solutions that would combine democracy with some continuation of strong social security provisions as the most plausible and likely option after the East European regimes failed.

However, especially in East-Central Europe, the collapse of these regimes released strong anticommunist and some anti-Russian reactions, as well as fostered hopes for a rapid capitalist approach to affluence. This reaction in the East was echoed and reinforced in the West, where the situation after the end of the Cold War was defined primarily as the failure of socialism in any form and as the triumph of neoliberalism. The first elections after 1989–1990 confirmed these responses.

Few observers anticipated that in the second wave of elections left parties would gain significantly in country after country. In Poland, where Solidarity fought its prolonged and finally successful fight against the communist regime, the Democratic Left Alliance—a transformed communist, now social democratic party—increased its share of the vote from 11.9 percent in 1991 to 20.4 percent in 1993, and led a left coalition to win an overwhelming majority of parliamentary seats against liberals and conservatives.

In Hungary, where the old regime itself had initiated liberalization, the Socialist Party, which also was created out of the old communist party, moved from just over 10 percent in 1990 to 33 percent of the vote in 1994 and, due to provisions guarding against party fragmentation, gained a majority of seats in parliament.

The Party of Democratic Socialism, another transformed communist party, nearly doubled its initial vote of 10 percent in eastern Germany, the former German Democratic Republic. Meanwhile, the Social Democratic Party gained steadily, increasing its vote from under 25 percent in 1990 to just over 30 percent in 1994.

The unreformed Communist Party in the Czech Republic retained only about one of every ten voters, but the newly founded Social Democratic Party rapidly gained ground against the dominance of liberal parties after it overcame initial difficulties by moving from 4.1 percent and 6.5 percent in 1990 and 1992 to 26.4 percent in 1996. By 1998, it became the country's strongest party, with 32.3 percent of the vote.

The essentially unreformed Communist Party of Russia became the strongest party in the Duma in 1995 with 22 percent of the vote. Although it had nearly doubled its share of the vote in 1993, it was unable to unseat Yeltsin as president, who, after the new constitution of 1993, could rule with vastly increased powers and whose actions were largely independent of parliament.

If nonsocialist governments were returned to power in Poland and Hungary after the elections in 1997–1998, the votes captured by parties of the left stabilized or even increased in all of the countries mentioned.[1] These developments parallel each other in ways that are important to explore. At the same time, even this most cursory overview suggests that the label "left" covers a range of very different parties.

At least three distinctions spring to mind: the difference between former communist parties that are dominated by reforming and democratically oriented elites (as in Poland and Hungary) and those led by rather unreconstructed cadres of the earlier regime (as in the Czech Republic); the distinction between reformed communist parties that now adopt the name of democratic socialism and social democratic parties that have deep historical roots but face the task of reconstituting themselves after forty years of destruction and forced absorption by their communist rivals (for which the German and the Czech Social Democratic Parties are the main examples); and the distinction between social democratic parties of either kind and parties of a different character that are likely to support left of center policies (the peasant parties in Poland and Russia, the left liberals in Hungary, and possibly the Christian and Democratic

Union [KDU-CSL] in the Czech Republic). These distinctions are sometimes fuzzy but they are not less important. We will revisit them throughout this book.

There are common elements in these different resurgences of the left, and at least for the East-Central European countries, they seem to add up to a common political meaning. We see here primarily responses to the unexpected hardships of the transition from the political economy of state socialism. These responses remain, as Mitchell Orenstein convincingly argues (Orenstein 1998), embedded in a party-transcending project of continued market-oriented reform.

Yet within this project, there is room for lively political debate, and the social issues at stake are in the eyes of many voters more important than the presence or absence of links to the past regime. Especially if a party establishes a credible commitment to political and economic reform, its organizational and personal roots in the past are treated by many voters with benign neglect. It is this unexpected weakness of a "postcommunist anticommunism"—which has a different and much more compelling meaning in the East than in the West—that makes the success of the communist successor parties so surprising.

The second and perhaps less obvious political meaning of the resurgence of the left in Eastern Europe is the strength of democratic life it signifies.[2] It is only an apparent paradox if the success of post- and excommunist parties is counted as a symptom of democratic strength. The different contributions in this book make it quite clear that voters weigh their interests, assess the state of their country, and cast their votes accordingly.

A vote for transition-oriented left parties, be they rooted in communist predecessor organizations or not, typically represents neither a nostalgic preference for the past nor a blind protest against a not understood frustration. It is true that the fairly shallow grounding of democracy in broad-based social and political participation gives politics in Eastern Europe an elitist character, leaving the formulation of political alternatives to small groups that are largely immune to input and pressure from "below."[3] But it is also true that at least the East-Central European countries give evidence of active political contestation and democratic turnover in government.

The case of Russia seems more complicated. The Russian political scene is not dominated by broad-based support for an incipiently successful market-oriented transformation, and democracy is problematic if for no other reason than that the readiness and capacity of the state apparatus to execute democratic decisions is seriously in question. The Communist Party of the Russian Federation is clearly not committed to the transition to a market economy that is wiping out the old system of social provisions, and its allegiance to democratic rule may be doubted as well. However, one may want to think twice before classifying its success among voters hurt by the transition simply as an irrational protest vote. Its representation of these interests is not effectively changing policy; but effective projects are a rarity across the Russian political spectrum, a situation that is due to political stalemate and administrative disorganization.

At the conference that brought together the contributors to this book at Brown University's Watson Institute for International Studies in the fall of 1997, a major point of doubt and disagreement was the characterization of communist successor parties as "left."

What do we mean when we characterize a party as left? We use the term in a quite ordinary sense. At the core of the common understanding of left is a simple idea—the principle of pursuing the interests of those who are socially weak. This tends to go together with a certain differentiation of appeal in terms of economic and social inequality, but this criterion must not be pushed too far. Confining a party's appeal to subordinate interests is in most political systems self-defeating. Successful left parties include the interests of socially weak groups in their policy goals but do not confine their appeal to them as they are broad-based but solidaristic. Nevertheless, focusing on representing the interests of groups and strata that are socially weak relates the current meaning of left to class analysis and the conception of democratic politics as a moderated version of the class struggle.[4]

Historically, the political meaning of left has always included other components than references to class interests, but these other components were typically related—if in complex and historically variable ways—to class positions. Such linkages with other issues indicate that the actually pursued class interests are themselves historical and political constructions defined by leaders, clubs, parties, unions, and other organizations.

Thus liberal and socialist ideas of progress and rational social reconstruction of society stood as left positions against the conservative claims that the right made for tradition and "organic" growth. Liberal individualism moved from left to right as subordinate interests successfully demanded social security against the workings of the capitalist market. Patriotic and national sentiments were often liberal—and in their context left—positions in early nineteenth-century Europe; only later did they become associated with the political right. The relationship of religion to politics, stereotypically seen as an alliance of religion with the conservative right, is similarly complex and variable across different historical constellations.

The upshot of these historical allusions is twofold. First, if in our analyses of Eastern European politics we encounter secularism, social and moral issues, nationalism, or other issue complexes that were historically related to the left-right continuum, it may be fruitful to make an attempt at understanding their meaning in relation to the newly crystallizing interests of strata and classes.

Second, focusing on the protection of subordinate interests as the core meaning of the term *left* does not entail the claim that class is the exclusively dominant causal factor—either in politics generally or in the politics of contemporary Eastern Europe in particular. An important dimension of politics in most countries concerns norms regulating social life—about abortion, about weekend work, or about treatment of children born out of or within marriage. Such issues seem of particular importance in postcommunist politics.

The communist regimes pursued on many of these issues antitraditionalist and secularist, often aggressively antireligious, policies. They had some success in this; but we now see in several countries a resurgence of traditional and religious positions in response to the collapse of communism. Some of these issues cut across social and economic divisions and mute the impact of different class interests on politics. Yet it is our claim that the resurgence of left parties in the sense we use the word here indeed represents a stronger articulation of divergent social and economic class interests.

How does the core meaning of left express itself in policy orientations, constituencies, and actual policies of the east European parties under consideration? Do these parties in fact promote left policy orientations? These questions may be asked especially about the offshoots of formerly ruling communist parties. Before 1989–1990, the core of these parties was strongly shaped by managerial concerns, and during the last years of East European state socialism, many intellectuals and state and party managers looked for market-oriented reforms as a possible solution to their systems' economic problems.[5] But this hardly redefined the character of their parties, nor did these ideas determine the policy orientations of the successor parties.

The wake of the old regime leaves us with complex questions. First perhaps is the puzzle of why these dictatorships chose to support socially weak groups and strata by adopting universal and comprehensive welfare provisions. That these provisions were limited by the severe economic problems of the East European countries does not solve, but only heightens, the puzzle. Some productivity problems were closely linked to such welfare provisions as the employment guarantee. Explanations based on a calculus of power and power maintenance compete with accounts that see intrinsic leftist impulses at work. Even if a full account involves both factors, many members and followers of the once ruling and now postcommunist parties will take these past policies as an inspiration for adopting left policy orientations now.

Correspondingly, much of the population takes the past social provisions for granted. They became inscribed in the codes of everyday life. Diminishing them by reducing pensions, eliminating job security, raising rents, and terminating enterprise day care centers for children is experienced by many as unjust public policy. That creates an electoral premium for those who promise—if not to retain the old system—to protect the interests of those hardest hit by restructuring the political economy.

This restructuring seeks to deal with the two central deficits of the old state socialist order—the productivity deficit and the liberty deficit. The option for such restructuring clearly still has the upper hand in East-Central Europe, and it is far from defunct even in the countries of the Former Soviet Union. But what form restructuring takes is increasingly becoming a matter of struggle between left and right.

The social democratic parties that could build on a historical tradition of social democracy present a different but similarly instructive picture. The European social democratic tradition had changed well before 1989–1990 from an anticapitalist socialism to the pursuit of welfare state policies that would modify capitalism and limit the impact of the market. The Czech social democratic party did so even before World War II, while the German SPD contained different orientations for many years, and changed as a party only with the Godesberg program in 1959.

The re-creation of social democratic parties in the Czech Republic and in the former German Democratic Republic after 1989–1990 was first dominated by civil rights activists, who sought to transform the legacy of the old regime and were little concerned with left policies. In both cases, but in different ways, the social democratic traditions reasserted themselves and the constituency of these parties acquired a more class-related profile (see Marilyn Rueschemeyer and Sharon Wolchik in this book).

The social and political contexts in which Eastern European left parties operate is very different from the typical situation in the West. As the different contributions to this book show, these contexts also differ strongly from country to country in the East, but there are some shared features. First, we observe that initially anticommunist opposition groups were not particularly pro-market, capitalist, and neoliberal (Szelenyi et al. 1997), nor did they move later toward these positions as concertedly and unambiguously as is sometimes assumed in the West.

Rueschemeyer and Wolchik note in their chapter that the center-right coalition with its neoliberal rhetoric, which dominated Czech politics until 1998, took its cues for actual policies more from the West Central European welfare states than from Britain's Thatcherite conservatives. The complex postcommunist history of Poland's Solidarity movement offers similar evidence, as Cook and Orenstein show in this book.

Another common feature of the postcommunist East European politics are the changing and unclear structures of interest. It is a mistake to assume that people's shared interests are plainly given and easily identified. The radical transformations of the economy, their direct and indirect impact on everyday life in family and community, and the opening of the political system changed the objective interests of people in complex and not immediately transparent ways. Diagnosing these changes and translating them into collective goals that are realistic and appealing to different constituencies are difficult tasks for political initiatives. Various associations, unions, and parties are involved in this process, which only after a while will settle into a new structure of politically relevant interests.

This restructuring of interests and constituencies relates to what was noted earlier about the fairly low level of social and political participation and the elitist character of East European politics. The fact that one's interests and their relation to politics are changing and unclear seems to be one major explanation for the comparatively low levels of civic engagement and for the elitist way in which political options consequently are formulated.

Do left orientations of parties lead to actual left policies? The following chapters offer complex answers to this question. Several factors seem especially important. The first is the consensus on economic and political restructuring that developed as a response to the productivity and liberty deficits of the past regimes, and that continues to be strong at least in East-Central Europe. This consensus does not deny left policy options, but it shapes the encompassing ideological climate. At the same time, the inheritance of the past has a tremendous impact on policy options.

On the one hand, past commitments to social provisions are very difficult to abandon, even for parties of the right; on the other, left politicians have to face the fact that under conditions of political pluralism and market economy, their countries are now too poor to afford extensive welfare provisions. Yet difficult as the restructuring of the old welfare systems is for either side, it is hard to imagine that it makes no difference in the long run which political coalitions shape the process of transformation.

Finally, some of the ideological and political developments in Eastern Europe are shaped by foreign influences. This is perhaps strongest in the countries of East-Central Europe that are now candidates for membership in the European Union. Receptivity for foreign influence is, of course, shaped by the history of national self-definition, and thus it is related in complex ways to the previous hegemony of Russia and the Soviet Union.

Foreign influence comes in different forms, flows through different channels, and involves different forms of leverage. The flow of ideas follows different dynamics than the flow of goods and services and, more importantly, capital, which specifically can be combined with explicit or implicit conditions that can effectively constrain domestic policy choices. It is questionable, however, whether foreign constraints outweigh domestic forces that shape policy options.

The future of Eastern Europe will be shaped, perhaps disproportionately, by policy options embraced and set in motion today. Comparative historical studies of social policies in different countries show clearly the long-term influence of past developments. Social policy is highly "path-dependent."[6] That gives the analyses brought together in this book a special weight. The impact of today's political constellations in Eastern Europe is likely to be felt for decades to come.

The editors of this book have brought together an ensemble of extremely interesting contributions that offer in-depth information and interpretations, while putting specific evidence and data into context. Geographically and politically, the book focuses on the East-Central European countries of Poland, Hungary, and the Czech Republic, but significantly includes also Russia, the hegemonic power of the old order, as well as the former German Democratic Republic, which is now part of unified Germany.

Dena Ringold presents on overview of social policy developments that is rich in comparative and systematic information. The following two chapters both compare a few countries in detail within the same framework of analysis. They demonstrate how much can be gained for analytic insight by combining the richness of a country case study with going beyond the boundaries of a single case. Linda Cook and Mitchell Orenstein discuss how the return of the left affects welfare state policies in Poland, Hungary, and Russia, while Marilyn Rueschemeyer and Sharon Wolchik do the same for the former German Democratic Republic and the Czech Republic.

While in these two chapters' attention to the parties and their development stands in the foreground, the next two chapters focus more on substantive policy issues. Michael Cain and Aleksander Surdej analyze stalled pension reform in Poland, and Robert Jenkins looks at the role of the nonprofit "third" sector in Hungarian social policy. Michael McFaul returns to the large case of Russia and asks why no post-Soviet Russian government has pursued a successful strategy for social policy reform. In the conclusion, the editors return to the broader themes that appear in different forms in the preceding chapters.

References

Esping-Andersen, Gosta. 1990. *The Three Worlds of Welfare Capitalism*. Princeton, N.J.: Princeton University Press.

Lipset, Seymour M. 1968. *Political Man*. Garden City, N.Y.: Anchor books.

Orenstein. Mitchell. 1998. "A Genealogy of Communist Successor Parties in East-Central Europe and the Determinants of their Success." *East European Politics and Societies* 12:3 (Fall 1998): 472–99.

Rueschemeyer, Dietrich, Marilyn Rueschemeyer, and Björn Wittrock, eds. 1998. *Participation and Democracy East and West: Comparisons and Interpretations*. Armonk, N.Y.: M.E. Sharpe.

Szelenyi, Ivan, Eva Fodor, and Eric Hanley. 1997. "Left Turn in Postcommunist Politics: Bringing Class Back In?" *East European Politics and Societies* 11:1 (Winter): 190–224.

Notes

1. For the different electoral results, see chapters by Cook and Orenstein as well as by M. Rueschemeyer and Wolchik in this book.

2. This is a point that Marilyn Rueschemeyer has made repeatedly in the many discussions we had about post-1989 Eastern Europe.

3. This is suggested by recent comparative work on social and political participation; see Rueschemeyer, Rueschemeyer, and Wittrock (1998).

4. Seymour M. Lipset titled chapter 7 of his classic book *Political Man* "Elections: The Expression of the Democratic Class Struggle."

5. That is also an observation of Szelenyi and his collaborators: "Ironically, economic liberalism, the program of 'capitalist restoration,' first was formulated by the technocratic fraction of the communist elite." (Szelenyi et al., 1997: 208, n. 28).

6. See for instance Esping-Andersen (1990).

2

Social Policy in Postcommunist Europe: Legacies and Transition

DENA RINGOLD*

Social policy is perhaps the most important neglected area of post-communist reform. Liberal reformers who came to power throughout much of Central and Eastern Europe after 1989 initiated radical structural changes in macroeconomic policy, property ownership, corporate governance, tax law, market regulation, and many other areas, but social policy has ranked relatively low on the policy agenda. Few of the transition plans crafted early in the transition addressed social sector reform as a priority focus. Reforms to date have been largely ad hoc and reactive, despite the dramatic changes in social welfare that have occurred during the transition period and the pervasiveness of the social sectors in terms of high levels of government spending and employment.

As a result, postcommunist social policy has been shaped both by the legacy of the inherited socialist welfare states, characterized by universalistic "cradle to grave" social policies and by a variety of critical decisions, nondecisions, and environmental changes made in the postcommunist period. Whereas many observers of the early transition period noted that the first days following the collapse of communism provided a unique opportunity for policy innovations and substantive reform, the absence of a coherent and coordinated approach to social policy reform has left an unfinished agenda for successive postcommunist governments to address.

This chapter provides an analytical and statistical introduction to the status of welfare and welfare states in Central and Eastern Europe, drawing upon data from primary and secondary sources such as governments and international organizations. The discussion focuses on Central and Eastern Europe, but trends and data from some of the countries of the Former Soviet Union are provided for contrast and comparison. Social policy is defined broadly throughout the chapter and encompasses social insurance, social assistance, health, and education.

Following an introductory background discussion, the second section provides an overview of aggregate changes in social welfare. The third section examines how governments have responded to the challenge of social policy reform in the context of rapidly expanding and divergent needs and increasingly tight budget constraints. It also provides an overview of aggregate trends in public social expenditures and examines the factors driving change, specifically focusing on health, education, and pensions.

Data Sources and Quality

Although the quality and availability of social sector data for the transition economies has improved substantially in recent years, quality remains variable and lacunae continue to exist. There have been significant improvements in the scope and reliability of data during the transition. For example, many of the countries in the region have implemented labor force surveys, which provide fuller and more reliable information on labor market trends than official registration statistics, as well as household income surveys. However, problems remain that impede comparability across countries and years.

One of the most challenging areas is social expenditure data. Accurate and comparable data on social sector spending are not widely available, as accounting systems differ and data are often fragmented across government ministries. In addition, trends toward privatization and decentralization of social services impede analysis of fiscal issues. In many countries, central governments have devolved fiscal responsibility for social programs to local governments. As local expenditures are not always reported back to the ministries of finance, it is frequently difficult to obtain full information on the sources and uses of local expenditures. Data on private expenditures on education and health are generally not available, other than through household surveys.

Increasingly divergent conditions among countries also compound the difficulty of capturing trends. Social conditions during the transition have varied widely across the region, due to a range of socioeconomic, geographic, and historical factors, as well as armed conflict in several countries. From the beginning of the transition, the countries of Central and Eastern Europe have fared better than the countries of the Former Soviet Union, due largely to differences in the depth of the output collapse and the starting points of transition. These initial gaps have widened during the transition, and differences between Central Europe and Central Asia, in terms of the severity of social indicators, are strong (see Table 2.1).

Not only has there been growing divergence between Central and Eastern Europe and the Former Soviet Union, but conditions within each region vary greatly as well. There are marked differences between the new OECD countries (Poland, Hungary, and the Czech Republic), and Southeastern countries, such as Bulgaria and Romania, where reform has been slower and growth more elusive. Health and demographic status, including trends in life expectancy, maternal and infant mortality, and fertility, also vary widely. In addition, conflict and the impact of economic sanctions have caused social conditions to deteriorate severely in some of the countries of the former Yugoslavia.

Finally, analyzing social sector change is particularly challenging because the linkages between policy design and welfare outcomes are ambiguous and the time it takes to implement reforms and produce outcomes is considerable. Many changes in health and education policy can take years to affect aggregate health status and educational outcomes. It is nearly impossible to disentangle the impact of the transition on health from changes rooted in the pre-transition period. In contrast, changes in social protection and labor market policies can have a more immediate impact on welfare through a direct impact on household incomes. These issues challenge both analysts and policymakers who attempt to implement difficult reforms with a long-term impact.

Background

Legacies

Social policymaking in the postcommunist countries has been shaped by the inheritance of socialist institutions and processes (Barr 1994). The achievements of the socialist regimes in social policy provision were notable. In particular, provision of health, education, and income security—through both employment and cash benefits—was comprehensive and largely equitable. On the other hand, institutional and organizational weaknesses were significant. Input-oriented central planning created vast inefficiencies in social services and distorted incentives, which persist in the transition period. In addition, high expectations created by vast and pervasive welfare states have limited the type and extent of reforms that have been adopted since 1989.

Large Welfare States.   The former socialist countries inherited welfare states that, relative to OECD countries and countries at similar levels of

TABLE 2.1   Subregional Trends in Social Welfare (% change 1989–96)[a]

	Central Europe	Southern Europe	Baltics	Western FSU	Caucasus	Central Asia	FYR Yugoslavia
Real Wage	−16.4	−35.3	−5.2	−50.4	−76.0	−60.6	—
Crude Birthrate	−23.7	−21.3	−38.9	−36.7	−37.2	−30.0	−6.3
Life Expectancy (male)	2.3	−1.9	−2.5	−5.6	−1.7	—	—
Infant Mortality Rate	−32.5	−11.7	−0.1	1.6	−20.3	−19.7	−45.5

[a]Central Europe (Czech, Slovakia, Hungary, Poland); Southern Europe (Albania, Bulgaria, Romania); Baltics (Estonia, Latvia, Lithuania); Western FSU (Belarus, Moldova, Russia, Ukraine); Caucasus (Armenia, Azerbaijan, Georgia); Central Asia (Kazakhstan, Kyrgyz Republic, Tajikistan, Turkmenistan, Uzbekistan); FYR Yugoslavia (Croatia, Slovenia, FYR Macedonia, FR Yugoslavia)

SOURCES: TransMONEE Database, UNICEF-ICDC, Florence, Italy, World Bank

NOTE: Unweighted averages, data are for latest available year when 1996 was not available.

development, were large in terms of total expenditures. When transition began, spending on the social sectors, including health, education, social insurance, and social assistance, ranged from 15 to 25 percent of GDP. Janos Kornai has termed the transition countries "premature welfare states," because their level of social spending is disproportionate to their resources (Kornai 1992).

While liberal-minded reformers and Western advisors perceived high social spending as a potential drag on growth in the early 1990s, few governments adopted measures to cut social spending. Instead, social expenditures have grown across the region, as subsidies for social spending have been made explicit and governments have attempted to preserve existing social services. Stopgap policy measures, such as the encouragement of early retirements to prevent massive unemployment, have also increased expenditures on social programs. Whereas systemic social insurance reforms designed to scale back social insurance spending are moving forward in Hungary, Poland, and other countries, the impact of these measures will take time, and most countries are likely to retain large welfare states over the long term.

Full Employment and Universalism. The socialist welfare states were among the most extensive in the world, providing "cradle to grave" benefits for all. From birth, individuals were eligible for a full range of universal social programs, including birth grants, child allowances, maternity leave, pensions, and disability benefits, among others. Most benefits were granted at the workplace, as full employment was a virtual guarantee. State-owned enterprises provided their workers subsidized housing, child care, health care, and often vacation facilities. Subsidies have been scaled back and enterprises have divested themselves of social services, but much of the legacy remains and continues to shape social policymaking in the region.

Policy Directions and Indirection

Liberal Revolution versus Socialist Conservatism. A critical aspect of reshaping social policy in postcommunist Europe is the region's quest for a new welfare state model. From the beginning of the transition, there was widespread consensus, among policymakers and theorists alike, that the former communist welfare states were intellectually bankrupt, mismatched with the objectives and principles of a market economy and illegitimate in the eyes of the public. They incorporated elements of state paternalism, social control, subsidization, and class differentiation that rapidly became anachronistic in the postcommunist period. While economists and practitioners worked to ensure that macroeconomic policy in the transition countries corresponded with market principles, social policy was left subject to immediate fiscal and political concerns. Policy changes have not corresponded to strategic ideas of what social policy should be in the future, and have therefore been ad hoc and contradictory.

Liberal ideas have had an important, but ambiguous impact on postcommunist social policy. Parties that espoused liberal platforms early in the transition included the Liberal Democratic Congress and the Democratic Union in Poland, and the Civic Democratic Party in the Czech Republic. Liberal economic programs in the postcommunist states have tended to ignore welfare state development both because they prioritized other aspects of reform, and because liberal efforts to reduce the role of the state did not leave much room for constructive thought about its new role.

Some liberals hoped the socialist welfare states would fade away altogether. More constructive ideas about state restructuring appeared after the initial thrust of reform, when the importance of the state became an inescapable reality, and after illegal state and nonstate activity in Russia and other countries emerged (Sachs and Pistor 1997; W. B. 1996a). Besides a strong initial effort to delegitimize the role of the state in the economy, the contributions of liberal thought to social policy were minimal.

Liberal neglect of welfare state restructuring has often had the unintended effect of making social policy more expensive. Liberal welfare-state philosophy advocates welfare states that are residual and provide only minimal benefits to those who are stigmatized as being permanently or temporarily in need (Esping-Andersen 1990). Liberal reformers have pushed for greater targeting of social benefits, with only moderate success. One major and widespread liberal innovation was the introduction of systems of unemployment insurance. Liberals wanted to create a safety net for those who lost their jobs, partly to provide a cushion for those temporarily out of the labor market, and partly to provide incentives for companies to rationalize their allocation of labor (see Cain and Surdej in this volume).

In conjunction with this targeting effort, several countries, including Hungary and Poland, began to use the pension system to reduce pressure on the labor market. Older workers who found themselves unemployed were offered early retirement or disability pensions, vastly expanding the pension rolls (Andrews and Rashid 1996). As a result of misguided "targeting efforts," imbalances in the social system are just as great, if not greater, in countries that have made the most progress in liberalization and other reform areas, such as Poland and Hungary.

Socialist conservatives, who have sought to preserve the inherited welfare state, are opposed to liberals in most countries. Resistance to liberalism generally has been led by interest groups tied to the old system, especially workers in troubled industries such as steel and coal, who were the heralded heroes of socialism. Conservative communist successor parties have emerged in many countries in the region, including the Communist Party of the Russian Federation, and the Communist Party of Bohemia and Moravia. As with liberal reformers, interest groups seeking to maintain the existing system have lacked a strategic vision for social policy development. Consequently, social policymaking has taken on a rather ad hoc character, with periodic radical liberal efforts at reform thwarted by resistance from socialist conservatives (see McFaul in this volume). These groups have attempted to preserve the largely universalistic benefits characteristic of socialism, and moreover adhere to egalitarian standards and benefit levels.

A third trend deserving mention in the postcommunist context is Christian Democracy. A number of parties in postcommunist Europe adhere to a vision of conservative, pro-family social policies that would uphold accepted Christian moral standards and norms. This strain of thought has played an important role in many countries (see Kulczycki 1995), although none of the welfare states appears to be moving decisively in this direction.

Liberal reforms have been promoted by liberal parties and Christian Democracy by Christian Democratic parties, but left parties have played a more complex role (see Cook and Orenstein in this volume). Some communist successor parties remain tied to the legacies of communism, including normative support for an extensive and paternalist social welfare system. However, other left parties have taken on a substantial dose of liberalism and now seem to be attempting to reconcile social and liberal goals. No significant party is advocating a return to the social democratic models that have characterized some West and East-Central European countries in the past, and policy developments in the region reflect these contradictory trends. The direction of reform has been decisive nowhere, and postcommunist Europe continues to muddle through these controversial and challenging issues.

Transition in Context

Although the extent of the output collapse in Central and Eastern Europe has led to rapid changes in household welfare, such as falling incomes and the emergence of open unemployment and poverty, there have been positive developments in recent years. Real GDP growth has resumed in nearly all countries except for Bulgaria, Romania, and Albania, where economic crisis and conflict in the case of Albania have reversed earlier gains. In Poland, real GDP has now surpassed its 1989 level, with other countries to follow soon.

Living standards are closely linked to changes in macroeconomic developments. Some households have experienced notable improvements in opportunity and welfare in recent years. In many countries, wages have recovered alongside output, and incomes for some workers have surpassed pre-transition levels, particularly for well-educated workers in the private sector. The growth of the private sector, and the expansion of employment in areas neglected by the socialist regimes, including the service and financial sectors, have opened new career opportunities. Simultaneously, increased choice and options for continuing education, especially at the secondary and tertiary levels, are positive developments as returns to education have increased in the labor market.

However, adverse trends persist. Vulnerable groups, including low-skilled workers, the long-term unemployed, ethnic minorities, including Roma, and families with many children, continue to experience deterioration of living standards. Recent World Bank poverty studies illustrate the rapid and significant emergence of poverty in Poland, Hungary, Romania, and other countries (World Bank 1995; 1996b; 1997b).

Similarly worrisome is the increasing evidence of more slowly emerging trends that may have a longer-term, systemic impact. Recent evidence suggests that preschool and primary school enrollments, which were traditionally high in the region, have begun to decline. In addition, adverse trends in health, including declining life expectancy, increased mortality from preventable causes, and nutrition status from unhealthy diets, will inevitably have an adverse effect on societal welfare.

The urgency and complexity of the social policy agenda has increased during the transition. At the outset of transition, few countries were prepared for the pending emergence of open unemployment and the swift declines in real household incomes that came with transition and that continue alongside macroeconomic reforms and restructuring. These unanticipated and rapid changes directly affected household welfare and have had political consequences in many countries.

The near-universal coverage of services and benefits, which often were provided at the enterprise level, was eroded by the dismantling of full employment and the elimination of state subsidies, while administrative structures to redistribute benefits independently from employment were only weakly developed. Benefit systems under socialism were largely fixed and categorical, and lacked the flexibility to adapt to the changing needs of the transition period. Throughout the region, the need for income support and benefit systems for the unemployed and poor emerged rapidly. However, growing need coincided with shrinking budgets and fiscal crises, and existing institutions proved inadequate and unable to respond effectively.

Social policy developments have been shaped considerably by financial considerations and attempts by governments to address the marked declines in real resources available for social services. In health and education, where real expenditures have declined by as much as 70 percent of pre-transition levels in some countries, alternative financing mechanisms have been adopted, including the introduction of health insurance and fees for education. In both sectors, the decline of the public sector has led to increased private and informal activity as well as widespread decentralization of social services to local governments.

These developments have been mostly ad hoc and have failed to address underlying systemic constraints to quality and efficiency and the overall lack of resources. As for pensions, efforts to protect the rights of existing pensioners, and poor policy choices, such as the easing of eligibility criteria for early retirement and disability pensions, which led to significant inflows of beneficiaries into social insurance, have led to explosions in costs and have exacerbated inherited problems.

Social Welfare

Transition has had a rapid and direct impact on household welfare across the region. The unprecedented collapse of output that accompanied macroeconomic stabilization measures led to an immediate and, in some cases, dramatic fall in real wages that directly affected household incomes. Corresponding employment shocks led to the emergence of open unemployment, a phenomenon virtually unknown in the socialist economies, which had based their welfare policies on full employment.[1] In a very short time, previously remarkably equal societies, at least in terms of living standards, have evolved into countries with inequality comparable to many Western European OECD countries. This has occurred despite the fact that the transition countries remain at lower levels of GDP per capita.

The increase in inequality was anticipated, but not necessarily undesirable, as wages under socialism were artificially compressed. Communist ideology encouraged homogenization of living standards. The concern is how much evolving inequality is linked to the emergence of deep and stagnant pockets of poverty. Some groups have been able to take advantage of new opportunities provided by the transition, but others have experienced continued declines in living standards. In general, the rapid change and uncertainty associated with the transition have brought about considerable socioeconomic stress. Whereas individuals previously relied on the state for employment and other basic needs, access to and availability of many free services, including health and education, has deteriorated. This section examines overall changes in social welfare as observed in incomes, labor markets, health status, and access to education.

Incomes and Inequality

Across the region, the output shocks of transition led to dramatic declines in wages, especially for low-skilled workers and workers at the bottom of the income distribution. Falling incomes among some groups have led to the emergence of poverty, in both absolute and relative terms. In the early years of the transition, real wages in the region fell by approximately one-third. In general, low-paid workers lost the most—between 10 and 45 percentage points in the early years of transition—while higher-paid workers fared better (Figures 2.1 and 2.2).

Recovery of growth has been accompanied by increased wages for some groups of workers, while incomes of others, most often the poorly educated and low skilled, continue to decline. Real wage dynamics are closely related to macroeconomic developments. In the rapidly reforming countries, Poland, the Czech Republic, and Slovenia, wages for workers at the top of the earnings distribution fell less than 10 percent, whereas in countries where recovery has come more slowly, such as Bulgaria, Romania, and Slovakia, wages have fallen between 20 and 25 percent (Rutkowski 1996).

Increased income dispersion reflects the overall growth of inequality in Central and Eastern Europe. Under socialism, due to wage compression, inequality was remarkably low by international standards. In addition, because of the high number of universal social benefits attached to employment and widespread consumer subsidies, there was little variation in living standards among households. This situation dramatically changed during the transition, with the elimination of guaranteed employment, and wage and price liberalization.

Within a remarkably short period, income inequality, as measured by the Gini coefficient for many countries in Central and Eastern Europe, was close to that of middle-inequality OECD countries, including Finland, the Netherlands, and Australia. Inequality in the Former Soviet Union has continued still further. In 1994, the average Gini coefficient in Central and Eastern Europe, a standard measure of inequality, was 27, a level close to the OECD mean. Growing inequality reflects growing differential returns to productivity, and the movement away from artificial wage compression.

Education, in particular, has become an increasingly significant determinant of labor market status and earnings potential. Financial returns to education were notably low under socialism because wages were set centrally, with no relation to productivity or skill level. In the Czech Republic and

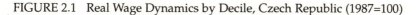

FIGURE 2.1 Real Wage Dynamics by Decile, Czech Republic (1987=100)

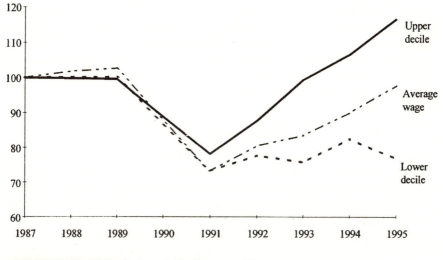

SOURCE: World Bank, Social Challenges of Transition Database

FIGURE 2.2 Real Wage Dynamics by Decile, Poland (1987=100)

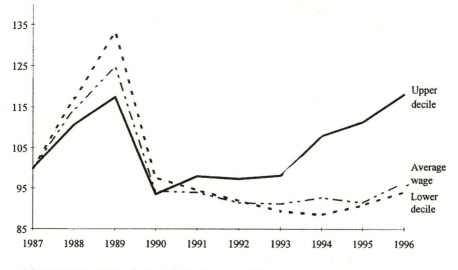

SOURCE: World Bank, Social Challenges of Transition Database

Poland in just three years, the earnings differential between a university-educated worker and a worker with basic vocational training more than doubled for male workers (Rutkowski 1996). There is also increasing evidence of divergent trends in earnings in the private and public sectors. These developments are similarly linked to education. In Poland, for example, educated workers in the private sector have the highest earnings of all workers, while poorly educated workers in the private sector have the lowest (Rutkowski 1998).

Employment and Unemployment

Unemployment is another critical factor behind the growth of inequality and poverty in the region. From a near-zero level during the socialist period, unemployment rates in Central and Eastern Europe climbed rapidly in the early 1990s, generally peaking in 1993 (see Figure 2.3). This has resulted from dramatic declines of public sector employment and shifts in demand for different types of labor and skills (Allison and Ringold 1996). In recent years, unemployment has stabilized but registered unemployment rates in 1996 remained high at 13–15 percent in Bulgaria, Croatia, and Slovenia.

In contrast with other countries, registered unemployment rates in the Czech Republic have remained surprisingly low, between 3 and 4 percent. The low unemployment in the Czech Republic has been attributed to a range of factors, including high labor force attrition, low agricultural employment, labor hoarding of state-owned enterprises, and the rapid growth of the private sector. Another key factor was the aggressive program of active labor market measures that the government launched in 1990.

Labor market dynamics vary considerably across countries, and particularly between Central and Eastern Europe and the Former Soviet Union, where unemployment rates have remained low throughout the 1990s. In 1996, despite continuing declines in output, registered unemployment rates were 3.4 percent in Russia and 1.5 percent in Ukraine. Rather than leading to layoffs and unemployment growth, adjustment in the Former Soviet Union has largely occurred through wages and informal sector activity. Instead of firing workers, firms have retained their employees, paying them reduced wages and benefits, or nothing at all.

Unemployment is distributed unevenly across age groups. As is the case in many OECD countries, youth unemployment is high in Central and Eastern Europe, with unemployment rates for new school graduates nearly double or triple that of any other age group. In 1995, youth unemployment was 38 percent in Bulgaria, 33 percent in Poland, and between 20 and 30 percent in Hungary, Romania, and Slovakia.

FIGURE 2.3   Registered Unemployment Rates (1990–96), Percent of Labor Force

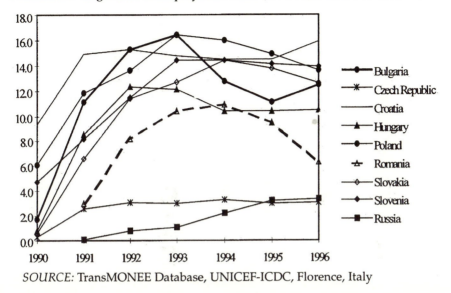

SOURCE: TransMONEE Database, UNICEF-ICDC, Florence, Italy

Even in the Czech Republic, youth unemployment was nearly twice the overall rate for the population for that year. High youth unemployment reflects the overall decline in the size of the youth labor force. On the one hand, the tightening of labor markets may have discouraged young people from entering the labor force, while others may have chosen to delay entering the labor force to continue their studies. Conversely, unemployment for the working age population between 25 years and retirement age has been lower, ranging from 14 percent in Poland to 3 percent in the Czech Republic in 1995.[2]

As already mentioned, education has emerged as a determinant of labor market status. Unemployment is highest for those with primary education and lowest amongst the university educated (see Figure 2.4). Overspecialization of vocational secondary education has limited the flexibility of the labor force, resulting in significantly high unemployment rates. In Poland, unemployment for workers with vocational secondary education exceeded that of all other education levels. This reflects the excessively specialized curricula, which were tailored to the needs of specific industries and enterprises. Under socialism, vocational schools in Poland prepared students in over 250 specializations. With sectoral shifts in employment and the introduction of new technologies, workers with narrow training have found it difficult to adapt to changes in the labor market.

FIGURE 2.4   Unemployment by Education Level, 1997

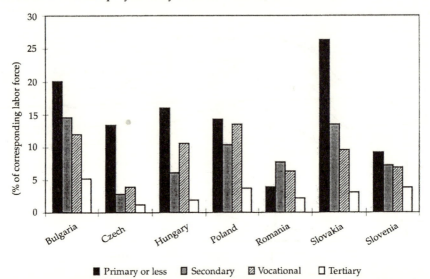

SOURCE: OECD-CCET Labour Markets Database

Unemployment among university graduates has been stable or declining (see Figure 2.4). As is the case in the OECD countries, a university education provides the best insurance against unemployment. In Central
and Eastern Europe, low unemployment rates for the university educated and the growing financial returns to education have been accompanied by increasing enrollments in higher education (Laporte and
Ringold 1996).

The growth of long-term unemployment has been one of the most serious developments accompanying the transition from plan to market in
Central and Eastern Europe. Throughout the region, long-term unemployed individuals, who have been out of work longer than one year, now
constitute the largest proportion of the unemployed. The growth of long-
term unemployment is not a phenomenon unique to the transition
economies. However, the situation in Central and Eastern Europe is particularly worrisome because of gaps in the safety net, and the lack of effective
labor market measures targeted to the needs of the long-term unemployed.

Long-term unemployment in Central and Eastern Europe now resem-
bles, or even exceeds, levels found in Western Europe (see Figure 2.5).
The share of unemployed who were out of work for over a year in 1996
comprised nearly 64 percent of total unemployment in Bulgaria. This rate
is higher than that of Spain, which has experienced chronically high

FIGURE 2.5   Long-Term Unemployment, 1992–1996, as Percent of Total Unemployed

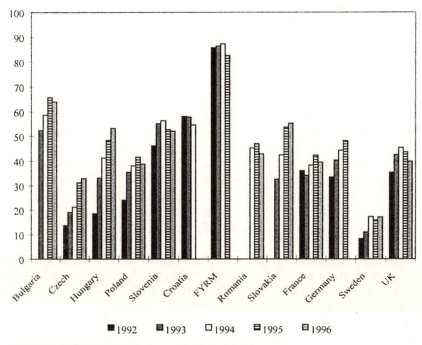

■1992   ▨1993   ☐1994   ▤1995   ▨1996

SOURCE: OECD-CCET Labour Markets Database

long-term unemployment. Long-term unemployment in FYR Macedonia is also high, at 81 percent in 1996. In Central and Eastern Europe, long-term unemployment is linked to job transition patterns in the region. Individuals are more likely to be hired out of the public sector into the private sector, or between firms, than out of unemployment or right out of school. As a result, there is very little movement out of unemployment and the pool of the unemployed has become increasingly homogenous.

Health Status

Growing poverty and unemployment, declining real incomes and living standards, and increasing uncertainty have adversely affected social welfare and health status. Although determinants are difficult to establish, evidence illustrates that socioeconomic stress is severe and related to transition shocks. A 1997 study of health in Russia by the President's Commission estimated that over 70 percent of the Russian population was under severe stress associated with depression, heavy smoking, alcoholism, drug use, poor diets, and unsafe driving practices. There was also growing evidence of increased suicides. Between 1989 and 1996, suicide rates for Russian males between the ages of 5 and 19 increased from 7.4 to 13 percent (UNICEF 1998).[3]

Across countries, much of the decline in health status can be linked to unhealthy behavior and lifestyles. Health status has also been affected by lax regulation of environmental and occupational risks and the breakdown in basic health services (Goldstein et al. 1996). In addition to changes in more traditional demographic and health indicators, there is growing evidence that the transition has affected health and social cohesion indirectly through trends in family formation, including rapidly increasing numbers of divorces and births out of wedlock in many countries, as well as increased abandonment and institutionalization of children (UNICEF 1997). Increases in noncommunicable diseases have been accompanied by a startling rise in incidence of some communicable diseases, including tuberculosis, diphtheria, and sexually transmitted diseases such as syphilis (Staines 1998).

Declining Life Expectancy. Although health status has deteriorated greatly in several transition countries, most striking has been an increase in the crude death rate in some countries and a decrease in life expectancy for males. Conversely, life expectancy for females has remained constant. The most dramatic declines in male life expectancy have been in Bulgaria, Moldova, Russia, and Ukraine (see Table 2.2). A recent study for Russia attributed much of the decline in life expectancy to alcohol abuse (McKee and Leon 1997).

Erosions in health status and declining conditions in health facilities point to the need for systemic health system reform in the region. Lack of investments in health and isolation from Western developments in medicine led to increasing obsolescence in technology and clinical systems. In addition, inherited inefficiencies such as overstaffing of health personnel and an excessive emphasis on specialist tertiary level care, at the expense of preventative medicine, limit the quality and effectiveness of health care. In nearly all countries in the region, the ratios of doctors and hospital beds to the population exceed OECD levels, and in some cases, have increased during transition.

Access to Education

Without exception, the countries of Central and Eastern Europe inherited education systems that provided full and equitable access to education at the preschool and primary levels. However, the legacy of central planning distorted patterns of access, especially at the secondary and tertiary lev-

TABLE 2.2   Life Expectancy at Birth for Males (1989–1996)

	1989	1990	1991	1992	1993	1994	1995	1996	% change (1989–96)
Czech									
Republic	68	68	68	69	69	70	70	70	3.3
Hungary	65	65	65	65	65	65	65	66	1.0
Poland	67	67	66	67	67	68	68	68	2.0
Slovakia	67	67	67	68	68	68	68	69	3.0
Bulgaria	69	68	68	68	68	67	67	67	–2.2
Romania	67	67	67	67	66	66	66	65	–1.8
Slovenia	69	69	70	69	69	70	70	71	2.9
Moldova	66	65	64	64	64	62	62	63	–4.0
Russia	64	64	64	62	59	58	58	60	–6.7
Ukraine	66	66	66	64	63	63	62	—	–6.4

SOURCE: TransMONEE Database, UNICEF-ICDC, Florence, Italy

els. Education was tailored to the demands of the socialist state and, as a result, was biased toward highly specialized vocational training at the expense of more flexible programs.

Seven years into the transition process, there is increasing evidence of deterioration in quality and access to education, particularly in the poorer countries. Fiscal constraints and systemic inefficiencies threaten both the ability of countries to maintain the coverage of their systems and the capacity of families, especially the poor, to send their children to school. This section assesses access to preschool and basic education.

Preschool education was a critical element of the social contract in the formerly planned economies. High levels of participation in preschool education reflected not only the state's overall commitment to educating the workforce but also a means of ensuring full labor force participation. In 1993, the share of women in the labor force was nearly 50 percent, compared with 25 percent in the European OECD countries (Laporte and Ringold 1996). Women, especially, were encouraged to work by access to preschools and day care centers located at the workplace. As a result, preschools served a child-care and an educational function. In some cases, preschool systems were maintained outside of the education ministries; in the former Czechoslovakia the Ministry of Health administered preschools until 1990, and in FYR Macedonia the Ministry of Labor and Social Policy continues to oversee part of the preprimary education system.

Under socialism, access to preschool education was often provided in government-subsidized schools and day care centers attached to large state-owned enterprises. Tightening budget constraints have led firms to cut benefits, including those for child care and education. This trend has been compounded by the decentralization of fiscal responsibility for education. Local governments and families have assumed a growing share of financing for preschool education, as ownership and administration of preschools have been transferred to municipalities, churches, or the private sector. Parents increasingly have had to pay for school lunches, textbooks, and other education materials that were previously subsidized by the state. In the early stages of transition, access to preschool was protected, with enrollments increasing slightly in some countries. However, enrollments have fallen in most countries since 1989 (UNICEF 1998).

Enrollment rates in basic education, generally grades one through eight, have remained high, although there are some indications of deterioration. Data show notable declines in access in some countries, including Bulgaria, Croatia, and FYR Macedonia, although it is unclear whether these are statistical artifacts resulting from unreliable demographic data due to migration or conflict (see Figure 2.6).

Enrollment statistics also may mask emerging problems, as actual school attendance may be suffering due to the increasing direct and indi-

FIGURE 2.6   Enrollments in Basic Education (1989–1996), as Percent of 6/7 to 14/15 Age Group

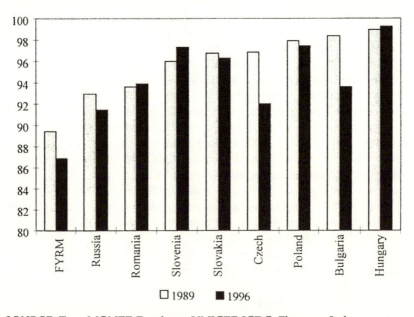

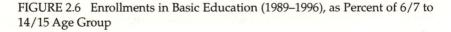

□ 1989   ■ 1996

SOURCE: TransMONEE Database, UNICEF-ICDC, Florence, Italy

rect costs of sending children to school. The loss of subsidies for transportation, school meals, and services that were previously provided free to students has made it difficult for poorer households, especially those in rural areas, to continue sending their children to school (UNICEF 1997).

Declining minority enrollments have been another source of basic school attrition, particularly in countries with large Romany populations. Legislation on compulsory enrollments was eliminated at the outset of transition in a number of countries. A UNDP report on Bulgaria estimates that somewhere between 40 and 70 percent of Romany children do not attend school. These are serious developments as education becomes an increasingly important determinant of earnings potential and labor market success.

Policy Responses

Changes in social welfare have brought about an overwhelming increase in need and demand for social services. Before the transition, few countries had policies in place to address unemployment, and programs targeted to the needs of the poor were weak and rarely utilized. However, the legacy of the universalistic paternalist state left an inheritance of high expectations and, in many countries, a consensus that it remains the role of the state to provide a full range of social policies, services, and programs. This section examines trends in aggregate social spending, and then analyzes its roots in spending on health, education, and income transfers. It notes major policy developments and future policy directions.

Social Expenditures

The state in Central and Eastern Europe has extricated itself from public life in many ways since 1989. Previously, the state orchestrated all economic activity, but now the majority of output and employment are generated in the private sector (EBRD 1996). However, the state has not abdicated its responsibility in the social sectors. Opinion polls show that many in Central Europe continue to believe that the state has a major role to play in alleviating poverty and ensuring living standards. Basic social rights, such as the right to health care, are provided in the postcommunist constitutions of many countries.

This consensus surrounding the role of the state in the social sectors is clearly reflected in social expenditure patterns in the region. Across countries, social expenditures have grown as a share of GDP during the transition, in some cases quite significantly. In the most dramatic case of Poland, the share of GDP devoted to social expenditures expanded from

17 percent in 1989 to 32 percent in 1995 (see Figure 2.7). This trend has been borne out to varying degrees in other countries, with social expenditures comprising between 25 and 30 percent of GDP in the Czech Republic, Slovakia, and Hungary.

Romania has been the exception to this trend. Before the transition, Romania maintained very low social expenditures and depressed living standards to repay foreign debts and to finance its large-scale industrial investment program. Following the collapse of the Ceausescu regime, limited democratization constrained popular pressures for increased social expenditures. Only since 1996, with the election of Constantinescu's reformist government, have decisions been made to raise expenditures on health and family benefits.

The growth of social spending largely reflects the shift from subsidies to explicit social spending. Under socialism, much of the extensive safety net was linked to employment and was supported through subsidies to state-owned enterprises and consumers. States supported full employment and provided social services, including child care, health services, pensions, and a wide range of family benefits through enterprises. Subsidies for

FIGURE 2.7   Total Social Expenditures as Percent of GDP, 1991–1995

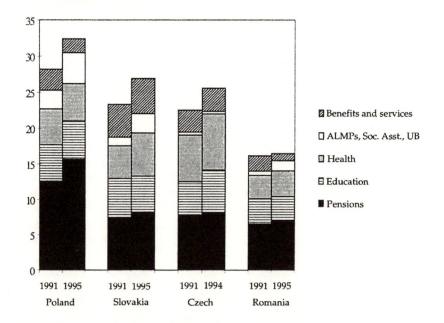

SOURCES: OECD, World Bank

housing, utilities, and consumer goods also were provided directly to households.

The elimination of subsidies and the closure of many large enterprises eroded the enterprise-based benefit system, and the need for income support and unemployment benefit systems for the unemployed and poor emerged rapidly. Milanovic (1996) called the establishment of unemployment benefit systems and the renewed emphasis on cash benefits in the early years of the transition the "monetization of social transfers." Although much of the reduction in spending on subsidies was redirected toward explicit spending, the growth of social expenditures measured in shares of GDP has exceeded the reduction in subsidies (Kramer 1997).

Growth in aggregate social spending stems from different sources across countries. In Poland and FYR Macedonia, pension expenditures clearly have been the driving force behind increased social expenditures. In other countries, such as the Czech Republic, pension spending has remained stable, while health and education expenditures have grown. In general, pension expenditures consume the largest share of social expenditures in all countries. Health expenditures have grown as well, most notably in the Czech Republic, Hungary, and Slovakia—countries that have established health insurance and now finance health care out of payroll contributions and general revenues.

Two trends that have become increasingly prevalent across countries are decentralization and privatization of social policy. Local and municipal governments have been granted increased autonomy in the administration and implementation of health, education, and social assistance. Whereas this was an expected and necessary development following decades of rigid central control, decentralization proceeded unplanned in many cases, and local governments found themselves without the fiscal basis to fund their new found responsibilities. For example, in Bulgaria the central government devolved responsibility for health and education finance to municipal governments without granting localities the necessary revenue raising authority. Although a law adopted in 1991 helped to clarify intergovernmental roles and responsibilities, tax regulations have limited, and even decreased, municipal revenues by scaling back the share of income tax revenues granted to municipalities and setting caps on local fees.

Another response to tightening budget constraints has been growing formal and informal privatization of social services. While the Central and East European countries remain committed to maintaining public financing of health and education systems, there have been movements toward privatization. In particular, health services, including pharmacists and dentists, have been increasingly privatized. Privatization in education has occurred largely at the university and secondary levels. Most notably, by 1994, nearly 25 percent of secondary schools in the Czech Republic and 12 percent in Slovakia were private (UNICEF 1998).

There is also evidence that informal payments for health and education services have become more common. Before the transition, private "under-the-table" payments to public providers for health services were prevalent but not well documented. These payments have continued, although few regulatory mechanisms are in place for overseeing emerging private sector activities. In addition, there is growing evidence that the collapse of public systems has led to ad hoc and unplanned privatization. The most extreme examples have occurred in countries of the Former Soviet Union, including Georgia and Azerbaijan, where public financing for health care has completely collapsed, and private financing now makes up the majority of health expenditures (Staines 1998).

The following sections investigate changes in health, education, and pension spending patterns in more detail, analyzing how countries have responded to changes in demand in the context of fiscal constraints. Despite wide variation in approaches, there are broad commonalities. All countries have introduced new programs to cope with the fast emerging problems of unemployment and poverty. Both passive and active unemployment measures have been adopted across the region, and means-tested social assistance programs have been implemented. Existing programs and policies have also been modified to address changing conditions, for example, by expanding access to higher and general secondary education and implementing curriculum reform to adjust education systems to the needs of a market economy. The scope and innovativeness of policy reforms vary notably across countries and sectors as well as within countries.

Health

Without exception, the former socialist countries inherited fully developed health systems, offering universal access to care and broad coverage. Following socialist industrialization in the 1950s, these systems, combined with adequate nutrition and rising incomes, substantially improved health status (Goldstein et al. 1996). As a result, life expectancy rose and infant mortality rates fell rapidly in the 1960s and early 1970s. However, the systems suffered from structural weaknesses that ultimately limited their effectiveness in such things as a lack of incentives for efficiency and quality of care, highly centralized management structures, and narrowly trained health personnel. Among other weaknesses were excess physical capacity, such as beds and hospitals, a lack of capital investments, an overemphasis on tertiary level care, and poor public health programs.

These structural inefficiencies, isolation from medical and organizational innovations, and stagnating economic growth contributed to a widening gap in health status compared with the West. During the late 1970s, the long-term trend toward improvements in health status in Central and Eastern Europe slowed and even reversed in many countries. The gap in health status was due largely to rapid increases in premature death, mostly from chronic diseases that tend to be associated with unhealthy lifestyles and environments.

The impact of the transition on regional health systems has been severe, particularly due to dramatic declines in real resources available to the health sector. In the early years of transition, fiscal collapse led to real reductions of between 10 and 70 percent of health expenditures (Goldstein et al. 1996).

Alongside the financial collapse, the increase in the burden of disease associated with noncommunicable diseases and the additional health costs of the transition have strained health systems to their limits. Countries have adopted measures and coping strategies to address the new challenges. Most have sought to adopt Western models of health care financing and reimbursement, such as establishing new provider payment mechanisms, decentralizing services, privatization, and introducing out-of-pocket user charges. Despite these changes, there has been little systemic reform of health systems in the region. Most financing remains public and centralized, and resource allocation mechanisms remain that often reinforce inherited inefficiencies, such as overstaffing of personnel and emphasizing specialized hospital care.

Because of the severity of the fiscal crisis, financing reforms have dominated the health reform agenda in many countries. Under socialism, health systems were, with few exceptions, financed out of general revenues. They offered universal coverage with comprehensive benefits. In several important ways, these countries have not broken with the past during the economic transition. Despite the real declines in resources available to the health sector, most countries have protected, or even increased, health expenditures as a share of GDP. In the Czech Republic, Hungary, FYR Macedonia, and other countries, growing health expenditures have been a driving force behind increased social expenditures.

However, fiscal pressures have prompted most countries to adopt measures to contain expenditures, including scaling back benefits, allowing for local privatization of services, and decentralization. Initial exclusions of benefits have focused on relatively uncontroversial, nonessential services, such as cosmetic surgery and some prosthetic devices or health sanatoria. Ongoing economic crises have since led most countries to consider more profound reforms of benefits, or reduce service supply without restructuring or prioritizing spending.

The introduction of national health insurance, based on payroll contributions, has been one of the most significant health reforms across the region. The republics of the former Yugoslav federation had adopted health insurance before the transition, while Hungary, the Czech Republic, and Slovakia adopted such systems in 1991, 1992, and 1993, respectively. Bulgaria, Romania, and Poland have all passed health insurance regulations and are currently planning their implementation.

The adoption of Western European health insurance models is not surprising in the postcommunist countries, as the solidaristic insurance principle and promise of continued universal coverage resonates in countries where full benefits were provided by the state. In addition, health insurance has appealed to interest groups, most notably physicians groups, who expected insurance to provide increased revenues to the health sector. However, due to unique aspects of the transition, including declining numbers of contributors and the growth of substantial informal sectors, its implementation has been problematic.

Contrary to expectations, financing through insurance contributions has not increased available resources to the health sector. High unemployment rates, informal sector activity, and poor compliance by both employers and employees did not yield the expected revenue base for health insurance (Goldstein et al. 1996). Rather than substitute for general revenue expenditures, insurance contributions have been supplemented by general tax revenues, increasing total public resources for health. As a result, the adoption of health insurance has had a visible impact on health expenditures.

The Central and Eastern European countries that spend the highest proportion of GDP on health (6–8 percent) are those that have either historically relied on, or recently adopted, a national health insurance system financed by payroll taxation. This includes the former republics of Yugoslavia, which had a decentralized payroll-based health insurance system before the economic transition, as well as Hungary, the Czech Republic, and Slovakia. In contrast, countries that still rely on general revenues to finance health care, Poland, Bulgaria, and Romania, spend much less on health care (see Figures 2.8 and 2.9).

In addition to the impact on aggregate expenditures, the introduction of insurance-based systems has had serious implications for the cost of labor and, hence, the competitiveness of the transition economies. Payroll contributions for health insurance alone range from around 3.5 percent of net wages in Albania and Lithuania, to 6 percent in Bulgaria, to nearly 20 percent in Hungary and Croatia. Payroll taxation as a whole greatly increases labor costs. Payroll taxation for pensions, unemployment, and other social security programs ranges from around 30 percent of net wages in FYR Macedonia to over 60 percent of net wages in Bulgaria and Hungary.

FIGURE 2.8 Total Public Health Expenditures as Percent of GDP, 1991–1997

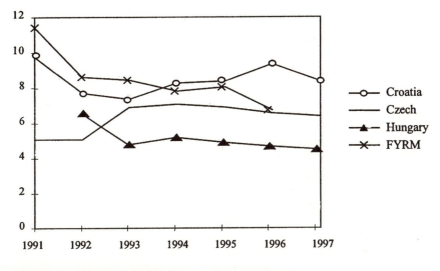

SOURCES: OECD, World Bank

FIGURE 2.9 Total Public Health Expenditures as Percent of GDP, 1991–1997

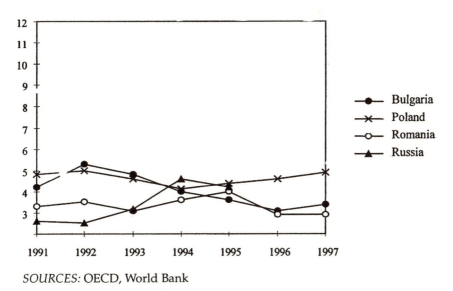

SOURCES: OECD, World Bank

In this context, phasing in new contributions for health insurance requires careful planning and coordination to ensure the fiscal viability of the system.

Changes in health financing models have left most existing incentive and resource allocation mechanisms untouched. Despite the declines in real resources, there have been few efforts to rationalize facilities and personnel in line with funding realities. Systemic inefficiencies inherited from the socialist past persist and continue to constrain the efficacy of the health sector. Overstaffing and capacity remain high in contrast with OECD countries (see Table 2.3). Similarly, there is continued emphasis on higher levels of care including an oversupply of specialists at the expense of the primary care system.

Some countries have adopted reforms. In 1995, Hungary embarked upon a three-year program to eliminate or convert to chronic care about 20 percent of acute care beds. Croatia, which had a 40 percent real reduction in public spending for health, has also experienced downsizing. Romania had a 6–7 percent reduction in public sector physicians and nurses and an 11 percent reduction in beds. The average length of hospital stay has declined by nearly 40 percent since 1987 in the Czech Republic, Slovakia, and Poland. In contrast, the number of health care personnel increased by nearly 10 percent in Bulgaria between 1992 and 1996.

Not many adjustments in health systems have been made to address the changes in health status in several transition countries. Increased emphasis on public health is needed to improve lifestyles and ensure the preventive measures and basic health care to arrest the development of diseases that are now becoming the predominant causes of male mortality. Public education programs are needed to inform the population about nutrition, exercise, and the risks of smoking and other dangerous behavior.

TABLE 2.3 Health Services in Comparison, 1996

	Doctors per 1,000 population	Inpatient beds per 1,000 population	Average length of stay (days)
Bulgaria	3.3	10.0	13.0
Czech Republic	2.9	6.7	10.0
Hungary	3.8	9.0	10.3
Poland	2.4	6.2	10.6
Romania	1.8	7.4	10.2
United Kingdom	—	4.5	9.8
United States	2.6	4.1	7.8
Spain	4.2	4.0	11.0
Sweden	3.1	5.6	7.5

SOURCES: OECD; TransMONEE Database, UNICEF-ICDC, Florence

The socialist systems had an impressive record in preventive health care, especially in providing immunizations, but health education emphasizing the importance of lifestyles on health outcomes was lacking. Financial developments have led to significant changes in the health sector, including privatization, decentralization, and the introduction of insurance-based provision, but the health reform agenda remains in its early stages in other respects.

Education

Developments in education mirror trends in the health sector in many ways. Although changes have been made to financing arrangements, the underlying structures of the system have not evolved significantly. With few exceptions, education systems before transition were almost exclusively financed by central governments out of tax revenues.

Financing responsibilities were assumed largely by ministries of education, with other ministries involved in certain areas. Ministries of industry, communication, and transportation financed various streams of vocational education, and ministries of health often participated in providing medical education and some early childhood education programs.

During the socialist period, all of the countries in the region succeeded in establishing extensive and relatively equitable education and training systems. However, these accomplishments came at the expense of efficiently allocation and use of resources. At the outset of transition, investment levels stagnated and fiscal pressures grew, making maintaining equity and quality in education increasingly difficult.

The fiscal crisis that accompanied liberalization further burdened education budgets and threatened the abilities of countries to sustain pretransition spending levels. Countries have adopted various policy responses to adapt education budgets to changing economic constraints, such as privatization, decentralization, and the adoption of alternative funding arrangements. Moreover, schools and universities have experimented with new options for cost recovery and financing for academic research. Research and education were separated in most socialist countries, but many countries in Central and Eastern Europe have reunited them in recent years. However, these developments have had varied impact on quality and equity of access to education.

Expenditures on education during the transition have been protected in many countries. Although real expenditures on education have declined with declines in output, as a share of GDP, education expenditures have grown in Romania, the Czech Republic, Hungary, FYR Macedonia, and Slovenia (see Figure 2.10). Education expenditures in some countries now equal or exceed the proportion of education expenditures in the

OECD countries. Yet fiscal data for the education sector are particularly problematic because of the trend toward decentralization that has hampered collecting data.

As in the health sector, systemic inefficiencies plague the education sector, due to the absence of appropriate incentives for resource allocation and use. In particular, overstaffing and ineffective use of facilities remain two of the most daunting obstacles. Not only did countries inherit education systems characterized by overstaffing, but there is also evidence that the problem has worsened during the transition. Employment in education has increased in many countries and student to teacher ratios, which were low by international standards before the transition, have decreased even further (see Figure 2.11). It is important to note that low ratios of students to teachers do not necessarily translate into smaller class sizes. Rather, large classes are common, as teachers' time has been ineffectively allocated through low teaching loads and high numbers of single-subject teachers.

Overstaffing has been financed by the erosion of teachers' wages, and the crowding out of nonpersonnel expenditures. Teachers' wages have

FIGURE 2.10   Total Public Education Expenditures as Percent of GDP, 1990 and 1996

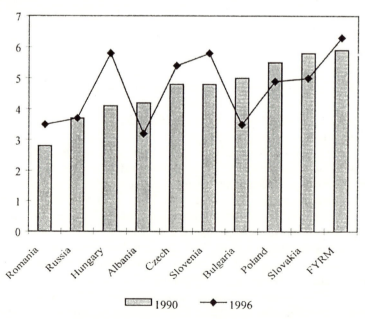

SOURCES: TransMONEE Database, UNICEF-ICDC, Florence, Italy, World Bank

FIGURE 2.11   Students per Teacher (1989–1996)

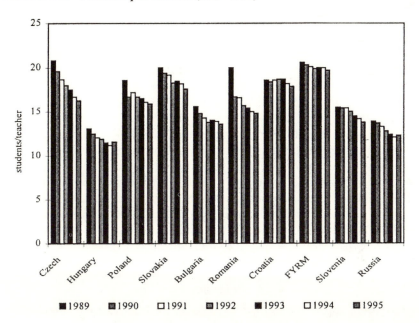

SOURCES: TransMONEE Database, UNICEF-ICDC, Florence, Italy, World Bank

declined more sharply than the average wage in the transition economies, implying a decline in the competitiveness of the teaching profession. With economic returns to education increasing, teachers with marketable skills will increasingly leave the teaching profession for more lucrative teaching or other employment opportunities in the private sector. A severe scarcity of certain types of teachers has already emerged in some countries, especially of foreign language teachers. There is a risk that the quality of teaching will decline further as highly qualified teachers leave the profession.

Another challenge to the education system has been effective use of facilities. Due to price liberalization and the loss of the CMEA trading block, energy prices have skyrocketed. As a result, many countries have had difficulty affording utilities and maintaining facilities. For example, the high cost of heating and electricity in Bulgaria led the Ministry of Education to close many schools for short periods during the winter months. In addition, traditionally low levels of capital investment under socialism led to the deterioration of many educational buildings.

Despite this legacy, there is change in the education sector. Countries have attempted to adapt to the needs of a market economy, responding to changes in student choice, particularly at the secondary and tertiary levels. The socialist systems placed a high emphasis on vocational and technical secondary education, at the expense of more general academic programs. Governments trained students for employment in socialist industry, and usually set enrollment targets centrally. Since the transition, there has been an attempt to shift the emphasis away from narrow technical and vocational schools, since individuals with more flexible, academic backgrounds adapt better to changing labor market demands (UNICEF 1998).

Similarly, as demand for university educated workers has expanded, and opportunities for post-secondary education have increased, overall enrollments in tertiary education have grown. Student choice has responded to changing labor market demands. While there has been a noticeable decline in enrollments in engineering programs, which were heavily emphasized under socialism, there has been a clear movement toward the social sciences, such as law and economics, and business disciplines that were previously ignored or infused with socialist ideology.

Pensions

Pension spending has been the driving force behind increased social spending in several countries, including Poland, FYR Macedonia, Hungary, and Slovakia. These increases have their roots in the extensive and generous pension systems inherited from the socialist era, as well as policy measures adopted during the transition, particularly the increase in early retirements and disability pensions. For decades under socialism, workers who contributed into the social insurance systems during their lifetimes could expect to live comfortably following retirement. Pensions were relatively generous as measured by the ratio of pension levels to the average wage. When the transition began, governments sought to protect pension expenditures, to shelter the elderly who were predicted to be hard hit by the social costs of transition from the effects of inflation.

Social insurance schemes were viewed as a safety net for those affected by economic restructuring. Early retirement and disability pensions were encouraged by many governments as a way of avoiding open unemployment. However, the rapid increase in pension expenditures, and the overall pressure of pension costs on aggregate social expenditures have called into question the sustainability of these systems, leading countries to consider substantial reforms of their pension systems.

Similarly, the ability of pension systems to provide adequate income support to the elderly has been threatened by high inflation, which reduced the real value of pension benefits. Efforts to maintain, or in some cases, increase the real value of pensions led to rapid increases in pension spending in some countries, as in Poland and FYR Macedonia (Andrews and Rashid 1996). Reform of pension systems poses difficult political and economic challenges, and political parties representing the interests of pensioners have emerged in some countries.

Pension expenditures consume the largest share of social spending in all countries, but have not increased uniformly or consistently in the region. In some countries, including Poland, FYR Macedonia, Hungary, and Slovakia, pension expenditures grew rapidly as a share of GDP and led to a rise in total social expenditures (see Figure 2.12). Since then, expenditures have leveled off or declined as a share of GDP. In Slovakia and Bulgaria, pension expenditures declined after a peak in 1993, and in Poland, recent data show a slight fall in 1996.

Conversely, pension spending has been maintained or reduced in the Czech Republic and Romania since 1989. In proportion to their aggregate income levels, most transition countries are spending far more on pensions than other countries. Pension expenditures in most countries matched, or exceeded, the level of spending in Western European countries and are much greater than in Latin American and Asian countries at similar income levels.

FIGURE 2.12   Pension Expenditures as Percent of GDP, 1989–1996

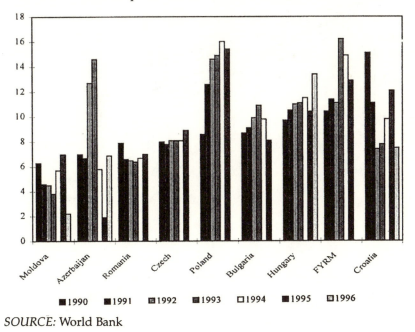

SOURCE: World Bank

Escalating pension costs in many countries have resulted from a combination of factors, including aging populations, more pensioners due to early retirement ages, and fewer contributors. As a result, the ratio of contributors to pensioners has declined in all countries since 1989, exerting an upward pressure on pension costs and threatening the sustainability of the social insurance system (see Figure 2.13). In addition, the inclusion of many nonpension expenditures in pension fund budgets, such as spas, and special programs for the disabled has threatened the fiscal viability of the pension system.

Fewer contributors to the pension system is a side effect of contracting labor force participation. Growing open unemployment and declining employment rapidly reduced the pool of contributors to social insurance programs. Also, growing employment in the informal sector sharply reduced the tax base of pension funds. A study of the informal sector estimated that activity in the unofficial economy in 1995 ranged from 36 percent of GDP in Bulgaria to 30 percent in Hungary and 11 percent in the Czech Republic (Johnson et al. 1997). The ratio of contributors to working age population declined in all countries in the region.

FIGURE 2.13   Ratios of Contributors to Beneficiaries, (1990–1993)

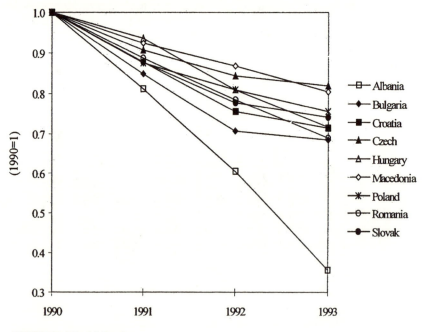

SOURCE: World Bank

In response to tightening fiscal constraints and growing pension fund deficits, many countries in the region have made initial steps toward pension reform. Both Poland and Hungary have passed the initial legislation necessary for systemic reform, which will eventually lead to the creation of three-pillar systems, incorporating mandatory and voluntary private pensions. Other countries have taken smaller steps toward reform, such as gradual raising of retirement ages, tightening of eligibility requirements—including scaling back early retirements, and developing the regulatory framework for private pensions.[4]

Conclusions

Social welfare regimes in the transition economies are caught between the legacy of the broad-based universalistic systems they once were and high expectations for what is to come. There are contrasting pressures to maintain existing services, adjust to fiscal constraints, address diverging needs, respond to shifting political dynamics, and adapt to European Union norms. These pressures have elicited piecemeal social reforms that, while incorporating neoliberal characteristics, still retain much of their pre-transition features.

Most countries in the region have struggled to maintain elements of the universalistic welfare state by preserving social insurance entitlements and maintaining national health coverage through the introduction of health insurance. Despite real declines in spending, the share of government expenditures devoted to social policies has been protected and, in most cases, increased. Given fiscal constraints, countries are finding that maintaining the full range of social benefits may no longer be feasible and that they will have to scale back benefits or undertake reforms to improve fiscal management.

Despite overall efforts to maintain existing systems, major trends in the administration and financing of social policy, such as the shift away from enterprise-supported social benefits, decentralization, and privatization, have left large policy gaps. These trends are the natural outcomes of the transition from central planning and ultimately may improve the coverage and quality of social services.

The absence of a coherent and concerted approach toward social policy has often left or even exacerbated systemic distortions inherited from the past. The elimination of state subsidies to state-owned enterprises to provide benefits and services, such as child care and subsidized housing, has created holes in the safety net. Decentralization and privatization of health and education may have similar consequences. The transfer of responsibility for the administration and financing of social policy to local governments may create large gaps in coverage and quality, if regional authorities have different levels of resources available to them. Similarly, when taken too far, privatization of social services can negatively affect equity and quality.

Postcommunist Europe remains faced with a difficult search for a new welfare state model that addresses current challenges and improves upon the legacies of the past.

References

Adeyi, Olusoji, Gnanaraj Chellaraj, Ellen Goldstein, , Alexander Preker, and Dena Ringold. 1997. "Health Status During the Transition in Central and Eastern Europe: Development in Reverse?" *Health Policy and Planning* 12:2, 132–145.

Allison, Christine, and Dena Ringold. 1996. "Labor Markets in Transition in Central and Eastern Europe: 1989–1995." Technical Paper No. 352. Washington, D.C.: The World Bank.

Andrews, Emily, and Mansoora Rashid. 1996. "The Financing of Pension Systems in Central and Eastern Europe." Technical Paper No. 339. Washington, D.C.: The World Bank.

Barr, Nicholas, ed. 1994. *Labor Markets and Social Policy in Central and Eastern Europe: The Transition and Beyond.* New York: Oxford University Press.

Boeri, Tito, and Stefano Scarpetta. 1994. "Dealing with a Stagnant Pool: Policies Coping with Long-Term Unemployment in Central and Eastern Europe." Paris: OECD.

Commander, Simon, and Fabrizio Coricelli, eds. 1995. *Unemployment, Restructuring, and the Labor Market in Eastern Europe and Russia.* Washington, D.C.: The World Bank.

EBRD (European Bank for Reconstruction and Development). 1996. *Transition report.* London.

Esping-Andersen, Gosta. 1990. *The Three Worlds of Welfare Capitalism.* Princeton, N.J.: Princeton, University Press.

Goldstein, Ellen. Alexander Preker, Olusoji Adeyi, and Gnanaraj Chellaraj, 1996. "Trends in Health Status, Services, and Finance: The Transition in Central and Eastern Europe, " Vols. I and II. World Bank Technical Papers Nos. 341 and 348. Washington, D.C.: The World Bank.

Johnson, Simon, Daniel Kaufmann, and Andrei Schleifer. 1997. "The Unofficial Economy in Transition," Brookings Papers on Economic Activity, 2, Washington, D.C.: The Brookings Institution, 159–239.

Kornai, Janos. 1992. "The Postsocialist Transition and the State: Reflections in the Light of Hungarian Fiscal Problems." *American Economic Review* 82:2, 1–21.

Kornai, Janos. 1997. "Reform of the Welfare Sector in the Post-Communist Countries: A Normative Approach." Pp. 272–298 in Joan Nelson, Charles Tilly, and Lee Walker, eds. *Transforming Post-Communist Political Economies.* Washington D.C.: National Academy Press.

Kramer, Mark. 1997. "Social Protection Policies and Safety Nets in East-Central Europe: Dilemmas of the Postcommunist Transformation." In Ethan B. Kapstein and Michael Mandelbaum, eds. *Sustaining the Transition: The Social Safety Net in Postcommunist Europe*. New York: Council on Foreign Relations.

Kulczycki, Andrzej. 1995. "Abortion Policy in Postcommunist Europe: The Conflict in Poland. *Population and Development Review* 21:3 (September): 471–505.

Laporte, Bruno, and Dena Ringold. 1996. "Trends in Education Access and Financing during the Transition in Central and Eastern Europe." Technical Paper No. 361. Washington, D.C.: The World Bank.

McKee, Martin, and David Leon. 1997. "Understanding the Russian Mortality Crisis." *Eurohealth* 3:2.

Milanovic, Branko. 1996. "Poverty and Inequality in Transition Economies: What Has Actually Happened?" In Bartolomej Kaminski, ed. *Economic Transition in Russia and the New States of Eurasia*. New York: M. E. Sharpe.

Milanovic, Branko. 1998. *Income, Inequality and Poverty During the Transition from Planned to Market Economy*, Washington, D.C.: The World Bank.

OECD (Organization for Economic Cooperation and Development). 1995b. *Employment Outlook*. Paris.

OECD (Organization for Economic Cooperation and Development). 1995c. *Review of the Labour Market in the Czech Republic*, Paris.

OECD (Organisation for Economic Cooperation and Development). 1996a. *Education at a Glance: OECD Indicators*. Paris.

OECD (Organization for Economic Cooperation and Development). 1996b. *Labour Market and Social Policies in the Slovak Republic*. Paris.

Rutkowski, Jan. 1996. "Changes in the Wage Structure during Economic Transition." Technical Paper No. 340. Washington, D.C.: The World Bank.

Rutkowski, Jan. 1998. "Welfare and the Labor Market in Poland: Social Policy during Economic Transition." Technical Paper No. 417. Washington, D.C.: The World Bank.

Sachs, Jeffrey D., and Katharina Pistor, eds. 1997. *The Rule of Law and Economic Reform in Russia*. Boulder: Westview Press.

Schöpflin, George. 1993. *Politics in Eastern Europe*. Oxford, UK: Blackwell.

Staines, Verdon. 1998. *A Health Sector Strategy for the Europe and Central Asia Region*. Human Development, Health, Nutrition and Population Series, Washington, D.C.: The World Bank.

UNICEF. 1993. *Crisis in Mortality, Health and Nutrition*. Economies in Transition Studies. The MONEE Project Regional Monitoring Report, No. 2. Florence: UNICEF International Child Development Center.

UNICEF. 1995. *Poverty, Children and Policy: Responses for a Brighter Future*. The MONEE Project Regional Monitoring Report, No. 3. Florence: UNICEF International Child Development Center.

UNICEF. 1997. *Children at Risk in Central and Eastern Europe: Perils and Promises*. The MONEE Project Regional Monitoring Report, No. 4. Florence: UNICEF International Child Development Center.

UNICEF. 1998. *Education for All?* The MONEE Project Regional Monitoring Report, No. 5. Florence: UNICEF International Child Development Center.

World Bank. 1995, *Understanding Poverty in Poland, A World Bank Country Study*. Washington, D.C.: The World Bank.

World Bank. 1996a. *World Development Report, 1996: From Plan to Market*. Washington, D.C.: World Bank.

World Bank. 1996b. *Hungary: Poverty and Social Transfers*. Washington, D.C.: World Bank.

World Bank. 1997a. *World Development* Indicators. Washington, D.C.: World Bank.

World Bank. 1997b. *Romania: Poverty and Social Policy*, Vols. I and II. Washington, D.C.: World Bank.

Notes

*I am grateful to Mitchell Orenstein, Michael Cain, Linda Cook, and Maureen Lewis for their comments on earlier drafts of this paper.

The findings, interpretations, conclusions, and all errors in this paper are those of the author, and should not be attributed to the World Bank.

1. Unemployment was illegal in many countries and Barr (1994) note that in 1989 the unemployment office in Warsaw had five clients.

2. Retirement ages generally ranged from 50 to 55 for women and 55 to 60 for men.

3. Suicide rates measure deaths per 100,000 population.

4. The Hungarian and Polish pension reform programs are discussed in this volume in chapters by Cook and Orenstein, and Cain and Surdej, respectively.

3

The Return of the Left and Its Impact on the Welfare State in Poland, Hungary, and Russia

LINDA J. COOK AND MITCHELL A. ORENSTEIN

Since the revolutions of 1989, political scientists have recognized the potential incompatibility between democratization and simultaneous economic reform in postsocialist states. In one commonly proposed scenario, the social costs of reform produce a popular backlash that translates into electoral victory for parties promising relief. Once in power, these parties seek to modify or abandon reform policies. The theory proposes that in the initial stages, voters may have accepted reform because they recognized the bankruptcy of the preexisting system and blamed past leaders for their hardships, because they expected future benefits, or because they were caught up in a period of "extraordinary politics," in which they placed the perceived common good above individual goods (Balcerowicz 1995b:161). But once voters feel the painful effects of reform, a fierce electoral protest—or backlash—becomes likely. As Joan Nelson has pointed out, "The political challenges tend to be greatest in the medium term . . . [when] reforms are more vulnerable to dilution, delay, and derailment" (Nelson 1995:49–50).

Electoral protest against reform has in fact materialized. In Poland in September 1993, in Hungary in 1994, and in Russia in December 1993 and more decisively in December 1995, electorates rejected strongly reformist parties in favor of others, mainly communist successor parties, that promised less severe economic policies and more social welfare. This chapter examines whether these parties actually modified reform policies. Have the parties that won these elections responded to constituents, delivering on their campaign promises to improve welfare and cushion the effects of newly established markets?

As parties that have come to power through democratic means for the first time, left parties must establish credibility with their electorates to consolidate support. But they also face considerable constraints. Left parties may want to ameliorate the effects of reform, but find themselves with little room to maneuver between reform policies already set in motion, international pressures to stay the course, and constituency pressures for relief. Can these parties deliver enough to their constituents without gutting reform or causing a damaging economic crisis? Are these parties becoming effective representative forces, or are they dominated by cynical cabals that sell out their voters once they reach the seat of power?

Defining What Is Left

In answering these questions, we need to turn to a literature that has expressed manifold doubts about the meaning of "left" as a political term in the postcommunist states. A number of authors have asserted the meaninglessness of the left-right distinction in postcommunist states, arguing that it has been replaced by a liberal-conservative axis or a postmodern fragmentation of society along multiple dimensions. Echoing the arguments made in Dietrich Rueschemeyer's introduction to this volume, we find the left-right distinction central to the politics of our cases. We concur with Szelenyi, Fodor, and Hanley (1997), who argue that while the first postcommunist elections were dominated by a liberal-conservative split, a left-right cleavage asserted itself in subsequent elections. These authors propose a "theory of two axes" to define postcommunist politics, to which we subscribe:

> *Theory of the Two Axes.* No one seems to question the importance of cultural conflicts, the significance of the Liberal/Conservative cleavage in contemporary Eastern Europe. Some sociologists, political scientists, and social commentators, however, insist that the Left/Right divide also exists—that two axes of postcommunist politics exist. While the Liberal/Conservative cleavage is created by differences in values, the Left/Right axis is based on economic interests. (Szelenyi, Fodor, and Hanley 1997:205)

Still, what do we mean by left in the particular postcommunist context? As Rueschemeyer notes, we use the term "left" in a quite ordinary way, to indicate parties that seek to represent those who are socially weak. These parties may also represent other social groups and therefore may advocate a multiplicity of policy approaches, from communist recidivism to the policies of New Labor. Indeed, despite their common leftist roots, the parties that won backlash elections in 1993–1995 presented very different programs, ranging from a "softening" of radical neoliberalism in the Polish case to a frontal assault on market reforms in Russia. Both the politics of reform and the politics of reaction will vary considerably across the postcommunist states.

Programmatic differentiation among left parties may reflect differences in their activist and voter constituencies, both current and prospective. While all the left parties gained much of their electoral support from reform's losers, including less-educated workers and pensioners, the shape of their electorates also varied considerably, as did the extent of their alliances with trade unions, other societal organizations, and business elites. In seeking to define their partisan policy preferences, it is important to ask more precisely whom these parties represent. Parties may favor some constituencies at the expense of others. In their post-election programs, left parties may focus on delivering benefits only to limited groups that were key to their election, or to the most organized of their supporters, pursuing agendas that affect only limited aspects of reform. Or they may gear their policies to the median voter, in an attempt to win mass support in a majoritarian system.

Left party electoral programs may also differ significantly from their coalition government programs. In the cases we consider, only the Hungarian Socialist Party, in 1994, won enough seats to govern alone, and even they formed a parliamentary alliance with another party that had its own constituency and its own agenda on economic reform. The Russian Communist Party needs support from other parties in the Duma to pass or block legislation. It would be wrong to measure the impact of left parties without taking account of their particular constituencies, agendas, and alliances.

Parties, moreover, do not simply reflect the interests of their constituencies. Much of the literature on transitions assumes that electoral protest against reform will necessarily be translated into policy through the medium of a backlash party, but parties are substantially autonomous from societal interests and are subject to many conflicting pressures and constraints. As Adam Przeworski notes in *Sustainable Democracy*, "the causal chain that leads from individual discontent to organized reactions against the effects of reform and from organized reactions to their abandonment is contingent and complex" (1995:80).

In power, parties will confront economic realities that they could ignore in the election stage as well as strong pressures from international financial actors and domestic markets to continue reform policies. Possible costs of eschewing reform, including inflation and reductions of investment and foreign aid, may be very costly to their constituencies.

Left party programs in postcommunist Europe may also be defined by what Orenstein (1998) calls their "genealogy," a term that encompasses their historical origins, family traits and commitments, and development paths chosen by party leaders during the transition. What influence do path-dependent historical features and prior leadership choices have on the programmatic positions of left parties? Left parties can be grouped into three distinct families, each implying distinct policy preferences, based on their historical relation with the previous regimes.

Among the communist successor parties that dominate the left or center-left of the political spectrum in the states we discuss, there are now two different party types that resulted from divergent evolution during the transition period. In the first place are social democratic successor parties in Hungary and Poland, led by former reform communists who remain reform-oriented and have rejected the former regime while embracing membership in the Socialist International. Second, there are unreformed successor parties in Russia and the Czech Republic, led by former hard-liners that cling to the name and many ideals of communism.

Historic left parties form a third genus of the postcommunist left. These parties were typically suppressed under communism, but often played a significant role in previous periods of democratic rule. They managed to reestablish themselves in only a few cases after 1989, particularly in the Czech Republic. Policy preferences may vary systematically across party types. For instance, one valence issue for the postcommunist left is NATO expansion in East-Central Europe: hard-line successor parties oppose it (Russian and Czech communists), while social democratic successor parties (Polish Social Democrats and Hungarian Socialists) and historic parties (Czech Social Democrats) support it. This reflects the parties' very different attitudes towards the West and Western-oriented reform. Such inherent and inherited preferences of party leaders may dictate the types of constituencies they choose to canvass and the types of policies they pursue, rather than the other way around.

In assessing the impact of left parties on changing the course of economic reform, their technical competence in legislative politics also needs to be considered. Parties may try to alter the course of reform and fail. Most of the parties are new to the democratic game, and even if they are committed to clear agendas that respond to constituency interests, they may be ineffective in legislative politics. We will need to see how successful these parties have been in gaining control of critical legislative committees and governmental positions, in maintaining party discipline, and in realizing the potential for alliance-building on issues central to their agendas. Some analysts have suggested that people voted for communist successor parties in part because of their perceived political competence and experience (Marody 1995:268; Kornai 1996:970), but these parties' effectiveness in a democratic context remains to be demonstrated.

Do backlash parties generate coherent programs that address social problems, battle for these programs, set reasonable priorities, make compromises, and translate their initiatives into effective policy? Do these parties manage to maneuver in a space between the fiscal demands of reform and the social needs of their constituencies in crafting policies, drafting budgets, and getting both through a complex legislative process? In part, the answer to these questions depends on how we understand left party preferences, but in part on how severe we judge the constraints to be.

Constraints on Left Party Programs

International Economic Pressures

Constraints on left party economic programs may arise from the internationalization of economic pressures. Garrett and Lange (1991) provide an important theoretical exploration of the dilemma faced by left parties that seek to advance their partisan preferences in an open economy, one that is subject to ever greater forces for integration. The authors note in regard to Central and Eastern Europe and the Former Soviet Union that the transition to market economies gives "apparent testimony to the pervasive pressures toward convergence in the increasingly interdependent world economy" (Garrett and Lange 1991:541).

International pressures clearly had much to do with the breakdown of communism and the design of subsequent reform efforts. How much room does any postcommunist government have to maneuver? While Garrett and Lange concede that both left and right governments around the world are increasingly constrained in their fiscal and macroeconomic policies by international pressures and expectations, they argue that other economic policy areas remain to be manipulated. "Governments not only of the right but also of the left continue . . . to be able to shape supply-side policies affecting industrial innovation, investment, and labor markets in accordance with their partisan preferences" (Garrett and Lange 1991:541).

How much room for innovation and change is there in the postcommunist social policy? Do left parties have the opportunity to introduce major changes? Or will their inherent partisan preferences be constrained by a desire to be reelected that may cause parties to renege on promises to support costly social measures? Garrett and Lange reason that this may happen when partisan preferences are unsustainable in a given international environment. Parties will therefore face powerful incentives to choose policies that prevent an economic crisis, since economic crises often cause governments to fall. How much do left social policies reflect

inherent partisan preferences, and how much do they reflect the caution-
ary influence of the international environment?

Political Institutions

Garrett and Lange and others also analyze how political and socioeconomic institutions may influence effective policy efforts. Political institutions have a major impact on how backlash elections are reflected in
policy. Analysts normally expect electoral protest to have a greater impact on the course of reform in parliamentary systems such as Hungary,
and in mixed parliamentary-presidential regimes such as Poland, where
parliamentary victories translate directly into control of the government
and policymaking. In presidential systems such as Russia's, where parliament has limited powers and the shakily pro-reform president governs
by decree in many areas, reform is often seen as largely insulated from
such electoral protest.

On the other hand, there may be good theoretical reasons to believe that
reform is more susceptible to backlash in presidential regimes such as
Russia, not less. Analysts have recently suggested that although presidential decrees are effective at initiating reform, the later stages of reform consolidation and institutional adaptation demand democratic consensus-
building, which may be better served in parliamentary and mixed
regimes. Haggard and Kaufman, chief proponents of this view, argue that
"debate and peaceful contestation offer the best hope for finding durable
compromises for the social conflicts and economic policy dilemmas" that
reform produces (Haggard and Kaufman 1995a:8). Without these compromises, reform is endangered over the medium term. Haggard and Kaufman further argue that the shape of the party system—in particular the
degree of party polarization and fragmentation, matters more than regime
type, whether presidential, parliamentary, or authoritarian.

Electoral laws have also played an important role in the return of the left
(Kaminski, Lissowski, and Swistak 1997). Between the first and second
postcommunist elections, many countries introduced changes in the electoral laws that favored larger parties, including thresholds for parliamentary representation that are now nearly standard across the region. The relative impact of political institutions, such as electoral laws, party systems,
and constitutional rules, on electoral backlash will also be considered.

Finally, the effectiveness of left parties, once elected to govern, will be
critically affected by the capacity and authority of the state structures
that must actually carry out the government's decisions. As Juan Linz
and Alfred Stepan (1996) observe in their book *Problems of Democratic
Transition*, "A reasonably strong state with a clear hierarchy of laws and
the capacity to extract a surplus and to implement the policies of the new
democratic government is crucial for democratic consolidation. Indeed,

many of the rights of democratic citizenship can only be obtained if there is a coherent state, an enforceable rule of law, and a usable state apparatus" (390). As will be obvious, the states under consideration in this book vary greatly in their capacities and lawfulness.

Social Policy and the Left

In sum, all three backlash elections—in Poland, Hungary, and Russia—constitute critical tests of responsiveness and accountability in newly democratizing political systems. The 1993 and 1994 elections brought the first transfer of power from the initial reformist coalition to its opponents. A comprehensive study of left party social policies provides an opportunity to answer important questions about the nature and responsiveness of these parties, and about the future directions that postcommunist welfare states are likely to take. It also provides a window on the stabilization and consolidation of democracy. If the protest registered in these elections does not affect policy, and if constituent demands are elided, the cost to party political stabilization may be great.

Furthermore, Rueschemeyer, Stevens, and Stevens have pointed out that the, "Consolidation of parties . . . is made particularly difficult in a situation where the political support of incumbent parties is more or less regularly decimated because of their inability to improve the economic situation or satisfy the aspirations of the large mass of the electorate" (Rueschemeyer, Stevens, and Stevens 1992:293). Left parties need to fulfill constituent expectations in their social policy agenda if they are to consolidate voter support, and contribute to the stabilization of electorally volatile postcommunist democracies (See Rose, Munro, and Mackie 1998:118–119).

All things being equal, we would expect left parties to advance social democratic or socialist conservative versions of the welfare state in Central and Eastern Europe and Russia. This chapter sets out to test whether left parties have produced substantial left alternatives in the postcommunist welfare state debate that correspond with, and effectively advance, the interests of their constituencies in the social dimension of reform or, alternatively, whether policy attempts have been overwhelmed by pressures of the international or domestic environment, or by backtracking, incompetence, and selling out of the parties themselves.

Russia

The Left's Election Victory

The Communist Party of the Russian Federation (CPRF) differs fundamentally from the social-democratically oriented East European successor parties. It grew from the antireform wing of the old CPSU, which opposed both economic liberalization and the breakup of the Soviet state. By far the dominant left party in Russia, the CPRF is flanked to the right by several small social democratic parties that have remained marginal in electoral politics. To the left stand orthodox Marxist-Leninist parties, of which the largest is Viktor Anpilov's militant and vocal Working Russia. The Communist Party itself is also internally differentiated into social democratic and orthodox tendencies and a dominant nationalist wing led by Gennady Zyuganov. It is allied with its post-communist rural analog, the Agrarian Party, and has cooperated at various points with other parties of leftist and nationalist proclivities (Fish 1995; Ishiyama 1996; Urban and Solovei 1997).

The largest mass party in Russia, the Communist Party has a membership of some half million, mostly older functionaries, veterans, academics, and others, well-organized and especially active in provincial areas. Its links with organized labor are weak. Some local unions have endorsed the party, but its efforts to form an alliance at the national level have been rebuffed by the major trade union federation and active membership among workers remains low (Urban and Solovei 1997:186–189; Cook 1997). In any case, the Communist Party defines its constituency not in class or socioeconomic terms but in nationalist and collectivist ones: it seeks to unite a "popular patriotic majority" to save the nation from Yeltsin and the reformist government. Under Zyuganov, the party has placed itself in the leadership of a diffuse "patriotic" movement that spans the political spectrum. At the same time, the party places popular welfare at the center of its platform, combining, as one scholar aptly notes, the social values of the left with the state-patriotic political values of the right (Vujacic 1996:122).

The CPRF condemns the reform program as a national disaster and national betrayal that has brought the collapse of Russia's production and destruction of its scientific potential, the impoverishment of its people, the selling off of its natural wealth, the humiliation of the country, and its subordination to foreign interests. The party's full program promises a radical "change in course," including a return to the social protections of the communist period as well as extensive state intervention to revive the economy. Its social policy is essentially restorationist—a promise to "reestablish the socioeconomic rights of the people," though with acknowledgment that this system must be altered "to exclude tendencies toward leveling and dependence" ("Za Nashu" 1995).

The CPRF Program for the 1995 Duma election specifically promised that the party would strive to return to citizens rights to work, relaxation, inexpensive housing, free education and medical care, and state regulation of prices for necessities ("Za Nashu" 1995). The Communists committed themselves to a nearly uncritical defense of the universalistic and paternalistic Soviet-era welfare state, and made unrealistic promises to bring it back, in some measure if they won the parliamentary elections, and in full measure if they won the presidency.

Electoral support for the Communist Party, as well as the Russian left generally, is concentrated among older, less-educated, and rural voters. Support from workers has also grown significantly (see Table 3.1), though it remains weak among the traditional class of industrial workers in large cities. In the 1995 Duma election the party gained votes disproportionately from those 55 and older, retired, with elementary or incomplete secondary education, and those living in the agricultural south of the country.

The strongest growth in support for the Communist Party over the previous two years had come from the older and poorly educated and low-skilled, and while the party made significant inroads into better educated urban groups in 1995, this also was mainly among older voters. Those who had lost most from reform clearly turned toward the left: the villages and small towns that provided most support for left parties had also experienced the largest declines in employment and family income, as well as the highest levels of wage arrears. Low regional wages generally correlated with the Communist Party vote, and low and moderate income households dominated among the party's supporters[1] (Clem and Craumer 1995:611–615; Hough et al. 1996:37, 56–58; Wyman 1997:120–121). In sum, the party's main constituency consisted of the socially weak, with pensioners especially central, both to the party's voting bloc and even more to its strong grassroots organization.

In the Duma election of December 1995 the CPRF placed first with more than 22 percent of the vote, nearly doubling its share of the electorate from the December 1993 level. The party's actual vote increased

TABLE 3.1 Votes Cast for CPRF by Occupation (in %)

	1993	1995
Self-employed, managerial, professional, clerical	9	12
Worker	9	25
Retired, housewife	21	32
Full-time student	0	4
Unemployed, disabled	4	19

SOURCE: Matthew Wyman, "Elections and Voting Behavior," in Stephen White, Alex Pravda, and Zvi Gitelman, eds., *Developments in Russian Politics* (Durham: Duke University Press, 1997), pp. 120–121. Calculations are by Matthew Wyman, from post-election surveys.

from 6.7 million to 14.4 million, and it gained a dominant position in the Duma. Three other left parties, the Agrarians, Popular Power, and the extremist Working Russia, together won 10 percent, marking a distinct left turn in the electorate. Because many parties failed to pass the 5 percent barrier for entry into the Duma, the Communists' vote translated into 35 percent of the seats, 157 of 450, nearly three times the number of the pro-government Our Home is Russia (NDR.)

The Communists formed a faction of 149 and delegated some members to give their much weaker Agrarian and Popular Power allies the 35 deputies needed to form separate factions (Urban and Solovei 1997:167; *FBIS* Jan. 11, 1996:32). This move was well-calculated to maximize the influence of the left parties in the Duma, as each faction could claim representation on the Duma Council, committee chairmanships and assignments, and seats on the conciliation commissions formed to iron out executive-legislative differences on the budget and other important legislation (Remington and Smith 1995). Members of these three factions chaired 13 of the Duma's 28 committees, including those for legislation, economic policy, and education and science.[2] They also had a total of 220 votes, just six votes short of the simple majority necessary to pass or reject legislation. The Communists and Agrarians had shown themselves to be disciplined parties, and in practice the left proved cohesive, especially on social policy issues.

The four other factions in the Duma were divided among Zhirinovsky's nationalist Liberal Democratic Party (LDP), the centrist Our Home and Russian Regions groupings, and the democratic-centrist Yabloko. They agreed on little. Effectively, the election gave the Communist-led left control of the lower house of the legislature and thus the possibility to pursue its restorationist social policy agenda through legislative initiative, bargaining over the federal budget, and blocking government initiatives to dismantle or "streamline" the welfare state.

Social Policy Legacies

The Communists confronted a social welfare system that was in shambles. The Soviet-era welfare state had provided nearly universal housing subsidies, health care, maternity and child benefits, pensions, etc., and laws mandating most of these remained on the books. Neoliberal reformers condemned the old system as too expensive and wasteful, but until the spring of 1997 they did not put forth a serious program of social policy reform. Rather, they cut subsidies and spending, left entitlements and basic services unfunded, made piecemeal policy changes, and let the system fall into disarray as the economy deteriorated.

Three major factors had combined to undercut past social protections:

1) Budgetary spending had fallen precipitously as a result of declines in both GDP and the per cent of GDP spent by all levels of government. Overall GDP had declined by about 40 percent from 1989–1995. The percent of that GDP expended by the Russian Federation's enlarged government budget declined from some 69 percent in 1992 to about 40 percent in 1995, and industrial subsidies that implicitly funded enterprise social services were severely cut. Explicit social expenditures were fairly well-protected at about 17 percent of GDP and continued to constitute the largest component of local budgets. However, they remained significantly below East European levels (see Ringold chapter) and fell in real terms as GDP declined (see Table 3.9) (OECD 1997:29; World Bank 1996a:21, 1996b:4–5). Expenditures could not keep up with mandated benefits, especially in regions hardest hit by the economic decline. For example, former Social Welfare Minister Lyudmila Bezlepkina reported that by 1995 there were "constant and massive months-long delays" in payment of child grants, and in many regions, these and other benefits were simply no longer provided (*Rossiiskie Vesti* Apr. 23, 1996:1–2).

2) A large part of social spending came from four extra-budgetary funds (EBFs), in which money was collected for social insurance, medical and unemployment insurance, and pensions, the last by far the largest of the four funds. Enterprises paid most of the contributions to the EBFs in the form of high payroll taxes, and a 40 percent decline in the level of real wages combined with mounting wage arrears and a shrinking labor force to produce deficits. The situation worsened as enterprises began to rely on barter transactions and illegal cash payments to avoid the high taxes, while the government scattered the EBFs resources among unreliable commercial banks (*Moskovskaya Pravda* Nov. 14, 1996:1; Stevenson 1998). Beginning in 1995, pensions arrears mounted, and in 1996 they more than doubled (see Table 3.2), while minimum pensions stood at less than half the minimum elderly subsistence level. By the spring of 1997, fewer than 25 percent of corporate entities were paying into the Pension Fund punctually, and it owed R15.7 trillion in unpaid pensions (*Rossiiskaya Gazeta* June 7, 1997: 2; Maleva n.d; World Bank 1996a:xviii).

3) In the communist period, many social services, including housing and utilities, were provided to workers and their families through the employing enterprise. In the post-privatization economy, both financial pressures and presidential decrees have pressed enterprises to shed some of these services, transfer them to local governments, or charge fees. Though there were patterns to these cuts (for example, kindergartens tended to go, housing to stay), overall, they were random, creating, as Dena Ringold

TABLE 3.2   Overdue Arrears to State Extrabudgetary Funds in Russia
(rubles trillion, in constant January 1995 rubles)

Year	Month	Arrears
1995	January	4.8
	December	9.0
1996	January	16.6
	November	38.7

SOURCE: Russian Economic Trends, 1997.1, p. 33. *Russian Economic Trends* is produced by the Working Centre for Economic Reform of the Russian Federation,
with the assistance of the London School of Economics' Centre for Economic
Performance team working within the Russian European Centre for Economic
Policy.

notes, "holes in the safety net." Virtually all employers scaled back social
provision, with enterprise directors and local governments deciding
which services would be continued and which terminated or privatized
(OECD 1996; Vinogradova 1996).

Unemployment has also emerged in Russia during the reform period.
While levels remained comparatively modest—about 10 percent of the
labor force in 1997—those affected lost not only wage income but also access to enterprise-based social services. In response, the Russian government added to its overburdened welfare system unemployment insurance and labor exchanges. But from the outset, relief was inadequate.
Benefits, set at a minimum of 15 percent of the subsistence level in 1995,
were too low, blocks to eligibility high, and only about one-third of those
eligible registered. Benefits were funded by a payroll tax paid into the
Employment Fund, an EBF that was subject to the familiar problems of
mounting payment arrears and misuse. Chronic deficits at the fund produced reductions and delays in paying benefits, even as the average du-
ration of unemployment increased. By 1997, a number of regions were
forced to abandon active labor market programs, such as counseling and
retraining, to concentrate all resources on direct benefit payments (Foley
and Klugman 1997; Maleva n.d.; Standing 1995).

In sum, the new Duma inherited a social welfare system that was drastically underfunded, faced with mounting deficits, and undergoing
piecemeal deconstruction. For many Russians, the social safety net had
collapsed: at least a quarter of the population lived in poverty, minimum
wages and pensions stood well below the subsistence level, and many
measures pointed to serious declines in levels of health, education, and
welfare (see Ringold chapter).

In considering the policy options available, both to the government
and to the left parties in the Duma, we must note here one critical feature
that distinguishes Russia from the postsocialist East European states. The

latter are law-governed states in which governments must either pay mandated welfare benefits or take decisions to cut or restructure those benefits. In Russia, a third option exists. As we have seen above, the government can simply fail or refuse to provide legally mandated benefits, or do so sporadically. The legal system is far too weak to enforce obligations, and citizens rarely seek to do so, though most believe strongly that the state is obligated to provide social welfare (Rose 1996). Since 1995, this third option has dominated in providing social services, divorcing policy debates from impacts on the population, and undercutting the accountability of both government and opposition.

The Left in the Legislature

Given both their rhetoric and the scale and complexity of the problem, the Communists' legislative agenda was modest, focusing mainly on increasing incomes among the poorer sectors of Russia's population (*Sovetskaya Rossiya* Feb. 17, 1996:2). The mainstay of their social policy was an effort to raise minimum pensions and wages, an effort into which they repeatedly put great legislative energy. Increasing the minimum wage was well calculated to shore up incomes at the bottom of society, because it formed the basis for calculating benefits to families, student grants, and other social payments. The focus on these issues also responded well to the interests of the Communists' relatively poorer and older constituency.

In February, March, April, July, November, and December 1996, and again in March, June, and September 1997, the Duma passed legislation to raise either minimum wages or pensions by 10–20 percent. In several cases they mustered the two-thirds majority needed to override a Federation Council veto, but Yeltsin finally signed only a couple of these measures: an increase in both wages and pensions in spring 1996, during the presidential race, when he also decreed large increases in payments to the poorest pensioners, and another increase in the minimum wage in December 1996, as part of a tacit deal to gain Communist approval of the 1997 federal budget. Yeltsin also vetoed Communist-sponsored legislation to establish a realistic uniform subsistence minimum (as it was, the Finance and Labor Ministries and the trade unions all used separate measures) to increase child benefits for single parents and to raise and index the wages of budget-sector workers in education and health care. The government condemned these legislative initiatives without exception as unaffordable and populist.[3]

Three conclusions may be drawn about the Communists' legislative agenda on social policy. First, they produced a large working majority at least on issues of poverty relief, with Yabloko and other non-left factions often supporting their initiatives.

Second, the presidential veto blocked much of their effort. The Communists were never able to put together the two-thirds majority in the more fiscally conservative Federation Council to override a presidential veto. When Yeltsin signed it was largely because of election-cycle pressures. The Communists' initiatives did contribute to putting pension increases and payment of wage and pension arrears at the center of the presidential election agenda, and the measures that passed produced some upward pressure on wages, as well as some improvement in real minimum pensions. These were modest achievements.

Third, the Communists' agenda offered virtually nothing to address the real underlying problems: the budget shortfall, the deficits of the EBFs, etc. They castigated the government for its failures but offered no real solutions.

The Left and Budgetary Politics

The 1997 draft federal budget was submitted to the Duma after years of fiscal austerity and radical declines in overall state spending (see Table 3.9). In the past, after months of criticizing the government's draft budgets the Communists and Agrarians had given their approval (Urban and Solovei 1997:110). But in 1996, the left was seemingly in a position to reject the draft and demand substantial changes, and if they were serious about restoring social protections, the budget was one place where they ostensibly had influence.

The budget that the government proposed at the end of August 1996 increased spending for defense and law enforcement while it decreased that for education, public health, and other social items (see Table 3.3). It assumed very low inflation, so allocated no funds for indexation of wages and other social payments. It projected a deficit of 3.3 percent of GDP, within IMF guidelines. Overall, this budget did not even hold steady in the social sphere.

TABLE 3.3   Budget Expenditures for Social Items (percent of GDP)

	1996 Confirmed Budget	1997 Draft Budget
National Defense	3.47	3.73
Law Enforcement	1.63	1.82
Education	0.66	0.62
Public Health	0.32	0.31
Culture and Art	0.12	0.11

SOURCE: *Rossiiskaya Gazeta*, Sept. 21, 1996, p. 9.

The Communists criticized the draft for its "antisocial bias," demanding more spending for investment, science, education, and health, provisions for indexing salaries and pensions, and allocations to repay 1996 wage and pension debts. The draft went back to the government for revision, then to a conciliation commission on which the left was strongly represented, but neither produced significant changes in social spending. Individual leftist deputies such as Communist Maslyukov and Agrarian Kulik pushed for higher deficits or currency emissions to provide for large spending increases, but Zyuganov did not move to unite the left behind either proposal.

In the end, the Communists supported a budget little different from that originally proposed, in exchange for a hodgepodge of "conditions," including prompt repayment of back wages and pensions, restructuring of enterprise debts, better access to the media for the Duma, and the promise of a large but elusive "development budget." The government proceeded to ignore most of these conditions. The Communists succeeded in gaining almost nothing for their social agenda from the budget process (*Rossiiskaya Gazeta* Oct. 19, 1996:1; Nov. 19:1–3; *Rossiiskie Vesti*, Dec. 7, 1996:3; *FBIS* Oct. 11, 1996; Oct. 30, 1996).

Why did the left fail to battle for its social agenda in budgetary politics? Its real options were quite limited. Increased currency emissions would produce inflation, hurting the Communists' large constituency of pensioners who lived mainly on fixed incomes. Higher government borrowing to fund a larger deficit would have raised interest rates and competed even more strongly with domestic investment, another Communist priority. In this important sense, economic constraints limited the Communists' options. In any case, the left must have realized that it could make little difference in actual spending patterns.

The fiscal condition of the Russian state, together with its extremely arbitrary enforcement of even those decisions that the Duma legally controls, rendered the Duma's apparent power over the budget nearly illusory. No matter what budget the Duma passed, it would have to rely on the state administration to collect the taxes that comprised the bulk of budget revenues, and the state's taxing capabilities were demonstrably weak.

But the problem extended beyond this: Yeltsin's government spent the money that it did collect largely as it wished, making unilateral changes in the allocation of budget funds. The Finance Ministry regularly refused to release allocated funds to other ministries, or to make required reports to the Duma. Auditors found gross violations of the Law on the Budget, and individual agencies, especially those in social services, often received a fraction of their allocated funds. For example, in September 1996, when overall budget allocations were met at 70–75 percent, the Health Ministry had received only 40 percent of allocated funds (*FBIS* Sept. 26, 1996). As a commentator in *Moskovskaya Pravda* aptly remarked,

> The passing or failure to pass the budget will not have a real impact on the economic situation. At the existing level of corruption of executive authority, no item is guaranteed. . . . The government finances expenditures as it sees fit, without consulting the State Duma. And often payments are made for items not foreseen in the state budget. The Government also "unceremoniously" cuts expenditures for other items (*Moskovskaya Pravda* Oct. 30, 1996:10, trans. in FBIS Oct. 30, 1996).

A combination of the state's weak administrative capacity, corruption, and arbitrariness undermines even those powers that the constitution gives the Duma and further limits its ability to influence social policy. Indeed, within a few months of the passage of the 1997 budget, the government was insisting that the Duma approve a "sequester" or cut of R108 trillion or 20 percent of the total budget, because of inadequate tax collections. The cuts were distributed unevenly over budget items, with the government initially proposing reductions of 55 percent in spending for agriculture, health, and culture (RFE/RL May 6, 1997). The Duma refused approval, a conciliation commission reached an impasse, and the cuts were nevertheless imposed. The 1998 budget was designed to incorporate the 1997 "sequester," providing even less in social spending, and the financial crisis beginning in mid-1998 rendered it irrelevant.

Comprehensive Social Welfare Reform

In the spring of 1997, the Russian government finally made the comprehensive restructuring of the social welfare system a policy priority. Under the leadership of newly appointed First Deputy Prime Minister Boris Nemtsov, Deputy Prime Minister Oleg Sysuyev, and First Deputy Minister of Labor Mikhail Dmitriyev, the government initiated a broad program to both streamline and rationalize social spending. Its central principle was the elimination of universal entitlements and their replacement with a system of means-tested benefits, a system that would both save money and target spending on the poor. Sysuyev, the major spokesman on these issues, identified social spending as a major source of the budget crisis and an intolerable burden on the economy. He argued that the existing system of universal benefits was neither justified, affordable, nor effective in alleviating poverty in the present context. Such benefit payments, Sysuyev argued, "made no sense for the prosperous, while for the needy they do not guarantee the necessary social protection" (*Delovoy Mir* June 18, 1997:2) and often went unpaid, helping no one. A number of government ministries and commissions, working with advisors from the World Bank and other international agencies, elaborated reform proposals in four major areas: housing and municipal services; social insurance benefits and state transfer payments; pensions; medical care; and education.

Housing and municipal service (or utility) subsidies constituted by far the largest item in local budgets, costing territories nearly 30 percent of their revenues, while users in most regions paid about one-third of real costs (World Bank 1996a:25; *Ekonomika i Zhizn* No. 13:27, March 1997). Subsidies were universal, benefiting households at all income levels. Beginning in 1996, the federal government, in one of its piecemeal efforts to deconstruct the old welfare state, had pressed cash-strapped municipalities to transfer charges to users, and a gradual shift had already begun (*Rossiiskaya Gazeta* July 11, 1996). Now it elaborated a comprehensive policy, including a timetable for transfer of costs to users over a five-year period with projected savings of more than R100 trillion (see Table 3.4), a system of means-tested reimbursements to families that met eligibility requirements, and measures to restrict "special" subsidies for government employees and veterans' families.

Implementation would have to be carried out locally and would be complicated, including calculations of both family income and amount of housing space per person. Nemtsov, placed in charge of housing sector reform, threatened that the federal government would withhold support from regions failing to implement the reform.

The system of social insurance and state transfer payments in Russia includes both universal entitlements and income-linked Social Insurance Fund (SIF) benefits. Overall it is not redistributive; nonpoor households receive benefits and transfers at higher rates than those below the poverty level, while 30 percent of the very poor receive no transfer payments from the government (World Bank 1995a). The major universal benefit is a system of child allowances, available to all families regardless of need (though with some variation in level). Reformers proposed to restrict eligibility for these payments through means testing and use some

TABLE 3.4　Planned Increase in User Fees as a Percent of Total Costs of Housing and Municipal Services in Russia

	1997	1998	1999	2000	2001	2002	2003
User Fees	35%	50%	60%	70%	80%	90%	100%

SOURCE: Ekonomika I Zhizn, No. 13, March 1997, p. 27; excerpts from the Russian Government Program "Structural Restructuring and Economic Growth From 1997 to 2000," "On Housing and Public Utilities Reform."

of the savings to raise benefit levels so that they would provide real poverty relief. In the case of the income-linked SIF benefits, including sickness and maternity for those in the labor force, reformers proposed restricting eligibility, reducing and capping benefits. Whereas the government could make some small administrative changes in these programs on its own, the proposed broad restructuring of the welfare system would involve changes in dozens of laws, each requiring the Duma's approval.

Reform of the system that provides pensions for 36 million Russians proved by far the most important and politically contentious aspect of reform. The pension system was mildly redistributive and had been relatively effective in keeping older Russians out of poverty, but accumulating pension arrears along with below-subsistence minimum payments were producing real hardship (Klugman 1997). Moreover, long-term demographic trends, similar to those illustrated by Ringold for Eastern Europe, would render Russia's pay-as-you-go system insolvent, even if short-term arrears could be eliminated.

To resolve immediate problems several proposals were generated, including raising the general age for eligibility, reducing payments for the seven million "working pensioners," eliminating special pensions and early retirement, raising workers' contributions to the pension fund, and expanding investment in nongovernmental pension funds (*Rossiiskaya Gazeta* June 7, 1997:2; *Rabochaya Tribuna* Sept. 24, 1997:2). Together, they would have reduced the entitlements of many in the current generation of pensioners. Development of a policy for long-term reform of the pension system proved more divisive within the government. After bitter debates, it rejected a "Chilean" model that would have left most Russians under the age of 30 entirely dependent on their own savings, and approved a three-tiered system with a state-run scheme as the key element, complemented by both state pensions and supplementary funded schemes (Maleva n.d.; *Trud* Aug. 16, 1997:1–2). All of these changes would require the Duma's approval.

Reforms of Russia's health and educational systems were also put on the drawing board at this time. In the summer of 1997, the government approved a concept for restructuring the public health care system, with basic medical services to be provided free and financed through mandatory medical insurance, while other services would become fee-based for all but the poor. These proposals took little account of Russia's failed experiment with mandatory medical insurance that was initiated in 1993 and produced a variety of unintended and dysfunctional consequences (Twigg 1998).

Finally, governmental reformers began work on an educational reform program that eventually produced proposals for the merger of higher educational institutions, replacement of universal stipends with means-tested assistance for the needy and student loans, and an increase in the numbers of paying students and commercially operated schools (*RFE/RL* June 30, 1998). These proposals would meet resistance from both the Duma and Russia's educational bureaucracy.

The government's reform program would have moved Russia far toward the model of the "liberal" welfare regime in which the state played a minimal role of providing means-tested benefits to the poor, while the bulk of the population provided for itself through private income and social insurance (Esping-Anderson 1990). The concept that the state should largely withdraw from social provision was, except when taken to an extreme, broadly accepted by governmental reformers. The proposed policy changes were formulated within the government through a policy process that included consultations with World Bank officials, who helped lay out both the principles of reform and many of the specific measures. The bank also supported the reform by providing an $800 million Social Adjustment Protection Loan (SPAL), with release of tranches contingent on progress in pension reform, establishment of poverty-targeted, means-tested benefit programs, and reform of the unemployment benefit system (Sederlof 1998). The argument that a poor state with weak taxing capacities should target benefits on those below the subsistence level seemed both compelling and humane.

But the reformers ignored or glossed over major technical and political problems. Means-tested benefits would require accurate information about household incomes, difficult in the Russian economy where at least 25 percent of activity was "unofficial" and unrecorded and administrative bureaucracies and procedures for testing were not in place. Local governments that had experimented with means testing found it to be expensive and cumbersome, and other studies have concluded that "means testing in partially monetized and fluid economies is unviable" (Deacon et al. 1997:136). Investment of pension funds in the highly unregulated Russian market would be extremely risky, as experience with nongovernmental pension funds had already shown. The reformers also ignored politics. Their approach was highly technocratic, barely acknowledging that large parts of Russian society, including many not far above the subsistence level, would lose claims to benefits and might demand or deserve some say in policymaking. They also took little account of the Duma majority's commitment to the old welfare state.

The Legislative Politics of Reform

Taken together, the government's program constituted a frontal challenge to the Communists and their leftist Duma allies, threatening to gut the social protections that the latter had committed themselves to defend. The proposed reforms would dramatically increase costs of housing and basic services, decrease state provision of medical care and education, and reduce the benefits of many of the pensioners who were so central to the Communists' constituency. The very comprehensiveness of the reform—the government's clearly stated intention to quickly remake Russia's welfare state in the liberal image—doomed it politically. Though the current system was patently unsustainable and the left had no real alternative, they met the government's reform package with nearly blanket rejection.

The first package of reform legislation was submitted to the Duma in May 1997, only weeks after Nemtsov and Sysuyev had been brought into the government. It was preceded by very limited consultation with the heads of relevant Duma and Federation Council committees. The legislation itself comprised a disparate group of several draft laws that would, among other things, have reduced sick pay and maternity benefits and replaced the universal system of child allowances. The government claimed that the changes would cut R30 trillion in spending, which would be used to pay pension and other arrears (*Rossiiskaya Gazeta* June 2, 1997:2; June Draft Leg. Pkg. 1997). The critical areas of general housing subsidies and pensions were not included in this legislative package, though major reform proposals in both areas were under active discussion.

The Duma rejected in the first reading all measures except reform of the child benefit system. The left bloc condemned the package as "antipeople," objecting especially to cuts in child and maternity benefits. Liberal Yabloko deputies were also skeptical, both of the government's savings estimates and of its promises that savings would be used to pay off arrears. Yabloko's Oksana Dmitriyeva, then chair of a budget subcommittee, urged deputies not to pass any of the measures until it was made clear "out of whose pocket this money is coming, and what there will be enough money [to pay] for, realistically speaking."

Ella Pamfilova, of the Russian Regions faction and former minister of social protection, called it a "collection of random elements that will not have any great impact, an attempt to allocate meager resources from the less needy to the more needy" (*Moskovskie Novosti* No. 25:22–29 June 1997:2). Deputies objected that there was no agreement on the "subsistence minimum," which would serve as a guideline, since the Duma's recently passed Law on the Minimum had not been approved by Yeltsin.

In the end, neither the government's bullying threats that pensions would remain unpaid unless the package passed, nor efforts at conciliation accomplished much. An amended version of the law on means testing child benefits did pass in the first reading, though this left it a long way from final approval.[4] The other measures were defeated by large majorities, with votes of 231 to 88, 226 to 70, and 200 to 122 (*Gosudarstvennaya Duma* 1997 N. 111 (253), I and II).

Of the parliamentary factions, only the pro-government NDR and Zhirinovsky's LDP supported the package. The left's opposition was a given. It was joined by Yabloko deputies who did not oppose rationalizing reforms as such but distrusted the government to carry them out honestly or efficiently, and by many others in the Duma who could not, morally or politically, support cuts in benefits to such a beleaguered population.

The executive-legislative conciliation commissions met through the summer, while the government continued to insist on the priority of social reform and to condemn the Duma for its irresponsibility. In the fall, Sysuyev submitted a new, elaborated package of social welfare bills, based on the same principles of eliminating beneficiary categories, capping benefits, and means testing (*Rossiiskie Vesti* July 22, 1997:2). Again the Duma passed only the measure on means-testing child benefits. The linchpin of the package, a draft federal law "On State Minimum Welfare Standards," which introduced a system of standards for wage and pension payments, education, health care, culture, social welfare, housing, and public utilities, was voted down 193 to 105 (FBIS Sept. 25, 1997, citing Itar-Tass). The Duma also demanded a two-year freeze on rent and utility payments, and it has rejected in principle any encroachment on the established rights of pensioners. Communist Party leader Zyuganov condemned the government's initiatives for "taking money away from children, sick women, the disabled," while at the same time noting the trillions of rubles of arrears in child benefit payments, clear evidence that the current system was also failing them (FBIS Oct. 1, 1997, citing Ekho Moskvy Radio).

In the aftermath of the government's fall defeat social policy reform lost momentum. Both government and Duma continued to work on "framework" legislation that would establish a subsistence minimum on which other payments could be based and define eligibility for welfare. In November 1997, Yelstin signed a federal law "On the Subsistence Minimum," that could lay the groundwork for social policy reform, but little further progress was made (*Rossiiskaya Gazeta* Oct. 29, 1997:1). At the beginning of 1998, the government acknowledged its failure in reforming the social sphere, while Zyuganov claimed success in blocking welfare cuts and reiterated his party's commitment to "restoring in full the people's guaranteed social rights." Yeltsin spoke more frankly, acknowledging that, "In the social sphere, a serious lack of money is still a bad problem. Free services are being replaced, without any controls, by paid . . . the poor are losing any real possibility of getting health care, education, and other services guaranteed by the state" (*Moskovskie Novosti* No. 1–2, Jan. 11–28, 1998:11).

Conclusion

How can we assess the effectiveness of Russia's Communists? Did they make a good faith effort to improve welfare and cushion the impacts of reform? Did they use their legislative resources effectively? How much were they constrained by political institutions and economic conditions? Did they produce a left alternative in welfare policy that advanced the interests of their constituents and consolidated support for their party?

The Communists used their resources well, translating a modest electoral victory into left dominance of the Duma and building broad coalitions around their legislative program to raise minimum wages and pensions, as well as to increase and index other benefits. Table 3.5 shows that their efforts contributed to some payment increases, though the minimum wage especially remained abysmally low in real terms.

Pressure from the legislature and Yeltsin's competition with Zyuganov for the votes of older Russians in the presidential race helped put payment of wage and pension arrears high on the list of governmental priorities in 1996 and 1997, producing substantial payoffs. In the end, most of the left's social policy initiatives met presidential vetoes and their impact remained small. In budgetary politics, too, we have seen that the left's influence was blunted both by economic constraints and by the poor capacity and corruption of the state administration. Moreover, the left's initiatives provided no solutions for the underlying structural deficits in the pension and other Social Insurance Funds. The payoff in pension arrears, for example, was accomplished mainly with funds from the World Bank and transfers from the federal government, and arrears mounted again in 1998.

TABLE 3.5 Minimum Wage, Minimum Pension, and Average Pension in Russia (% of subsistence level)

	Minimum Wage*	Average Pension*	Average Pension as % of Pensioner Subsistence Minimum**
1995	16%	69%	100%
1997	20%	80%	120%

SOURCE: *Russian Economic Trends*, 1998.1, pp. 46–47.

**T. Maleva and O. Syniyavskaya, "The Social Sphere," n.d., p. 37; data are for January 1996 and December 1997.

The Communists and their leftist allies were much more effective in blocking the government's reform program, which would have restricted the social rights and benefits of all social strata. Indeed, the left's real power in the Russian Duma is essentially negative because it cannot shape policy, but it *can* block change, and has done so, not only with social welfare but also with reform of the tax system and other critical areas. By blocking reform, the left has somewhat defended its constituency. There can be little doubt that the poorer and older sectors of society would be hurt most by increases in housing costs, cuts in payments to working pensioners, etc.—given that the government's promises of effective poverty relief are doubtful at best. At the same time, the system left in place is unfundable under current economic constraints, wasteful, often regressive in its distributive principles, and chronically fails to deliver mandated benefits (see Table 3.6).

The impasse over social policy in Russia both confirms and illustrates Haggard and Kaufman's (1995b) argument that consolidation of reform may be most difficult in a polarized party system in which major actors cannot reach, or will not seek, consensus. The reformist government's wholesale adoption of the liberal welfare state model confronted the Communists' socialist restorationism. Policy differences remained stark, with virtually no space for compromise or consensus building. Russia's constitutional setup contributed to this impasse. Even in the area of child benefits, where government and opposition essentially agreed on needed changes, legislation languished amidst broader conflicts.

At the same time, both policies are utopian and unfeasible. The Communists have no program for funding restored benefits. The government's promises that it would provide efficient, large-scale means testing and poverty relief in a reformed system were equally unrealistic, and were seen as such by Yabloko liberals, as well as many from other parties in the Duma. In a less polarized system, the left would presumably recognize some need for rationalization and spending cuts, working to maximize the claims of its relatively poor constituency in a reformed system, while liberal reformers would see the need for political compromises with the left.

TABLE 3.6   Child Benefit Arrears (rubles trillion)

	May 1997	October 1997	January 1998
Arrears	10	10.8	13

SOURCES: For 1997, *FBIS*, Oct. 1, 1997, citing *Ekho Moskvy* Radio; for 1998, *Country Year Report, Alfha Capital and Working Center for Economic Reform*, at http://www.securities.com.

It remains unclear whether the Communists consolidated support for their party from 1995 to early 1998, the period covered in this study. Polls report support for Zyuganov at 20–25 percent, about the level of the Communist vote in 1995. This percentage indicates that the party has retained a core constituency that is committed to it for several reasons. At the same time, overall approval of social policy outputs is low. In a fall 1997 survey, 97 percent of those polled thought that the government was doing a poor job of providing social protection for the needy (USIA 1998).

In the aftermath of the summer 1998 economic crisis, the left may be in a somewhat better position both to shape social policy in Russia and to be held accountable for it. The Primakov government was formed in the fall, with the support and participation of the Communist Party, at a time when economic constraints were especially severe and the official poverty level had increased to 30 percent. Zyuganov endorsed the goverment's proposals to increase state spending for social benefits and to introduce public works programs (*RFE/RL* Nov. 11, 1998). The coming months will tell whether the Russian left remains committed to its restorationist social policy or is forced by economic constraints to accept some of the cuts in spending and restructuring in social policy that it has rejected up to now.

Poland and Hungary

Poland and Hungary differ greatly from Russia in their social conditions and postcommunist social policies, but are similar enough to one another to be considered as a pair. In the first place, while Russia has experienced a collapse in state social spending during the transition and a collapse in state spending overall, Poland and Hungary have increased social spending since 1989, both as a percent of GDP and in real terms (Milanovic 1998). Second, Poland and Hungary have both pulled out of transitional recession and embarked on periods of dynamic economic growth, while Russia's economy remains in turmoil and decline. Third, although Russia's presidential institutions have prevented the CPRF from governing, social democratic successor parties won elections in Poland in 1993 and in Hungary in 1994 and governed their respective countries for four years, before losing elections in 1997 and 1998. In comparing the three cases, it is important to keep in mind these differences: whereas the Russian party has played an opposition role in a disastrous social and economic decline, the Polish and Hungarian successor parties—themselves very different from the CPRF—have conducted social policy in a far different set of circumstances.

Winning Coalitions

As discussed in the introduction and in Orenstein (1998), the social democratic successor parties of Poland and Hungary are different from restorationist, communist successor parties with their hard-line, old-timer constituency. These differences emerged in two stages between 1988 and 1991, as former communist parties in Central and Eastern Europe debated strategies for the future. The first stage of these parties' transformation consisted of battles between reformers and hard-liners over leadership in the post-communist era. In Hungary and Poland, reformers took control at party congresses in May 1988 and January 1990, respectively. They changed the parties' names and reorganized, losing most of their members in the process. The Hungarian Socialist Workers' Party became the Hungarian Socialist Party, dominated by reformers, while hard-liners split off to form their own Workers' Party (Agh 1995:494). In Poland, the communist party renamed itself the Social Democracy of the Republic of Poland and immersed itself in a coalition called the Democratic Left Alliance, which was made up of more than 30 left parties and associations.

New party labels and reform leadership went hand in hand with new programmatic designs and world outlooks. Both the Hungarian and the Polish parties applied for membership in the Socialist International, the international democratic socialist association founded in 1951 by West European left parties. Willy Brandt was its long-time president. After a few years of consideration and debate, the Hungarian and Polish successor parties were admitted to full membership in the Socialist International at its twentieth congress in New York in September 1996 (Socialist International 1996). In Russia and the Czech Republic, where hard-liners took control of the communist party organization, application for membership in the Socialist International has been out of the question.

A second stage in the transformation of communist successor parties in Hungary and Poland consisted of the establishment of electoral alliances with former official trade union movements. These proved crucial, for neither party had much of a working-class base. This became evident during the first fully free parliamentary elections, in Hungary in 1990 and in Poland in 1991, when social democratic successor parties failed to win a large share of the vote. Both parties won a surprisingly similar share, 10.9 percent in Hungary and 12.0 percent in Poland (see Figure 3.1), with disproportionate support coming from urban, middle-class professionals and managers associated with reform communism in the past (see Tables 3.10 and 3.11).

Social democratic successor parties realized that their political future lay with convincing blue-collar workers and other voters across the

FIGURE 3.1   Percentage of Votes for Communist Successor Parties in Parliamentary Elections

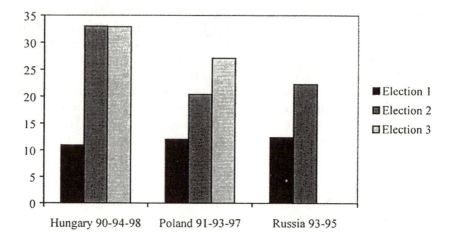

SOURCES: Richard Rose, Neil Munro, and Tom Mackie, *Elections in Central and Eastern Europe Since 1990*, Glasgow: University of Strathclyde Centre for the Study of Public Policy, 1998, for Poland 1991, 1993, 1997 and Hungary 1990, 1994. http://www.election.hu for Hungary 1998. Stephen White, Richard Rose, and Ian McAllister, *How Russia Votes*, Chatham, N.J.: Chatham House Publishers, 1997 for Russia.

socioeconomic spectrum to support their party. They wanted to become broad, left parties, representing diverse groups, with blue-collar workers being an important constituency. This provided the rationale for alliances with trade union movements that were forged in 1990 and 1991 in Poland and Hungary.

Trade unions in postcommunist Europe are relatively weak in broader European comparison. However, in extremely weak and demobilized postcommunist civil societies, trade unions remain among the strongest organizations. Furthermore, they are the only ones with broad, nationwide networks of branch offices that permeate the industrial working class, except perhaps for the church. In Poland and Hungary, these networks have proven their worth in electoral competition as a means of disseminating party messages and mobilizing working class support.

In short, the social democratic successor parties of Central Europe are catchall parties or cross-class alliances that include both nomenklatura

FIGURE 3.2   Percentage of Seats in Parliament for Communist Successor Parties

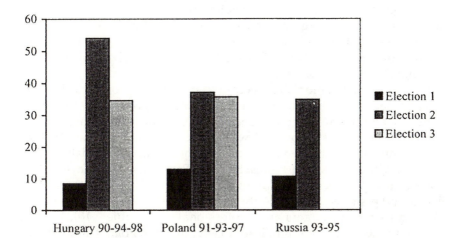

SOURCES: Richard Rose, Neil Munro, and Tom Mackie, *Elections in Central and Eastern Europe Since 1990*, Glasgow: University of Strathclyde Centre for the Study of Public Policy, 1998, for Poland 1991, 1993, 1997 and Hungary 1990, 1994. http://www.election.hu for Hungary 1998. Stephen White, Richard Rose, and Ian McAllister, *How Russia Votes*, Chatham, N.J.: Chatham House Publishers, 1997 for Russia.

elites who are winners of the transformation and many of its losers. In its 1997 electoral program, the Polish Democratic Left Alliance posed and answered the constituency question itself:

1. Who we represent. We are attached to the best tradition of the Polish left and European social democracy. We express the interests of various social groups, and at the same time we demonstrate the means and possibilities for their nonconflictual realization. We are particularly sensitive to the problems of those who benefit to a lesser extent than others from economic growth and who bear more than others the costs of transformation. In our activities, we direct ourselves to the principles of social justice and solidarity in the protection of the weakest social groups. (Sojusz 1997a:4, author's translation)

The Democratic Left Alliance continues to view the weakest social groups as potential constituencies. Upon taking leadership of the Democratic Left Alliance at its post-election party congress, Leszek Miller, a key engineer of the social democratic transformation of the party, announced that the party would attempt to mobilize those who did not participate in the 1997 elections. Nonvoters were disproportionately represented among the poorest and most socially disenfranchised segments of the population. Poland has suffered from high electoral volatility, in part because of the failure of all political parties to reach a sizeable segment of the eligible voter population.

Whereas social democratic successor parties have adopted a clear electoral strategy to appeal to relatively weak social groups, their core constituency and membership has been located among the managerial and professional groups associated with the communist regime. As Attila Agh points out, on the basis of a study of the Hungarian Socialist Party's membership database, the typical Socialist Party member in its first years "was a middle-aged, male, urban intellectual." Over half its members had a university education (Agh 1995). Its voter base was also heavily skewed toward managers and professionals (see Table 3.10). Working class votes became more significant to left parties in Poland and Hungary in the second postcommunist elections, which they won in 1993 and 1994, respectively.[5]

A reasonable degree of consensus has emerged from the survey literature, for instance that "the strong showing of the Hungarian Socialist Party in 1994 was the result of its ideological appeal to voters from across the spectrum of political parties and social groups" (Evans and Whitefield 1995: 1179), and that "left-right economic issues did not constitute the principal basis for voter discrimination among parties in 1994 but only a secondary, if highly significant component of it" (Evans and Whitefield 1995: 1198). In other words, the liberal-conservative divide remained prominent in 1993 in Poland and in 1994 in Hungary, with religion or religious practice being the most important determinant of party choice. But class voting increased, as predicted in Szelenyi, Fodor, and Hanley's "theory of the two axes." Class became an important determinant of left-party voting, with the working class especially moving to the left between the first two postcommunist elections in Poland and Hungary. However, neither the Polish nor the Hungarian successor party have become solely working-class parties. Both parties retained a high level of support among the managerial elite. These social democratic successor parties are cross-class, catchall alliances, united by a proreform vision that intends to also protect the interests of the less well-off.

This catchall nature provides a major part of the explanation why the social democratic successor parties have not engaged in a blanket rejection of market capitalism. The left parties' electoral programs in both Hungary and Poland supported a continuation of reform, desired by elites, and integration with the West. At the same time, the parties articulated a desire to guard some of most important social guarantees of communism and reduce the social costs of reform, especially for vulnerable groups. This was the cornerstone of their left identity and electoral strategy. As Kornai notes for Hungary:

> Many people voted for the Socialist Party hoping that it stood for socialist ideas. The party would be "left-wing." It would take sides with the poor, not the rich. It would soon set about improving the living conditions of the workers, the needy, and the pensioners. They hoped the party would defend the state system of paternalist care and perhaps even restore full employment and job security. (Kornai 1996: 970)

However, in contrast to Russia, the social-democratic successor parties did not promise to turn back the clock or move decisively away from market capitalism. In 1993, deputy chairman of the Democratic Left Alliance, Jozef Oleksy, said that, "The left can represent its voters properly only if it supports economic development . . . we are staunch supporters of a market economy" (*Reuters* August 31, 1993). At the same time, the alliance argued for a social market economy and used the slogan, "reforms must serve the people." Democratic Left Alliance chairman Aleksander Kwasniewski said that "Our program accepts . . . the rationalism necessary for the growth of the Polish economy, while bearing in mind the interests of working people" (*Polish Press Agency* August 10, 1993). Left parties in Poland and Hungary wanted to continue reform while reducing its social costs. Both elements were critical to their electoral success.

Social Policy Legacies and Challenges

Not only are the social democratic successor parties of Central Europe different from the Russian Communist Party in their constituencies, party genealogy, and election platforms, but they also inherited a completely different set of social conditions in 1993 and 1994. While Russia experienced a welfare state collapse under the presidency of Boris Yeltsin, left parties in Poland and Hungary came to power after a period of rapid, dramatic, and largely unplanned increases in state social spending.

Runaway Spending

These increases in state social spending arose for quite different social and political reasons in each country. Yet they are also part of a regionwide trend (see Ringold's chapter). Part of this trend is the "monetization" of social transfers after communism, in which widespread cuts in consumer subsidies and enterprise social benefits were replaced by increased cash

TABLE 3.7 Government Social Expenditures in Hungary

(1987 forint, bn per year, deflated by cost of living index)

	1987	1988	1989	1990	1991	1992	1993	1994	1995	1996
Pensions	110	113	116	116	111	106	111	112	101	100
as % of GDP	8.9	9.2	9.3	9.7	10.6	10.4	10.9	10.8	9.6	9.2
Family allowances	23	32	39	37	35	32	31	25	19	14
as % of GDP	1.9	2.6	3.1	3.1	3.3	3.1	3.1	2.4	1.8	1.3
Child allowances	2	10	11	10	11	13	11	10	8	5
as % of GDP	0.2	0.8	0.9	0.8	1.0	1.3	1.1	1.0	0.8	0.5
Sick leave	13	15	16	14	12	10	10	14	11	6
as % of GDP	1.1	1.2	1.3	1.2	1.1	1.0	1.0	1.3	1.0	0.6
Unemployment benefits		1	1	2	8	16	21	16	12	
as % of GDP		0.1	0.1	0.2	0.8	1.6	2.1	1.5	1.1	
Other: scholarships	2	1	1	1	2	2	16	17	15	
as % of GDP	0.2	0.1	0.1	0.1	0.2	0.2	1.6	1.6	1.4	
TOTAL CASH TRANSFERS	150	172	184	181	179	180	199	194	167	
as % of GDP	12.2	14.0	14.9	15.2	17.0	17.7	19.7	18.6	15.8	
Education	50	56	67	69	62	64	66	66	48	
as % of GDP	4.1	4.6	5.4	5.8	5.9	6.3	6.6	6.3	4.5	
Health	33	38	58	63	63	63	63	61	55	
as % of GDP	2.7	3.1	4.7	5.3	6.0	6.2	6.3	5.9	5.2	
TOTAL IN-KIND TRANSFERS	82	94	125	132	125	127	128	128	103	
as % of GDP	6.7	7.7	10.1	11.1	11.9	12.5	12.7	12.3	9.8	
TOTAL TRANSFERS as % of GDP	20	22	25	27	31	31	33	31	26	

SOURCE: Branko Milanovic, *Income, Inequality, and Poverty during the Transition from Planned to Market Economy*, Washington, D.C.: The World Bank, 1998, supplementary tables provided by author and own calculations. Reprinted by permission.
NOTE: Expenditure data here are derived from survey data and may differ from goverment budget data quoted elsewhere in this volume. See Milanovic for further details on methodology.

TABLE 3.8 Government Social Expenditures in Poland

(1987 zloty, bn per year, deflated by cost of living index)

	1987	1988	1989	1990	1991	1992	1993	1994	1995	1996
Pensions (gross)	1229	1293	1344	1271	1550	1787	1825	1978	2066	2137
as % GDP	7.3	6.9	6.5	8.1	12.4	14.7	14.9	15.8	15.5	15.1
Family allowances	187	294	415	223	231	257	185	169	131	145
as % GDP	1.1	1.6	2.0	1.4	1.8	2.1	1.5	1.4	1.0	1.0
Child allowances	13	15	6	16	28	25	22	19	17	17
as % GDP	0.1	0.1	0.03	0.1	0.2	0.2	0.2	0.2	0.1	0.1
Sick leave	14	13	9	113	140	47	64	84	80	110
as % GDP	0.1	0.1	0.05	0.7	1.1	0.4	0.5	0.7	0.6	0.8
Unemployment benefits				50	170	159	142	151	169	171
as % GDP				0.3	1.4	1.3	1.2	1.2	1.3	1.2
Other: scholarships	12	19	19	21	13	10	10	20		
as % GDP	0.1	0.1	0.1	0.1	0.1	0.1	0.1	0.2		
Social assistance				32	52	66	69	71	55	55
as % GDP				0.2	0.4	0.5	0.6	0.6	0.4	0.4
TOTAL CASH TRANSFERS	1453	1634	1793	1727	2184	2350	2317	2491	2519	2634
as % GDP	8.6	8.8	8.7	11.0	17.4	19.3	18.9	19.9	18.9	18.6
Education	607	636	760	750	529	530	507	555	581	324
as % GDP	3.6	3.4	3.7	4.8	4.2	4.4	4.1	4.4	4.4	2.3
Health	541	564	660	653	591	604	561	566	612	651
as % GDP	3.2	3.0	3.2	4.2	4.7	5.0	4.6	4.5	4.6	4.6
TOTAL IN-KIND TRANSFERS	1149	1200	1420	1404	1121	1134	1068	1121	1193	974
as % GDP	6.8	6.4	6.9	8.9	8.9	9.3	8.7	9.0	9.0	6.9
TOTAL TRANSFERS										
as % GDP	16.7	16.4	16.3	19.9	26.3	28.6	27.6	28.8	27.9	25.5

SOURCE: Branko Milanovic, *Income, Inequality, and Poverty during the Transition from Planned to Market Economy*, Washington, D.C.: The World Bank, 1998, 211–212, and own calculations. Reprinted by permission.

NOTE: Expenditure data here are derived from survey data and may differ from goverment budget data quoted elsewhere in this volume. See Milanovic for further details on methodology.

TABLE 3.9 Government Social Expenditures in Russia

(1987 rubles, bn per year, deflated by cost of living index)

	1987	1988	1989	1990	1991	1992	1993	1994	1995	1996
Pensions (gross)	30.9	32.2	32.3	36.3	29.1	18.7	25.5	21.5	17.1	17.0
as % GDP	6.2	6.1	6.0	6.4	4.8	3.9	6.0	5.8	5.1	5.6
Family allowances	8.4	9.2	10.7	10.8	5.0	1.3	2.5	2.6	0.2	2.6
as % GDP	1.7	1.8	2.0	1.9	0.8	0.3	0.6	0.7	0.1	0.9
Child allowancees					1.3	0.1				
as % GDP					0.2	0.01				
Sick leave							4.0	3.9	3.5	2.5
as % GDP							0.9	1.1	1.1	0.8
Unemployment benefits					0.1	0.2	0.3	0.5	0.7	0.5
as % GDP					0.01	0.04	0.1	0.1	0.2	0.2
Other: scholarships, bread subsidies, social assistance				0.6	5.2	4.7	5.4	1.5		
as % GDP					0.1	1.1	1.1			
TOTAL CASH TRANSFERS	39.3	41.4	43.0	47.1	36.2	25.5	37.1	33.9	21.6	22.6
as % GDP	7.9	7.9	8.0	8.3	6.0	5.4	8.7	9.2	6.5	7.4
Education	16.8	18.2	18.4	19.6	21.5	16.8	17.1	16.0	11.3	
as % GDP	3.4	3.5	3.4	3.5	3.6	3.5	4.0	4.4	3.4	
Health	10.1	11.1	11.8	12.9	14.5	11.6	13.4	11.5	8.1	
as % GDP	2.0	2.1	2.2	2.3	2.4	2.4	3.2	3.1	2.4	
TOTAL IN-KIND TRANSFERS	26.9	29.3	30.2	32.5	36.0	28.3	30.5	27.5	19.5	
as % GDP	5.4	5.6	5.6	5.7	6.0	6.0	7.2	7.5	5.8	
TOTAL TRANSFERS										
as % GDP	13.4	13.4	15.0	14.1	16.8	13.8	15.9	16.7	12.3	

SOURCE: Branko Milanovic, Income, Inequality, and Poverty during the Transition from Planned to Market Economy, Washington, D.C.: The World Bank, 1998, 199–200, and own calculations. Reprinted by permission.
NOTE: Expenditure data here are derived from survey data and may differ from goverment budget data quoted elsewhere in this volume. See Milanovic for further details on methodology.

FIGURE 3.3   Total Cash Transfers as Percent of GDP, 1987–1996

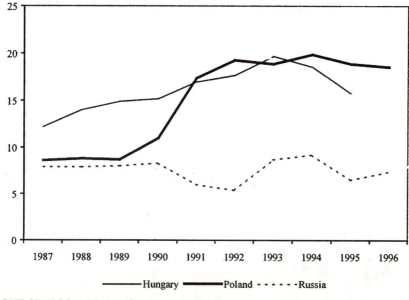

SOURCE: Tables 3.7–3.9 above.

FIGURE 3.4   Real Value Index of Total Cash Transfers, 1987=100

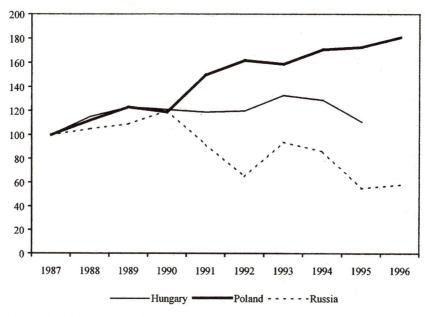

SOURCE: Tables 3.7–3.9 above.

benefits to individuals and households (Milanovic 1996). Cain and Surdej show in this book that a combination of historical legacies, transition social policies, and normal democratic politics explain spending increases.

A few general points: First, transition social policies played a major role in driving up welfare spending in Central and Eastern Europe. Second, these transition social policy decisions were mostly ad hoc (Offe 1993; Kornai 1996:966). Third, ad hoc policymaking dominated because reform governments did not prioritize social policy in the early years of transformation (Deacon 1997:92). This lack of emphasis reflected the advice of powerful international advisers and consultants at a time when the neoliberal "Washington consensus" was at its peak. Jeffrey Sachs, for instance, wrote that, "Although there are many submodels within Western Europe, with distinct versions of the modern welfare state, the Western European economies share a common core of capitalist institutions. It is that common core that should be the aim of the Eastern European reforms" (Sachs 1993:5). While crafting a common core of stabilization, liberalization, and privatization policies, social policy was largely ignored.

Postcommunist social policy was therefore rudderless in the first stage of transition, subject to policy drift, policy failure, and mistakes of omission and commission. As Ringold points out, this relative neglect seems odd when one considers that social expenditure now accounts for 15–25 percent of GDP in most postcommunist countries. That neglect furthermore should have produced rapid increases in social spending seems doubly odd, especially when one considers that Poland was implementing at the same time a radical shock therapy program that aimed to reduce the role of the state in the economy. Indeed, chief reformer Leszek Balcerowicz has acknowledged that the failure to reform the social sector was the greatest mistake of the Polish transformation (see Cain and Surdej in this book).

Part of the failure of neoliberal social policy in Central Europe can be explained by policy neglect. On the other hand, where typically liberal social policies were introduced, such as efforts to "target" social benefits to only the very poor and those temporarily in need, these resulted in surprising policy failures. Liberal social policy in postcommunist Europe was directed largely toward solving the unemployment problem, which was expected to be the main social problem of transition, and the main potential source of mass opposition to reform. Much attention was paid to setting up systems of unemployment benefits in countries where unemployment had not formally existed under communism. Yet Boeri (1998:1–3) find that these unemployment benefit and assistance policies generally failed to serve important social assistance and labor market goals.

Poland

Poland's experience is perhaps the most extreme. One component of the fight against unemployment in Poland was the use of early retirement as a means of reducing the labor force; but this backfired badly. First, many people took early retirement and then continued to work, often in the same jobs as before, simply using their early retirement income as a supplemental wage. Second, because the Polish pension system is not very redistributive, and became less redistributive during the early years of transition (Rutkowski 1998:54), early retirement has disproportionately benefited those less in need at great expense. A policy of means-tested social minimums, as in the Czech Republic, or a social citizenship wage would have better served vulnerable social groups. However in Poland, high pension spending crowded out better-targeted social programs.

Poland also created a system of unemployment benefits. Unemployment benefits have been extensive and reasonably well targeted, but not well coordinated with social assistance programs. They have not played the same role as unemployment benefits in the West, providing a means for support between jobs, but instead have proved a dead end. Most Poles who run out of unemployment benefits end up on some other form of social assistance. Meanwhile, Poland has spent little on active labor market policies designed to retrain, reeducate, and relocate workers in new jobs and has developed alarming pockets of long-term unemployed, half of whom would refuse retraining even if it were offered them.

In short, introduction of liberal, targeted, welfare state measures in Poland had the perverse effect of being extremely costly, ineffective, and largely misdirected. As one major World Bank report on Poland concludes, "the growth in pension spending has overshadowed what was assumed to be the major focus of the social welfare budget during the transition, namely a social safety net to protect vulnerable groups from emerging risks" (Rutkowski 1998:6).

Neoliberal social policy measures were ill conceived, ill executed, and ill performing. They caused Poland, a leader in neoliberal transition policy, to develop a misshapen and rapidly expanding welfare state between 1989 and 1993. This formed an important part of the legacy that the Democratic Left Alliance inherited when it took office.

Hungary

In Hungary, dramatic increases in social spending had different programmatic and political sources. It was not mainly pensions in Hungary, but better-directed social assistance programs, that fueled spending increases.

Policymaking in Hungary was not dominated by liberal reformers who introduced misguided efforts at targeting, but by communist and later conservative governments that increased spending to avoid an outbreak of social protest.

Both Hungary's last communist governments and the first postcommunist center-right government, led by the Hungarian Democratic Forum from 1990 to 1994, wanted to maintain as far as possible the social benefits of communism, rather than shift policies in a liberal direction. "Hungary, in its economic policy priorities, placed great weight on raising today's material welfare and, in the subsequent period of mounting economic problems and stagnating or declining production, on curbing the fall in living standards" (Kornai 1996:944).

Goulash communism was set in this mold, and Kornai argues that policies of moderation or consumer appeasement continued after 1990. They were reaffirmed in response to the Budapest taxi drivers' strike of 1990, after which center-right governments "never again took action that would elicit mass opposition" (Kornai 1996:951). There was no radical liberal break in economic policy in 1989 or 1990.

Such a cautious stance toward market reform, ongoing since the 1960s, spawned social policies that aimed to continue socialist-era guarantees and cushion the transition to a market economy. Hungary developed an extensive set of social assistance measures, which by 1993 included a half-year pregnancy allowance at full pay for working mothers, a child care fee that replaced 65–75 percent of previous gross wages until a child's second birthday, a fixed child care allowance paid until a child's third birthday, a family allowance for all children until their sixteenth birthday, a third child allowance for poorer families, social assistance for the long-term unemployed, and other local benefits (World Bank 1996c:26–27).

During the transition, these guarantees were not relinquished, even though in addition to pension and health insurance rates, this meant pushing payroll tax contributions for social security up to 54 percent of gross wages. Hungary began to spend far more on social welfare than it could possibly afford, running ever higher budget deficits, that reached 7 percent of GDP in 1994.

Evaluating Constraints

Against the background of a rapid increase of state social spending in both countries, left parties in Poland and Hungary faced a peculiar set of social policy challenges in 1993 and 1994. In both cases, living standards had fallen mostly as a result of declines in aggregate output, so these parties had to be dedicated to restarting growth if they were to improve social conditions. On the other hand, major restructuring of the social welfare state, postponed or botched by previous communist and center-right governments, needed to be launched. Yet spending levels and payroll tax levels had seemingly reached an absolute maximum, having grown sharply in previous years. Fashioning international credibility for left parties was a further restraining factor in countries that hoped to join the European Union.

Because they came to power after a dramatic increase in state social spending, left governments in Central Europe cannot be judged by their impact on spending alone. In most cases, spending had to be brought under control. They must also be judged according to their contribution to long-term structural change, their contribution to improving the living standards of the worst off in society, and in relation to their stated policy goals, which were very different than the restorationist policies advocated by the Russian communists.

The Polish Left in Government, 1993–1997

The left government formed in Poland in 1993 articulated a strategy for continuing Poland's transformation that differed substantially from the liberal Balcerowicz Plan's "stabilization, liberalization, and privatization" (Blazyca and Rapacki 1996:89). Its 1994 program, "Strategy for Poland," proposed to continue with market-oriented reform while focusing more on the social dimension of change. The left government stabilized and gradually increased social budgets, implemented a wide range of structural changes, and defined a broad center ground on social policy issues, that seemed geared to appeal to the median voter. Inclusion of social rights in the 1997 Polish constitution and the launching of a major reform of the pension system were big steps. Although not radically redirecting spending priorities, the Democratic Left Alliance made reasonable steps toward fulfilling its social policy agenda. It furthermore played an important role in reestablishing legitimacy for the social functions of the state, after years of rhetorical attack from the right.

Constraints. In its social policy, the Democratic Left Alliance was severely constrained by domestic political factors—in the first place its coalition with the Polish Peasant Party. After winning parliamentary elections in September 1993, the Democratic Left Alliance initially proposed a coalition with the liberal Freedom Union, the number three vote-winner (Zubek 1995:300–301). This would have allowed the Democratic Left to better establish its pro-reform credentials and avoid being isolated as a communist successor party. However, the dissident-based Freedom Union refused cooperation.

The Democratic Left was thus forced into a coalition with the Polish Peasant Party (PSL), the second-largest vote winner. Together, the two parties held two-thirds of the seats in the lower house of parliament,

TABLE 3.10   Votes Cast for Left Parties* in Poland by Occupation (in percentages)

	1991	1993
Managers	26.3	41.0
Professionals	19.0	28.8
White Collar	33.0	46.6
Blue Collar	28.3	51.1
Farm Workers	29.2	51.6
Inactive	29.2	41.8
Total	31.1	44.8

*Includes vote for all left parties, not just Democratic Left Alliance.

SOURCE: Ivan Szelenyi, Eva Fodor, and Eric Hanley, "Left Turn in PostCommunist Politics: Bringing Class Back In?" *East European Politics and Societies* 11:1, Winter 1997, p. 219. © 1997 by ACLS. Reprinted by permission.

which should have facilitated major legislative initiatives. However, the Peasants proved to be a difficult coalition partner, especially from the point of view of economic reform. They were skeptical of structural change. The Peasant Party wanted instead to pump up subsidies to rural areas and fill posts in local and regional administrations, the bread and butter of its party life. All reform initiatives originated from the Democratic Left, with the Peasant Party normally demanding political payoffs in return for accepting change.

Strategy for Poland.   Despite these conflicts within the government, the coalition enunciated a major shift from the priorities of previous center-right governments on social and economic policy. The centerpiece of this effort was a medium-term economic program, Strategy for Poland (Blazyca and Rapacki 1996:89). The document was drafted by Grzegorz Kolodko's Finance Ministry and approved by the coalition government in June 1994 (Hausner 1998:18). The strategy stressed the social dimension of reform, labor relations, and state administrative reform, in contrast to the liberal economic program of stabilization, liberalization and privatization. It enunciated ten strategic goals:

Decrease the social costs of reform;
Create a strategic concept of economic development;
Establish a partnership system of labor relations;
Achieve fast economic growth;
Achieve microeconomic and system stabilization;
Improve living standards;
Improve competitiveness of Polish exports;

Quickly join the European Union;
Reform the central economic institutions of the state;
Improve stability and security, including lasting social peace.

These goals are broadly similar in content to those outlined by the Democratic Left Alliance in its 1993 campaign platform, "Our Program for Poland," although they also bear the imprint of a politically independent finance minister. How far was the Strategy for Poland implemented? And how much of a difference did it make?

On face value, the left government made significant progress in pursuing the Strategy for Poland. One of the government's first acts in office was to increase the minimum wage as well as minimum pensions and pension indexation (see Cain and Surdej in this book; Sojusz 1997b:101). Although these increases were small, they decreased the costs of reform (goal 1) to vulnerable social groups. The left government also took steps to establish a "partnership system of labor relations" (goal 3) with the creation of a Tripartite Commission on Socio-Economic Issues in February 1994. This commission did not have sufficient power to develop into an effective wage-bargaining mechanism at the national level (Hausner 1995:116–117), but it was brought into existence and took on a life of its own. The government launched a successful reform of the economic administration of the state (goal 9) that consolidated a multiplicity of economic ministries into the new Ministries of Treasury and Economy.

Although the left government cannot take full credit for rapid economic growth between 1993 and 1997 (goal 4), its macroeconomic policy of running a near-3 percent budget deficit (the Maastricht treaty maximum) and increasing public spending in real terms helped fuel growth. Fast growth contributed to an increase in living standards (goal 6) and to an improvement in Poland's prospects for membership in the European Union (goal 8) between 1993–1997. The Strategy for Poland also included a proposal to overhaul Poland's expensive and misdirected pension system, which sparked a major reform in 1997–1998.

Policies did change under the left government, but they did not improve living standards as much as the Democratic Left Alliance promised or expected. In its own evaluation of its record in government in fulfilling its campaign promises, the Alliance notes that, "The determination of the Democratic Left Alliance parliamentary club in aiming to reduce the social costs of reform and improve the living standards of citizens, brought gradual (although not yet to the extent expected) effects" (Sojusz 1997b:70). Poverty and unemployment rates in Poland remained high throughout the period. The left government had its greatest successes elsewhere, especially in passing a new Constitution of the Republic of Poland in May 1997, a document that included declaratory social rights. However, in actually delivering increased social spending, radical restructuring of the social safety net, or improved living standards for the poorest in society, the record of the Democratic Left is equivocal.

Social Spending. Let's take social expenditures first. Looking closely at Figures 3.3 and 3.4, we can see two interesting trends in social expenditures under the Democratic Left-Peasant Party government. First, social spending decreased slightly as a percentage of GDP. Second, social spending increased in real terms. This reflected the basic budgetary principle of the Strategy for Poland, to increase state spending moderately in real terms, while shrinking the public sector share in the total economy. This way, the left government in Poland managed to satisfy both social and liberal goals simultaneously.

The same approach was used to elevate public sector wages, which had fallen sharply under previous austerity budgets, driving talent out of the civil service. Doling out small, but consistent, budgetary increases to numerous groups was the preferred budgetary strategy of the Democratic Left-Peasant Party government. The relatively rapid growth that Poland enjoyed between 1993 and 1997 no doubt contributed to this policy's success, since it gave considerable scope for increased state expenditures while still cutting the state budget as a proportion of GDP.

However, the left did not significantly reorient social spending toward poverty reduction, or reverse increases in inequality. The major social spending issue in Poland was necessarily pension spending, which at 15 percent of GDP by 1993, was crowding out other forms of social spending that were better targeted to the poor. Any effort to redress poverty would have to involve cutting pension expenditures. Yet the trade-offs between the interests of pensioners and the poor became the source of intense political infighting within the Democratic Left Alliance, as was the issue of the farmers' pension insurance fund, where contributions covered only a miniscule proportion of benefits. Left government policies changed over time, at first increasing minimum pension levels and indexation in 1994, and later cutting indexation in 1996 in preparation for a major reform that would substantially reduce pension costs over time.

Meanwhile, in 1995, the government engaged in a liberal policy to target family benefits to families earning less than one-half the average. More than one million families were cut from the roles (UNICEF 1997:100). Some of the savings generated by the reduction in family benefits in 1995 were used to increase unemployment benefits, which were found by the World Bank to be better targeted to the poor in Poland than family benefits (World Bank 1995b:42–45), while the rest was eaten up by pensions (see Table 3.8).

However, none of these spending changes had as radical an impact as the ones introduced in 1989–1993, at least in the present. In its current social expenditures, the left government did not significantly shift from the priorities of previous liberal and center-right governments, although its 1996 changes in pension indexation and 1997 legislative overhaul of the pension system will have enormous long-term impact.

Structural Change. In tandem with gradual shifts in the budget, the left government promoted structural change in many key social policy areas. The government created a Guarantee Fund for Workers' Services in 1994, to finance claims of workers against insolvent enterprises. It mandated the creation of Social Service Funds in all enterprises, both public and private, to finance enterprise social benefits. Whereas the range of benefits is decided by the management of each enterprise itself, the amount is a mandated share of employee wages, 37.5 percent of the average monthly wage per employee each year (Pietrzak-Paciorek 1996). The government introduced 200 amendments to the Polish Labor Code in early 1996, discussed in tripartite negotiations, that were interpreted as going "further than the statutory regulations of other European countries, where more beneficial terms for employees are decided by collective agreements" (Pietrzak-Paciorek 1996).

The government introduced some major changes to unemployment policy, including a Program for Promoting Labor Productivity and Decreasing Unemployment in November 1995 and a Program for Youth Career Activation in December 1995. The latter changed the practice of awarding unemployment benefits to those leaving school and instead encouraged further education and internship programs. The left government also went ahead with a sweeping health reform, created in cooperation with the World Bank, based on new regional health insurance funds, central state oversight, and competition among health care providers (Sojusz 1997b:97–108).

Pension Reform. Undoubtedly the most important social policy initiative of the left government was a radical reform of the pension system launched in 1995–1997. Various pension reform proposals had been bounced around in Poland since 1991, but those included in the Strategy for Poland in 1994, and elaborated in 1995, reflected a new start. Pressure on the pension system had been mounting, from skyrocketing costs between 1989 and 1993 and a series of Constitutional Tribunal decisions that forced the government to end its practice of making ad hoc adjustments in pension indexation to reduce pension fund deficits (Hausner 1998:17). However, the Democratic Left Alliance was split on how to proceed. This split underlined divisions between liberal and traditional leftist policy orientations in the alliance.

The independent, liberal Finance Minister Grzegorz Kolodko and the leftist Labor Minister Leszek Miller divided over two issues: pension indexation and broader structural reform of the pension system. Miller, a popular politician, took it upon himself to represent the interests of pensioners. He supported restoring full pension indexation, where previous governments had been forced to cut it, and advocated a moderate reform of the pension system that would limit special privileges, raise contributions to the farmers' system, introduce new disability rules, and gradually increase the retirement age.

Finance Minister Kolodko wanted to reduce pension indexation by linking pensions to prices rather than wages and to introduce a more radical structural change, including a mandatory, funded, private insurance system to supplement the state pay-as-you-go system (Hausner 1998:18). Miller viewed these as potentially unpopular measures, being more attuned to the concerns of left party constituencies. The policy standoff between the two men lasted until the middle of 1996.

In 1996, after a government reshuffle, Miller was transferred to the Ministry of Interior, while the new prime minister and minister of labor both supported the more radical version of pension reform. Finance Minister Kolodko introduced price indexation of pensions in October 1996 (Hausner 1998:18). Labor Minister Andrzej Baczkowski, a former Solidarity activist, made pension reform in Poland a bipartisan affair.

Appointed the first plenipotentiary for Social Security reform, Baczkowski forged alliances between the most politically independent members of government, representatives of Solidarity, the opposition Freedom Union, and The World Bank, all of whom worked together in the plenipotentiary's office. This gave liberals a major say in drafting reform, but the office was under the political direction of the left, which tempered reform proposals by a strict view to how they would sell. In doing so, the left government was guided heavily by public opinion polls that showed that the Polish population wanted more radical reform than that proposed by Miller in 1995 (Hausner 1998:18).

The left government also prepared the way by gaining the support of trade unions and business associations in tripartite negotiations in autumn 1995 (Hausner 1998:18; interview with Ryszard Lepik, July 1998). Extensively public-opinion tested, negotiated, and legislated by disparate political forces, pension reform in Poland became the keystone of a new centrist consensus on social policy.[6]

The new pension system links benefits more clearly and transparently to contributions, but reduces levels of redistribution. It guarantees a minimum pension to those working a minimum service period, but also provides incentives for workers to retire later as replacement rates fall. A mandatory second pillar was created under the new system through which mandatory payroll contributions will be channeled to private pension funds of the employee's choice. Workers under 30 must participate in the new system; those 30–50 can choose; and people over 50 neither contribute to, nor benefit from, the new system. For them, a reformed state system remains in effect.

Employees under the new system will have 12–22 percent of their gross wages channeled to the reformed state system and 7.3 percent to the private, funded system. An additional 17.48 percent will continue to fund state disability pensions and other benefits, including injury, sickness, and some family benefits (Gora and Rutkowski 1998). In its early stages, the new pension system will be extremely expensive for the state, which will have to continue funding its commitments under the old system and replace that part of payroll tax revenues now directed to private funds.

In the long term, the creation of large, private pension funds is expected to spur the development of Polish capital markets, provide more funds for investment, and fuel growth, improving the health of the economy, producing more tax revenues and enabling higher wages and pensions overall. Especially striking in Poland's new pension system is the level of bipartisan support for the program and its widespread public acceptance. Together with the principles enunciated in the Polish Constitution of 1997, pension reform seems to signal a new social policy consensus in Poland that combines liberal and social democratic elements.

Constitution and Consensus. The 1997 constitution, which was pushed through parliament and a victorious national referendum largely by the Democratic Left Alliance and President Aleksander Kwasniewski, included a substantial list of declaratory social rights, among them the right to state-provided health care and housing. However, these social rights were the product of complex bargaining between the four parties that supported the new constitution: the Democratic Left Alliance, the Polish Peasant Party, the Union of Labor, and Freedom Union.

Social rights were included at the request of the Democratic Left Alliance, while the liberal Freedom Union opposed them and instead lobbied for the constitutionalization of certain monetary and fiscal targets, including the Maastricht criteria for accession to the European Monetary Union and a restriction on government borrowing from the central bank. Right parties now grouped in the Solidarity Electoral Alliance lobbied for, but did not obtain, a ban on abortion.

Part of the overall political settlement on the new constitution was the ratification of the concordat signed with the Vatican in 1993 by a right government, something that much of the secular, and partly anticlerical, Democratic Left opposed. Among other things, the concordat allowed local priests to exclude certain individuals, including communists and abortion rights advocates, from burial in local cemeteries, when sometimes the Catholic cemetery is the only one in town. It also gave church marriages legal standing without approval from the civil authorities (*Polityka* December 5, 1998).

Whereas the importance of declaratory social rights in a constitution is always disputable, in the case of Poland, had the Democratic Left not pushed for the concept of social rights, the constitution would have enunciated quite different social principles. In the battle to redefine the social character of Poland, the Democratic Left has played a critical role, positioning it within the context of a social Europe.

In the pension reform and the 1997 constitution, a new middle ground has emerged in Polish social policy as a direct result of political compromise. Liberal principles have a great deal of weight in this middle ground, but so do state commitments to provide a certain level of social welfare and conservative values of work and family. Although the Democratic Left Alliance can be criticized for not having pursued a strongly partisan left social policy, it did something different. It geared policies toward the median voter and tried to forge durable compromises between the three perspectives that dominate Polish politics—liberalism, social democracy, and Catholic conservatism—while asserting some traditional left objectives. The Democratic Left Alliance did this mainly out of necessity of coalition government in a parliamentary system, where relatively broad alliances are required to make fundamental changes in policy.

Conclusions.   The Democratic Left Alliance followed a moderately left policy on social spending and introduced a range of structural reforms that were intended to strengthen the Polish welfare state. Its coalition government did not radically change spending priorities in the short term, but did tackle the main long-term expenditure issue—pensions—toward the end of its electoral term. Pension reform in Poland was heavily influenced by liberal ideas, but it had majority support in public opinion polls and signaled state commitment to reform, rather than dismember, the social safety net.

The left made Poland's 1997 constitution rearticulate a commitment to social rights in the future and played an important role in relegitimizing the welfare state after years of liberal attacks. The left government made minor improvements in the well-being of many groups through its budgetary policies. Living standards were raised and unemployment reduced, mostly because of high growth during its term in office. In sum, the Polish left in government did basically what it said it would do, trying to reduce the social costs of reform while bringing Poland into line with European market economies.

In pursuing its agenda, the Democratic Left Alliance was constrained by domestic political factors, especially coalition politics and median voter or majoritarian considerations, although international factors also played a role. International influences did not cause the left government to reduce spending or reverse its stated policy goals, but did dictate the limits of a spending policy that increased social spending in real terms while reducing it as a percent of GDP. International agencies, particularly The World Bank and the EU, played an important explicit and implicit role in policy formulation. Many of the left government's policies were oriented toward future membership in Europe and, therefore, largely, but not entirely, pointed in a liberal direction.

The Hungarian Left in Government

The return of the left in Hungary had the most paradoxical impact of our three cases. The Hungarian Socialist Party came to power in the summer of 1994, after winning a majority of seats in parliament in elections in May. Despite its strong showing, with 37 percent of the vote and 54 percent of the seats, the Socialists decided to enter into a coalition with a liberal former opposition party, the Alliance of Free Democrats (AFD), that had not participated in the center-right governments of 1990–1994. Whereas this alliance signaled a more liberal orientation for the Socialist Party-led government, the Socialists had campaigned on a platform of greater social harmony and care for the poor.

Furthermore, during the election campaign, the party explicitly promised to negotiate a comprehensive "social pact" that would reconcile disparate social interests in pursuit of transition. For a few months after the elections, the Socialist Party seemed to be trying to live up to this promise. It initiated negotiations toward a social pact in the Interest Reconciliation Council (IRC), a tripartite body that brings together representatives of government, business, and labor for regular discussions on social policy and employment-related matters (Hejthý 1995).

TABLE 3.11   Votes Cast for the Hungarian Socialist Party by Occupation (in percentages)

	1990	1994
Managers	13.2	36.1
Professionals	10.4	30.4
White Collar	9.6	30.3
Blue Collar	7.9	32.6
Farm Workers	2.6	27.5
Inactive	9.8	29.8
Total	9.6	30.9

SOURCE: Ivan Szelenyi, Eva Fodor, and Eric Hanley, "Left Turn in PostCommunist Politics: Bringing Class Back In?" *East European Politics and Societies* 11:1, Winter 1997, p. 219. © 1997 by ACLS. Reprinted by permission.

These negotiations proved short lived. When Hungary was threatened by a major financial crisis toward the end of 1994, the socialist-liberal government changed tack and implemented the most radical structural adjustment program ever attempted in Hungary, including deep cuts in social spending. This signaled the end of goulash communism (Kornai 1996) and the start of neoliberal shock therapy in Hungary (Stark and Bruszt 1998:174). The left proved more liberal than the right.

What caused this dramatic reversal? Did it reflect international economic pressures or sudden changes in domestic policy preferences? Can we still speak of the Socialist Party as a left party in Hungary, or is it a party of liberals in left clothing?

In essence, three factors combined to account for the policy shift: 1) risk of a serious international financial crisis arising from Hungary's fiscal and current account deficit; 2) failure to reach a transition social pact; and 3) outcomes of factional struggles within the Socialist Party and the coalition government that ended with a victory for liberals within the socialist-liberal coalition.

International pressures did not significantly constrain Hungarian social policy in the years after 1990, but were brought to bear on Hungarian economic policy toward the end of 1994 in the wake of the Mexican financial crisis. At that time, investors and the international financial community began to examine countries that might prove vulnerable to a similar run on the currency, and Hungary topped many lists.

After years of increased budgetary spending, primarily to fund social expenditures during the transition and to cushion the fall in living standards for a majority of the population, Hungary had reached the limits of the possible. Its current account deficit in 1994 reached 9 percent of GDP and its budget deficit, approximately 7 percent of GDP, depending on the means of measurement. Whereas Hungary's foreign obligations were mostly longer term than the "hot money" flowing out of Mexico, the potential consequences of a loss of confidence in the economy impressed themselves on Hungarian policymakers in 1994 (Kornai 1996:972).

Another factor behind the shift was the failure of the government to reach an expected agreement on a transition social pact. Such a social pact was seriously pursued within the Interest Reconciliation Council (IRC), with the support of both the Socialist Party and its Free Democrat allies (Hejthý 1995:362). However, the two political parties had quite different ideas about what a social pact should be. And the six trade union federations and nine business associations involved in the IRC pushed for a broad agenda for the talks, including employment, wage, regional development, transport, and macroeconomic policies. The agenda continued to broaden during the talks, making them practically interminable (Hejthý 1995:366–368).

Hungarian trade union federations initially wanted to be rewarded for their participation in a social pact by a favorable reform of labor legislation and labor institutions, including pro-labor collective bargaining mechanisms, but these proposals met with stiff resistance from the business associations represented on the IRC. After backing down early on, and agreeing to compromise measures, the trade unions returned to their earlier stances on labor law after accepting cuts in the 1995 budget.

This reversal, in mid-December 1994, combined with similar reversals in business association bargaining positions to throw a wrench in the gears of the IRC talks (Hejthý 1995:368). As 1994 closed with no agreement in sight, the government grew tired of talks that had dragged on inconclusively for half a year, while the Hungarian economy veered toward crisis. On February 2, 1995, the government declared talks on an economic and social agreement terminated (Hejthý 1995:369) and on March 12 launched a radical plan for economic restructuring without agreement from the IRC, although the terms of the package were discussed in the council in April.

A third factor—the outcome of internecine party struggles—strengthened the hand of economic liberals within the socialist-liberal coalition. Like the Democratic Left Alliance in Poland, the Hungarian Socialist Party was divided on economic policy between liberals, who supported market economic reform, and leftists, who sought to temper that reform by a firm adherence to state social guarantees. These two groups were bound together in the Hungarian Socialist Party by political pragmatism and an election program that combined elements of both. The two sides' coherence and relative strength were subjected to harsh tests once the party was in power.

As in Poland, the left faction of the Hungarian Socialist Party was strongest at the start of the parliamentary term, but was shunted aside in March 1995 with the launch of radical reforms. Marking a rapid and complete reversal from previous Socialist programs, the so-called Bokros package strained relations to the breaking point between the left and the liberals. Two government ministers from the Socialist Party, including the leftist Minister of Welfare Pal Kovacs, immediately resigned in protest over the announcement of the package in March (*Financial Times* March 14, 1995), while the liberals celebrated their ascendancy.

Stark and Bruszt suggest that the timing of the policy reversal reflected a personal struggle for supremacy within the Socialist Party between Prime Minister Horn and his first Finance Minister Laszlo Bekesi, who was seen as the leader of the liberal wing of the party (Stark and Bruszt 1998:172–173). Horn had campaigned on themes of national reconciliation and concern for the poor, and he continued to sound these themes until he had managed to force his rival, Bekesi, to resign in February 1995 through a series of maneuvers that undermined the latter's ability to run the Finance Ministry (Stark and Bruszt 1998:240ff).

Once Bekesi resigned, Horn appointed two other well-known liberals with very similar views, but less political clout, as finance minister and president of the National Bank—Lajos Bokros and Gyorgi Suryani, respectively (Stark and Bruszt 1998:173). Horn apparently was willing to go ahead with liberal austerity measures, but not so long as Bekesi could take the credit and threaten Horn's supremacy in the Socialist Party.

The Bokros Package.   In early 1995, Bokros began feverishly preparing a set of economic reforms that would stabilize the Hungarian economy. These reforms met with approval from the IMF, which had a delegation in Hungary at the time of their preparation (*MTI Econews* March 17, 1995). On March 12, 1995, Bokros announced a long list of radical changes. The most important measures were a 9 percent devaluation of the Hungarian forint (HUF) and the introduction of a monthly "crawling-peg" devaluation that would shave 28 percent off the currency's value by years' end; the introduction of an 8 percent surcharge on imports; and major cuts in social expenditures.

The package aimed at greatly reducing real wages, mainly by cutting public sector wages (Kornai 1996:968). Bokros projected that his measures, in total, would produce a drop of 9 percent in real wages, while the trade unions estimated they would drop by 15–20 percent (MTI *Econews* April 5, 1995). The finance minister also announced plans to cut civil service employment by 15 percent (*East European Markets,* April 14, 1995). In total, the Bokros package intended to cut Hungary's budget deficit in 1995 to 3 percent of GDP, down from the 5.4 percent target included in the 1995 budget (*Finance East Europe* April 21, 1995). The Bokros package met with hostility in the Interest Reconciliation Council, but was ultimately accepted as inevitable.

Although cuts in social expenditures, mainly in family and child benefits, were not the only, or even the most severe, elements of the austerity plan (macroeconomic changes had a bigger impact on welfare), they were the most politically controversial. In part, this was because family benefits not only had played a large role in preventing poverty in Hungary during the transition (World Bank 1996c) but also because many Hungarians felt they had a right to government social transfers.

The Bokros package intended to save money by targeting family benefits only to families earning less than HUF 25,000 ($208) gross per capita per month (*Reuters* March 30, 1995). Bokros fueled controversy by attacking Hungary's "premature" welfare state and by arguing that Hungary was too poor to afford generous welfare state provisions. He argued for targeting by stating, "Given the poor state of government finances, we can no longer afford the generous payments, especially to the people who are relatively well-off" (*Reuters* March 12, 1995). Bokros became known for his unwillingness to compromise.

Protest arose over numerous specific features of the Bokros package, including some reasonable tax changes that intended to broaden the basis of social security tax collection by forcing self-employed persons to pay social insurance contributions (*Heti Vilaggazdasag* June 10, 1995). In this way, the Bokros package hit relatively high-income earners as well as the poor. As a result, one public opinion poll found that two-thirds of Hungarians were "outraged" at the reform package (*The Economist* April 1, 1995). Some 12,000 students demonstrated against new tuition fees in March (*Reuters* March 30, 1995); thousands took part in a demonstration organized by the Hungarian Teachers' Union on May 1 against welfare and education cuts (*MTI Econews* May 2, 1995).

Evidence of the deep splits within the Socialist Party emerged, as the head of the teachers' union organizing the protest was a Socialist Party Member of Parliament Ilona Szollosi (interview with Szollosi in *Budapest Business Journal* May 12, 1995). Szollosi complained that, "The economic philosophy the government is pursuing is a wild-liberal, not a socialist policy," but added that she and other leftists would not leave the party: "We won't leave; it is not us who should leave."

Still, when it came time for parliament to vote on the Bokros package of twenty-one laws and amendments on May 30, the majority of Socialist and Free Democrat parliamentarians supported the package. The only issue on which Bokros was clearly defeated was on the introduction of social security contributions to be paid on employee food vouchers, a common benefit in Hungary. Parliament approved Socialist MP Sandor Nagy's amendment to scrap this social security levy, trimming about HUF 4 billion from Bokros's planned increase in budget income (Vidos 1995). Nagy was the former chairman of the Hungarian Trade Union Federation, affiliated with the Socialist Party.

The amended 1995 budget, approved by parliament on May 30, expected to plug a gaping deficit by adding HUF 56 billion in revenue from introducing the 8 percent customs surcharge, and HUF 10.6 billion from expanding the social insurance contribution base. Cutting health care supplied by the social insurance fund was expected to save HUF 7 billion. Restricting the number of people entitled to family allowance and the new system of child allowances was expected to save HUF 17.4 billion. Restricting the use of home-building benefits would save HUF 6.4 billion. Furthermore, the telecommunications fund was slated to pay HUF 16 billion to the central budget.

Transfer to the bank of various funds not already handled by the National Bank of Hungary intended to save HUF 10 billion. The budget also expected the tax and financial bodies and the police to raise an additional HUF 16 billion through efficiency improvements. An HUF 2.7 billion loan to India was canceled (*MTI Econews* May 30, 1995).

Some of the social expenditure cuts were reversed on June 30, when the Hungarian Constitutional Court ruled that changes to the child and family benefit systems could not be made on such rapid notice. The court ruled that the constitution gave Hungarians property rights to certain social benefits and that the principle of legal security prevented the government from rapidly changing benefit schemes that played a part in the calculation of life strategies of individuals (Gero 1997:9). Moreover, the court mandated a 300-day transition period for changes to the family and child benefits, so that pregnant mothers and families contemplating having children would not be affected by sudden changes. The finance ministry calculated that these delays would cost the budget HUF 12 billion (*Finance East Europe* August 4, 1995). However, the government made up the difference with a second round of cuts; cuts to the family and child benefits were simply postponed until April 1996.

Impact of Targeting.   In the liberal discourse on social policy, targeting is presented as a more efficient means of social service delivery, a way of cutting overall costs while increasing benefits for the truly needy. Bokros argued for targeting by saying that reductions in the family benefit would have no effect on most families, except for the top 20 percent who would lose benefits through means testing. Most families would remain eligible, and families with three or more children would not be means tested at all. Critics of means testing in Central and Eastern Europe argue that means testing involves far greater administration costs than universal benefits and that savings are not used to improve benefits for the poor. World Bank simulations showed that reductions in the family benefits would indeed deepen poverty in Hungary:

> Given the acute problems associated with means testing in Hungary . . . and the close proximity of incomes, it is likely that very few households will be excluded from an entitlement on the basis of income (and wealth). As such, budgetary savings will be scant, and will continue to be derived from the loss in real value of the family allowance. (It is likely that the cost of administering the means tests will outweigh the financial gains from eliminating a few families.) (World Bank 1996c:xiv)

Similarly, changes in child care benefits were expected to have a "negative impact on poverty" (World Bank 1996c:xv). UNICEF was more damning in its assessment of the impact of targeting and family benefit cuts in Hungary (UNICEF 1997:100):

Unlike other Central European countries, Hungary abandoned its comprehensive and generous child support programmes at a time when real wages and family incomes were falling sharply. Since April 1996 universal entitlement to family allowances has been retained only for families with three or more children or with children with disabilities. For all other families, allowances have become means tested. No improved allowance has been offered to the most needy through the overall savings thus generated.

Cuts in family and child benefits were not a left policy. In this crucial phase of the Socialist-Liberal government, liberalism came to the fore in Hungary although trade unionists and self-described "leftists" stayed in the Socialist Party. They continued to fight against liberalism within the party, and eventually harried Bokros into resigning. Bokros resigned from the Finance Ministry in February 1996, when the government rejected measures to cut the social security deficit to levels agreed upon with the International Monetary Fund (*Financial Times* Feb. 27, 1996:2). He had been subjected to angry personal attacks at cabinet meetings, obstruction from Prime Minister Horn and leftist cabinet members, and stated that the government no longer supported his reform drive.

Pension Reform.   Before he left, Bokros initiated work on a major reform of the pension system, similar in many ways to the package introduced in Poland a year later. However, while most of Bokros's reform efforts were not subject to extensive discussion or compromise, even within the Socialist Party itself, pension reform was, and it bore the mark of these compromises when it came into being in January 1998.

Bokros was succeeded as Finance Minister by Peter Medgyessy, a noted economist and reform communist who had served as finance minister in 1987–1988 and then as deputy prime minister in the government of Miklos Nemeth. In contrast to Bokros, Medgyessy was a career civil servant, well versed in the ways of negotiation and compromise (*Financial Times* Feb. 27, 1996:2). Still, his immediate concern upon taking office was plugging a gaping hole in the pension and health insurance funds, both of which were run by independent, elected bodies, dominated by the Socialist-affiliated trade unions. Medgyessy was under pressure to continue with the sweeping pension reform plans started under Bokros and to deal with the structural causes of these deficits before the end of the electoral term.

Bokros had appointed Adam Gere, an American businessman and investment banker of Hungarian descent, head of a new Working Group on Pension Reform at the Ministry of Finance. Gere was a strong supporter of a Chilean-type reform that would have totally transformed Hungary's pay-as-you-go system into a private, funded scheme, under which the state would provide only a bare minimum pension guarantee.

Gere, like Bokros, was a controversial figure. He did not want to compromise. Severe clashes began to manifest themselves within the Working Group, with some of the more politically connected Socialist members unwilling to support a Chilean-type reform. A compromise was eventually reached in which the new system would be 50 percent public and 50 percent private. This is where the debate stood at the end of Bokros's term in office. However the private share of the pension system continued to decrease in stages between 1995 and 1998, when it was decided by the new center-right government that the private system would be funded by only a 6 percent payroll tax, approximately 20 percent of the total.

A new phase of work on pension reform in Hungary came with the appointment, under Medgyessy, of an interministerial working group on reform that broadened the debate beyond the Ministry of Finance. Medgyessy had been able to get the Ministry of Welfare to agree to the introduction of a private, funded pillar in principle in April 1996 and to enter discussions on particulars. A major effort was made to include as wide a range of pension experts as possible in the deliberations of the new Working Group, although the group excluded representatives of the Pension Insurance Fund board that opposed reform (Ferge 1997).

Despite continued opposition from some left groups and experts associated with the trade unions, radical pension reform won the support of the Socialist and Free Democrat parliamentary groups, after some important compromises were reached in the Interest Reconciliation Council in early 1997. Mainly, the size of the second pillar was reduced and current pensions were increased to offset a reduction in indexation rates that would be felt further down the road (Palacios and Rocha 1998). However, the concept of introducing a mandatory, private second pillar was maintained, and indexation was switched to a mixed price-wage formula. Once the Socialist-affiliated trade unions agreed to such a reform, parliamentary debate went quickly. Legislation was passed in 1997, and the reform came into effect January 1, 1998.

Conclusions.   In Hungary, former-communist liberals rose to dominance within the Socialist Party during 1994–1998. They were not absolutely dominant, since they were forced to bargain with trade union and other left groups. However, liberals were put in a far stronger position in 1995 because of the depth of Hungary's international debt and its shaky financial situation. In Central Europe, at least, international factors do constrain left party polices, although these constraints are especially evident during a crisis, or near-crisis situation.

Does the behavior of the Socialist Party in implementing the Bokros package mean we must categorize it as a liberal, rather than a left party? Trade unionists and an avowedly "left" faction stayed in the party, despite the impact the Bokros package had on their constituencies. The Bokros package significantly weakened left factions within the Socialist Party, but since his resignation, more pragmatic liberals have come to the fore, cutting deals with powerful trade union leaders on such important issues as pension reform.

One of the key problems of left factions within the Socialist Party, and the Democratic Left Alliance in Poland, is that the path of transition is relatively narrow and Western-oriented, a factor that tends to elevate liberals within the left parties because of the credibility they have with the West. The left party in Hungary had to show that it was capable of pursuing a reform agenda that would allow that country to enter the European Union and OECD. Taking a radical liberal approach to dealing with a dangerous fiscal and current account crisis, such as Hungary faced in 1994, is a part of that. European integration has become a party-transcendent program in Central Europe, with clear effects on internal power struggles within left parties.

Conclusion

This study has shown that the Communist Party of the Russian Federation and the social democratic successor parties of Central Europe have followed very different approaches to reforming the post communist welfare states. The social democratic successor parties of Central Europe are center-left parties that appeal to the median voter with a social market agenda. They contain both liberal and socialist policy streams. The Russian CPRF presents a restorationist policy agenda that promises to revive social guarantees provided by the communist system. The CPRF has been able to maintain this rather utopian agenda partly because it has been in opposition for the entire period covered in this chapter. After the formation in fall 1998 of a new government with the support and participation of the Communist Party, it will be interesting to see whether the Russian left stays committed to its restorationist social policy, compromises, or abandons this agenda.

Different partisan policy preferences reflect differences in party constituencies and genealogy. Whereas the Russian CPRF is a party that grew out of the hard-line wing of the former CPSU, and whose voters are mostly losers of reform, the Central European successor parties are social democratic parties led by former communist reformers, in alliance with trade unions, business managers, and a variety of interest groups that represent both winners and losers.

In addition to differences in partisan policy preferences, social conditions and welfare state conditions were substantially different in Central Europe and Russia, shaping the strategies and actions of left parties in

opposition and in government. Russia suffered from a severe and continuing output decline and collapse of parts of the welfare state, due to reduced real spending, while Central European states substantially increased welfare state spending during the transition. This presented
entirely different contexts for policymaking. We have compared two different types of left parties, facing different social policy problems with
different political opportunities and institutional constraints. Despite this
differentiation, we have shown that communist successor parties in all
three countries, whether social democratic or restorationist, have expressed policy preferences in their electoral campaign platforms, programs, and activities in opposition that are clearly and demonstrably left.

The critical goal of this chapter was to determine whether left parties
have translated partisan platforms into effective policy once in power.
The analytical problems herein become more complex since one must
evaluate the parties both in terms of their intent and in the context of
powerful constraints that may shape their behavior. We have found that
within these constraints, two of the three left parties examined here delivered on their promises in limited ways, while a third, the Hungarian
Socialist Party, has engaged in a major policy reversal.

While the Russian communist party was not in government during the
period covered in this chapter, the record of the CPRF in the Russian
Duma shows that the Communists have been willing to take a stand
against the cutbacks and restructuring of the welfare state by liberals.
The Communists also have attempted, but not successfully, to increase
social budgets. Once in government, the party may well try to restructure
the welfare state in a manner very different from previous liberal efforts.

In Poland, we found that the Democratic Left Alliance was sharply
constrained in its social policy by its coalition with the nonreform Polish
Peasant Party and by dramatic spending increases by previous center-
right governments, which reduced its room for maneuver. Still, the Democratic Left Alliance managed to increase social spending in real terms,
while reducing it as a proportion of GDP, a move that was made possible
by the rapidly growing Poland economy.

The left government furthermore launched a radical reform of the pension system in cooperation with liberals from a nongovernmental party, the
Freedom Union, and the World Bank. This reform, while animated by liberal principles, was tempered by negotiation with both major trade union
federations and between parties across the political spectrum and met with
widespread popular approval. Overall, the Democratic Left Alliance be-
haved as a center-left party seeking to negotiate a social policy platform
across different party coalitions at different points in its term in office.

Hungary provides a case study of policy reversal by a left party in
power. The Hungarian Socialist Party, with the launching of the Bokros

reforms, made deep cuts in social expenditure a major element of its austerity package. The Hungarian case shows that left parties in power can be powerfully constrained by economic crises. International pressures to deal with them in particular ways may force parties to abandon inherent partisan policy preferences, as Garrett and Lange (1991) have argued.

The experience of Hungary underlines that the social democratic successor parties of Central Europe are dedicated to liberal reform. When forced to choose between the two, their dedication to liberal reform will rank higher in their priorities than social goals. Left social policy in Central Europe is dominated by a tension between wanting to join the West, and thus implementing liberal policies, while at the same time providing a high level of social protection. In Central Europe, the reform agenda is heavily dominated by liberalism because of the deeply based, party-transcending project of attempting to join the European Union.

No party can achieve governmental leadership or stay in power long without a credible commitment to reform. Still, both the Polish and Hungarian parties remain committed to a level of social spending that would not be acceptable to radical economic liberals and in doing so, reflect a broad centrist commitment to maintaining some of the guarantees of socialism in a market economy.

International constraints, however, are not the only, nor the most powerful, set of constraints on postcommunist social policy. Our parallel case studies have shown that four sets of constraints have shaped postcommunist welfare state policy:

State capacity;
Political institutional structure;
International/Economic constraints;
Legacies.

In the case of Russia, state capacity has been the strongest factor limiting the possibilities of postcommunist social policy. In a situation where the state cannot collect sufficient tax revenues, no amount of international economic aid will reverse the decline of the welfare state. Indeed, the IMF has long been telling Russia that it should increase tax revenues in order to finance state expenditures across the board. Cases of welfare state collapse in the postcommunist countries are likely to be based in a broader collapse of state capacity, especially to tax and to enforce the rule of law, powers on which all welfare state models are based.

Political institutions create a further set of constraints, and here we are mainly thinking of constitutional regimes and the structure of political party competition and government formation. Presidential and parliamentary regimes structure the policy context quite differently. We have shown that in Russia, social policy made in the Russian Duma was often vetoed by the president, and similarly, presidential initiatives were blocked by Duma opposition. This sort of policy stalemate, and the lack of incentives to overcome it, provides evidence for a widespread critique of presidentialism, especially in developing countries without strong party systems.

Parliamentary regimes, and the usual necessity of forming a coalition government, constrain partisan policy preferences, but also commonly lead to negotiation of differences and the development of policies that reflect a broader range of constituencies. We have found that coalition politics played a crucial role in shaping social policymaking of left governments in Hungary and Poland. Hungary was able to move so far in a liberal direction in large part because of its alliance with the liberal Free Democrats, while Poland was restrained by its coalition with the Peasant Party. In areas in which it pursued a more liberal agenda, for instance in pension reform, this was enabled by an institutionalized, single-issue alliance with experts from the liberal Freedom Union.

International influences have had an important impact on postcommunist social policy, but only at a very high level. International pressure did not stave off a vast expansion in social spending between 1989 and 1993 in Poland and Hungary, nor did it force spending down in Poland. International pressures only became an important influence in Hungary because welfare state expenditures were causing a budget deficit more than double the Maastricht maximum of 3 percent of GDP. It seems that postcommunist welfare states have latitude to expand to the levels of their Western neighbors and are certainly under no significant international pressure to be reduced to Latin American or East Asian ones. Indeed, Central Europe may be under significant pressure from the European Union not to reduce social expenditures much below European Union norms to prevent social dumping and emigration.

Legacies of the communist welfare state and transition policies of previous reform governments create another set of constraints. All left governments are necessarily grappling with problems that have their roots in previous welfare state structures and transition policies of previous liberal and center-right governments. In Poland and Hungary, we have shown that center-right governments presided over a perverse and predominantly unplanned expansion of social spending, limiting the left's room for maneuver. In Russia, the left must confront ad hoc budgetary policies initiated by previous governments that have undermined coherent decisions on social priorities. Legacies of the past regime and transition policies constitute important constraints on left governments.

Despite finding evidence for the operation of all the aforementioned constraints, left parties have made a credible effort to present a left alternative to the most radical sort of liberal economic reforms, to regain legitimacy for the welfare state, and to restructure it rather than destroy it or allow it to degenerate. This study reaffirms the conclusion of Szelenyi, Fodor, and Hanley (1997) and others, that "left" is not a meaningless term in postcommunist societies. A left-right divide along lines of interest does exist, and left parties do pursue identifiably left policies, at least in regard to the social welfare state, which is historically one of the most important areas of left party concern and intervention in the economy. As inequality increases in postcommunist societies, the salience of the left-right divide can only be expected to grow, forcing left parties to better articulate and follow their constituencies' interests.

References

Agh, Attila. 1995. "Partial Consolidation of the East-Central European Parties: The Case of the Hungarian Socialist Party." *Party Politics* 1:4, 491–514.

Balcerowicz, Leszek. 1995a. *Socialism, Capitalism, Transformation.* Budapest, London, and New York: Central European University Press.

Balcerowicz, Leszek. 1995b. "Understanding Postcommunist Transitions." In Larry Diamond and Marc F. Plattner, eds. *Economic Reform and Democracy.* Baltimore: Johns Hopkins University Press.

Blazyca, George and Ryszard Rapacki. 1996. "Continuity and Change in Polish Economic Policy: The Impact of the 1993 Election." *Europe-Asia Studies* 48:1, 85–100.

Boeri, Tito, and Andreas Worgotter. 1998. "Introduction," Special issue on "Long Term Unemployment and Social Assistance." *Empirical Economics* 23:1–3.

Clem, Ralph S., and Peter R. Craumer. 1995. "The Geography of the Russian 1995 Parliamentary Election: Continuity, Change, and Correlates." *Post-Soviet Geography* 36:10, 587–616.

Colton, Timothy J. 1996. "Economics and Voting in Russia." *Post-Soviet Affairs* 12:4, 289–317.

Connor, Walter D. 1997. "Social Policy under Communism." In Ethan Kapstein and Michael Mandelbaum, eds., *Sustaining the Transition: The Social Safety Net in Post-Communist Europe.* New York: Council on Foreign Relations, 10–45.

Cook, Linda J. 1997. *Labor and Liberalization: Trade Unions in the New Russia.* New York: Twentieth Century Fund.

Deacon, Bob, Michelle Hulse and Paul Stubbs. 1997. *Global Social Policy: International Organizations and the Future of Welfare.* London: Sage Publications.

Diamond, Larry, and Marc F. Plattner, eds. 1995. *Economic Reform and Democracy.* Baltimore: Johns Hopkins University Press.

Esping-Andersen, Gosta. 1990. *The Three Worlds of Welfare Capitalism.* Princeton: Princeton University Press.

Evans, Geoffrey, and Stephen Whitefield. 1995. "Social and Ideological Cleavage Formation in Post-Communist Hungary." *Europe-Asia Studies* 47:7, 1177–1204.

Ferge, Zsuzsa. 1997. "The Actors of the Hungarian Pension Reform." Paper prepared for the Fifth Central European Forum of the Institute of Human Studies, Vienna (October 24–25).

Fish, Steven M. 1995. "The Advent of Multipartism in Russia, 1993–95." *Post-Soviet Affairs* 11:4, 340–383.

Foley, Marc C., and Jeni Klugman. 1997. "The Impact of Social Support: Errors of Leakage and Exclusion." In Jeni Klugman, ed., *Poverty in Russia: Public Policy and Private Responses*. Washington, D.C.: World Bank.

Garrett, Geoffrey, and Peter Lange. 1991. "Political Responses to Interdependence: What's 'Left' for the Left?" *International Organization* 45:4 (Autumn).

Gero, Barnabas. 1997. "The Role of the Hungarian Constitutional Court." Columbia International Affairs Online, https:wwwc.cc.columbia.edu/sec/dlc/ciao/conf/ece01/ece01geb.html. (March).

Gora, Marek, and Michal Rutkowski. 1998. "The Quest for Pension Reform: Poland's Security Through Diversity," mimeo, The World Bank.

Haggard, Stephan, and Kaufman, Robert R. 1995a. "The Challenges of Consolidation." In Larry Diamond and Marc F. Plattner, eds., *Economic Reform and Democracy*. Baltimore: Johns Hopkins University Press.

Haggard, Stephan, and Robert R. Kaufman. 1995b. *The Political Economy of Democratic Transitions*. Princeton: Princeton University Press.

Hausner, Jerzy. 1995. "The State Enterprise Pact and the Potential for Tripartism in Poland." In Robert Kyloh, ed., *Tripartism on Trial: Tripartite Consultations and Negotiations in Central and Eastern Europe*. Geneva: International Labour Organization.

Hausner, Jerzy. 1998. "Security through Diversity: Conditions for Successful Reform of the Pension System in Poland," mimeo, Cracow University of Economics.

Hejthy, Lajos. 1995. "Anatomy of a Tripartite Experiment: Attempted Social and Economic Agreement in Hungary." *International Labour Review* 134:3, 361–376.

Hough, Jerry F., Evelyn Davidheiser and Susan Goodrich Lehmann. 1996. *The 1996 Russian Presidential Election*. Washington, D.C.: Brookings Institution.

Ishiyama, John T. 1996. "Red Phoenix? The Communist Party in Post-Soviet Russian Politics." *Party Politics* 2:2, 147–179.

"June Draft Legislative Package." 1997. Xerox.

Kaminski, Marek, Grzegorz Lissowski, and Piotr Swistak. 1997. "The 'Revival of Communism' or the Effect of Institutions? The 1993 Polish Parliamentary Elections," mimeo, New York University, Warsaw University, University of Maryland.

Klugman, Jeni, ed. 1997. *Poverty in Russia: Public Policy and Private Responses*. Washington, D.C.: World Bank.

Kornai, Janos. 1996. "Paying the Bill for Goulash Communism: Hungarian Development and Macro Stabilization in a Political-Economy Perspective," *Social Research* 63:4 (Winter): 943–1040.

Kudiukin, Pavel. 1998. Member of the Presidium, Russian Social Democratic Union, and Senior Research Fellow, Institute for Comparative Political Studies, Russian Academy of Sciences. Interview with author. Moscow. (June 25).

Linz, Juan J., and Alfred Stepan. 1996. *Problems of Democratic Transition and Consolidation: Southern Europe, South America, and Post-Communist Europe*. Baltimore: Johns Hopkins University Press.

Maleva, T. (Bureau of Economic Analysis), and O. Syniyavskaya (Carnegie Foundation). n.d. "The Social Sphere" Xerox.

Marody, Mira. 1995. "Three Stages of Party System Emergence in Poland," *Communist and Post-Communist Studies* 28:2, 263–270.

McAuley, Alastair. 1979. *Economic Welfare in the Soviet Union: Poverty, Living Standards, and Inequality.* Madison: University of Wisconsin Press.

Mikhalev, Vladimir. 1996. "Social Security in Russia under Economic Transformation." *Europe-Asia Studies* 48:1, 5–25.

Milanovic, Branko. 1996. "Poverty and Inequality in Transition Economies: What Has Actually Happened," In Bartolomiej Kaminski, ed., *Economic Transition in Russia and the New States of Eurasia.* New York: M.E. Sharpe.

Milanovic, Branko. 1998. *Income, Inequality, and Poverty during the Transition from Planned to Market Economy.* Washington, D.C.: The World Bank.

Nelson, Joan M. 1995. "Linkages between Politics and Economics." In Larry Diamond and Marc F. Plattner, eds., *Economic Reform and Democracy.* Baltimore: Johns Hopkins University Press.

OECD. 1996. *The Changing Social Benefits in Russian Enterprises.* Paris: OECD.

OECD. 1997. *Economic Surveys: Russian Federation 1997.* Paris: OECD.

Offe, Claus. 1993. "The Politics of Social Policy in East European Transitions: Antecedents, Agents, and Agenda of Reform." *Social Research* 60:4.

Orenstein, Mitchell. 1998. "A Genealogy of Communist Successor Parties in East-Central Europe and the Determinants of their Success." *East European Politics and Society* 12:3 (Fall): 472–499.

Palacios, Robert, and Roberto Rocha. 1998. *The Hungarian Pension System in Transition.* Social Protection Discussion Paper No. 9805. Washington, D.C.: The World Bank.

Pietrzak-Paciorek, Malgorzata. 1996. "Changes to the Labor Code." *East/West Executive Guide* 8:6 (August 1).

Przeworski, Adam., et al. 1995. *Sustainable Democracy.* Cambridge: Cambridge University Press.

Remington, Thomas F., and Steven S. Smith. 1995. "The Development of Parliamentary Parties in Russia." *Legislative Studies Quarterly.* 20:4, 457–489.

Rose, Richard. 1996. "New Russian Barometer V: Between Two Elections." *Studies in Public Policy* 260. Glasgow: University of Strathclyde, Center for the Study of Public Policy.

Rose, Richard, Neil Munro, and Tom Mackie. 1998. "Elections in Central and Eastern Europe Since 1990." *Studies in Public Policy* 300. Glasgow: University of Strathclyde, Center for the Study of Public Policy.

Rueschemeyer, Dietrich, John Stevens, and Evelyn Huber Stevens. 1992. *Capitalist Development and Democracy.* Chicago: University of Chicago Press.

Rutkowski, Jan J. 1998. "Welfare and the Labor Market in Poland: Social Policy during Economic Transition." World Bank Technical Paper No. 417. Washington, D.C.: The World Bank.

Sachs, Jeffrey. 1993. *Poland's Jump to the Market Economy.* Cambridge, Mass.: MIT Press.

Sederlof, Hjalte. 1998. Program Team Leader for Social Protection in Russia, World Bank. Interview with author, Washington, D.C. (January 12).

Socialist International. 1996. http://www.socialistinternational.org/5Congress/ SICONGRESS/con6.html.

Sojusz Lewicy Demokratycznej. 1997a. "Dobrze Dziā—Lepsze Jutro: Program Wyborczy Sojuszu Lewicy Demokratycznej," Warsaw: Sojusz Lewicy Demokratycznej.

Sojusz Lewicy Demokratycznej. 1997b. *Klub Parlamentarny 1993–1997: Fakty, Dokonania, Opinie.* Warsaw: Biuro Klubu Parlamentarnego Sojuszu Lewicy Demokratycznej.

Standing, Guy. 1995. "Enterprise Restructuring in Russian Industry and Mass Unemployment: The RLFS Fourth Round, 1994." Labour Market Papers. Geneva: International Labour Organization.

Standing, Guy. 1996. *Russian Unemployment and Enterprise Restructuring: Reviving Dead Souls.* Geneva: International Labour Organization.

Stark, David, and Laszlo Bruszt. 1998. *Postsocialist Pathways: Transforming Politics and Property in East Central Europe.* Cambridge: Cambridge University Press.

Stevenson, Irene. 1998. Director, American Center for International Labor Solidarity. Interview with author. Moscow. (June 23).

Struyk, Raymond J., ed. 1997. *Restructuring Russia's Housing Sector, 1991–1997.* Washington, D.C.: Urban Institute.

Szelenyi, Ivan, Eva Fodor, and Eric Hanley. 1997. "Left Turn in Post-Communist Politics: Bringing Class Back In?" *East European Politics and Societies* 11:1 (Winter): 190–224.

Twigg, Judyth L. 1998. "Balancing the State and the Market: Russia's Adoption of Obligatory Medical Insurance." *Europe-Asia Studies* 50:4, 583–602.

UNICEF. 1997. *Children at Risk in Central and Eastern Europe: Perils and Promises.* Economies in Transition Studies Regional Monitoring Report No. 4. Florence, Italy: UNICEF.

Urban, Joan Barth, and Valerii D. Solovei. 1997. *Russia's Communists at the Crossroads.* Boulder: Westview Press.

USIA. 1998. "Opinion Analyses," Washington, D.C.: U.S. Information Agency. (February 9).

Vidos, Tibor. 1995. "Bokros Gets Passing Grades for First 90 Days," *Budapest Business Journal.* (June 2): 19.

Vinogradova, E. V. 1996. "Analiticheskaya Zapiska: Rossiiskie predpriyatiya: Zanyatost, zarabotnaia plata, sotsial'naia podderzhka rabotnikov." Xerox.

Vujacic, Veljko. 1996. "Gennadiy Zyuganov and the 'Third Road.'" *Post-Soviet Affairs* 12:2, 118–154.

White, Stephen, Matthew Wyman, and Olga Kryshtanovaksya. 1995. "Parties and Politics in Post-Communist Russia." *Communist and Post-Communist Studies* 28:2, 183–202.

Whitefield, Stephen, and Geoffrey Evans. 1994. "The Russian Election of 1993: Public Opinion and the Transition Experience," *Post-Soviet Affairs* 10:1, 38–60.

World Bank. 1995a. *Poverty in Russia: An Assessment.* World Bank Report No. 14110-RU. (June 13).

World Bank. 1995b. *Understanding Poverty in Poland.* World Bank Country Study. Washington, D.C.: The World Bank (July).

World Bank. 1996a. *Russian Federation: Toward Medium-Term Viability.* Washington, D.C.: World Bank.

World Bank. 1996b. *Fiscal Management in Russia.* Washington, D.C.: World Bank.

World Bank. 1996c. *Hungary: Poverty and Social Transfers.* World Bank Country Study. Washington, D.C.: The World Bank (May).

Wyman, Matthew. 1997. "Elections and Voting Behavior." Pp. 104–128 in *Developments in Russian Politics,* ed. Stephen White, Alex Pravda, and Zvi Gitelman. Durham, N.C.: Duke University Press.

"Za Nashu sovetskuyu rodinu." 1995. (For Our Soviet Homeland): Preelectoral platform of the KPRF. *Pravda Rossii,* No. 16 (30) (Sept. 7): 2.

Zubek, Voytek. 1995. "The Phoenix out of the Ashes: The Rise to Power of Poland's Post-Communist SdRP." *Communist and Post-Communist Studies* 28:3, 275–306.

PRIMARY SOURCES

East European Market
Delovoy Mir
Finance East Europe
Ekonomika I Zhizn
Financial Times
Foreign Broadcast Information Service: SOV (FBIS) at http://wnc.fedworld.gov
Gosudarstvennaya Duma: Stenograma zasedanii, 1997.
Heti Vilaggaz-dasag
Moskovskaya Pravda
MTI Econews
Moskovskie Novosti
Polityka
Polish Press Agency
Rabochaya Tribuna
Radio Free Europe/Radio Liberty Reports
Reuters
Rossiiskaya Gazeta
Rossiiskie Vesti
Russian Economic Trends
Rzeczpospolita
Sovetskaya Rossiya

Notes

1. This is not to imply that economic discontent alone drove the Communist vote—research by Colton (1996) and others has demonstated the great influence of political values—but to identify the socioeconomic correlates of the Communist vote.

2. They did not, however, get the critical chairmanships of the Budget Committee, which went to Yabloko's Mikhail Zadornov, or the Committe for Labor and Social Policy, which went to the LDP's Sergei Kalashnikov (*Rossiskaya Gazeta* Jan. 25, 1996, p. 4).

3. Information for this section of the chapter has been collected from a range of Russian press and documentary sources.

4. This was by far the biggest cost-saver of the package and the one measure with the potential to provide some real poverty relief, if benefits were actually raised and paid. Savings on child allowances were supposed to account for $25 trillion of the estimated $30 trillion in savings, though the government did not provide detailed calculations to back its projections; see *Del Mir* June 18, 1997, p. 2.

5. A note on the data: Unfortunately, good exit poll data is lacking for the complete set of postcommunist elections. Szelenyi, Fodor, and Hanley depend on exit poll data from the 1994 Hungarian elections and retrospective surveys for voting behavior in all previous elections in Hungary and Poland (1997:212–213). Agh relies on surveys conducted a few months before and a few months after the 1994 elections (1995:508–509). Evans and Whitefield (1995:1178) use a survey conducted just before the 1994 elections that asked retrospective questions about 1990. For neither country do we have high-quality, comparable exit poll data for all postcommunist elections. Therefore, a number of important questions are impossible to answer definitively, and certain disputes probably will continue.

6. The left government initiated, but did not complete, pension reform in Poland. It was unable to get the full package of legislation through parliament before the end of its term in office and passed only about half the necessary laws, while setting a deadline for further legislation to be passed. The subsequent center-right government completed the second half in November–December 1998, but the basic design of the program remained the same. The Democratic Left Alliance, however, voted against the second package of laws. This turnabout is explained, in part, by the fact that Leszek Miller, the stolid leftist opponent of three-pillar reform, was elected the new party leader after parliamentary elections in 1997 returned the Democratic Left to opposition.

4

The Return of Left-Oriented Parties in Eastern Germany and the Czech Republic and Their Social Policies

MARILYN RUESCHEMEYER AND SHARON L. WOLCHIK*

This chapter focuses on two social democratic parties that increased their support in postcommunist Germany and in the Czech Republic after the early years of the transformation. The Social Democratic Party in eastern Germany and the Czech Social Democratic Party in the Czech Republic stand out among the left parties in Eastern Europe. They did not exist under communism. Nor are they reformed versions of the communist parties that ruled during the communist era, such as those that were elected in the early 1990s in Hungary, Poland, and Bulgaria. Rather, they are parties with indigenous roots in their own societies that predate the communist era. They represent an old political tradition in their respective countries that is open to the market and at the same time retains a commitment to the weaker groups in the society. Both parties are alternatives to the more conservative coalitions that took over after the end of communism, as well as to the communists.

We will discuss the background to their increasing success, the problems they faced at the beginning of their efforts to gain electoral support, and their place in the current politics of the two countries. This includes in particular their relations to the major other parties on the left, the successors of the formerly ruling communist parties, which are quite different in the two countries. The German PDS (Party of Democratic Socialism) is in the middle of a process of reform and gains increasing acceptance, while the Czech communist party remains unreconstructed and is now limited to roughly 10 percent of the electorate. The social democrats then face a different political competition from other parties of the left in the two countries.

The rise of the social democrats leads us to the issues they presently confront as governing parties. Here, we focus on problems of social policy, which must be seen against the background of the social provisions developed during the communist period and in the context of the current transformations of economy and society in the two countries.

Although both social democratic parties received the largest percentage of votes in the 1998 elections, they have difficult years ahead. Neither party was able to form a majority government. Both must gain the support of other political forces if they are to enact policies based on their political agendas. And in their political strategies, both must find a way of combining policies that will foster the economic development, which ultimately will ensure their future with those that will provide a safety net that addresses the needs of those less able to make it in a market economy.

Eastern Germany is in many respects a special case among the former communist countries of Central and Eastern Europe. It has become part of one of the richer countries of the West. Thus, the argument that Central and East European countries are now too poor to pursue policies similar to the West European welfare states does not apply here, even though including eastern Germany in the generous system of social provisions developed in West Germany after World War II has created more serious problems for the political economy of unified Germany than anticipated by the Christian Democratic Union (CDU) led by Chancellor Kohl.

The fact that the five new German states joined the ongoing and fundamentally unchanged legal and political structure of the Federal Republic of Germany also sets them apart from other formerly communist countries in another way. Though west Germany supplied tremendous economic resources for the transformation, east Germans find themselves in a situation that they had little part in setting up or even influencing. This deficit in self-determination creates problems in the eastern part of the country that are reflected in the dynamics of party competition.

Despite these differences, there are many ways in which the experiences of citizens of what is now eastern Germany parallel those of citizens in other formerly communist states. These are evident in the area that is the focus of this book. Thus, eastern Germany shares with the other former communist countries of Central and Eastern Europe the historical experience of a comprehensive system of social provisions and supports that shaped life expectations, even if it was combined with poor economic productivity, political rigidity, and a lack of many important personal freedoms.

Although there was great variation among Central and East European countries, the foremost features of these state socialist political economies were similar. These systems included guaranteed employment, combined with some freedom of choice, which made employee-supervisor relations at work in some ways more equal than they are now with the threat of unemployment and the new demands of the market. These states also provided education, health care, housing, basic food, and clothing at nominal prices. These policies constituted a tremendous boon to the weakest strata of society.

At the same time, people in stronger socioeconomic positions were dissatisfied with the quality and availability of goods and services and with their limited choices. Communist states also adopted policies that encouraged and usually required both men and women to work. Particularly in the former German Democratic Republic (GDR), these policies empowered women in the household and at work, even though their access to leading positions in the economy, in education, and in politics was limited. These policies and the expectations they established continue to have important repercussions in Germany and the Czech Republic. In addition to conditioning the attitudes and expectations of citizens, they also left a legacy that leaders have had to take into account as they have attempted to transform these societies into modern market economies.

The Early Years of Transformation in Eastern Germany and the Czech Republic

The process of privatization of industry, the closing down of enterprises, the abolishment of positions in cultural and administrative sectors, and the forced early retirement of older workers resulted in dramatic changes for most east Germans. Seventy-five percent of the labor force left their original place of work and frequently saw a devaluation of their working potential.[2] According to one survey in 1991–1992, 22 percent of employees changed their vocation, 21 percent changed their place of work, 11 percent changed places within the workplace, 14 percent took measures to retrain, and 26 percent were unemployed at one time or another.

Furthermore, western advisors, educators, and administrative specialists of all sorts were employed in the east. It has been estimated that since unification, 20,000 civil servants from the west have been employed in the east (Welsh 1995). On the other hand, huge numbers of east Germans, especially the young and the skilled left for the western part of the country where they hoped for better work opportunities and improved physical conditions. But not only problems of employment and underemployment arose with the transformation; social provisions of all sorts were affected as well, and many social supports that once were taken for granted were no longer available in the united Germany. Some of these problems will be discussed in detail later. In 1990, many difficulties and frustrations were seen as temporary phenomena that would be resolved with real integration into the welfare state of the Federal Republic. They weighed more heavily as time went on.

The transformation in eastern Germany coincided with a growing concern in the Federal Republic about the problems facing its welfare system. It may be useful to give a thumbnail sketch of this social provisions system. Social security legislation in the Federal Republic includes Statutory Pension Insurance; its contribution rate is 20.3 percent of gross wages, jointly funded by employers and employees on an equal basis and in addition a grant from the federal government of 20 percent of the total expenditures. Statutory Health Insurance, which is not a uniform system in Germany,[2] is compulsory for all employees whose monthly income does not exceed a certain level and voluntary for people whose monthly income exceeds this level,[3] with an average contribution rate of 13.4 percent shared by employers and employees. Long-Term Care Insurance is organized by the health insurance funds and compulsory for everyone with a contribution rate of 1.7 percent. Unemployment Insurance is mandatory for those working 15 or more hours per week, with a present contribution rate of 6.5 percent and shortfalls covered by the federal government. Occupational Accident Insurance is compulsory for employers with rates depending on employee earnings and accidental risk level; those insured include all employees, home workers, students, and those in rehabilitation. There is also a means-tested income maintenance program—Sozialhilfe, which is administered mainly by state and local governments, funded by taxation (Palik 1998).

Problems of maintaining this social welfare system have been attributed to increasing structural unemployment, the expense of unification, an aging population, and increased international competition. Reductions in supports had been initiated, including gradually raising the pension age, cutting health benefits by reducing the stay in hospitals, increasing the contributions of patients toward the cost of medicine, lengthening the intervals between health cures, cutting back on the income benefit in case of illness (from 80 to 70 percent of gross wages), toughening the criteria requiring unemployed persons to accept job offers, reducing job creation measures, and abolishing of unemployment benefit payments for advanced vocational training.

Many east Germans, already faced with enormous problems and not quite adjusted to the institutions and policies of the Federal Republic, are wary of further cutbacks. The Social Democratic Party, especially, faces a number of dilemmas about how to address these difficulties. The initial effects of these policies in eastern Germany and subsequent political developments will be discussed later in the chapter.

The situation Czech leaders faced immediately after the end of communism in 1989 in some ways paralleled the experience of East Germans in social welfare policies and the legacy of communist rule. But the context of decisionmaking about social policy and the calculations by political leaders concerning the costs of changing the social welfare system differed. The most obvious of these differences resulted from the former GDR's incorporation into the Federal Republic of Germany.

In contrast to the German case, in which an established polity expanded and extended its institutions to the newly incorporated area, the actions of Czech and Slovak leaders were influenced by the fact that they operated in a polity in which central institutions were themselves in a state of transition. Certain aspects of transition politics, including the lack of certainty in the political system, the rudimentary nature of the party system, the instability of popular political preferences, and the lack of experience of most political leaders, were common to other postcommunist states. However, other factors, including the ethnic composition of the country, its precommunist political traditions, and its federal structure also conditioned the transition and led to developments that differed from those that occurred in other postcommunist countries.

The country's federal structure was one of the most important of these influences. The powers of the republic governments under the Czechoslovak federation that went into effect in 1969 were very limited under communism, and there was a great deal of dissatisfaction with the way the federation worked in both the Czech Lands and Slovakia (see Leff 1988; Wolchik 1991:124–125). Nonetheless, political life continued to be organized federally after the end of communism. As a result, federal decisionmaking was conditioned by the need to take both Czech and Slovak interests into account.

Because much of Slovakia's industrialization took place during the communist period, the Slovak economy was significantly more vulnerable to the dislocations caused by policies designed to recreate a market economy. Citizens in Slovakia felt these dislocations earlier and to a greater extent than their counterparts in the Czech Lands. Most evident in the difference in unemployment rates, which were under 3 percent for most of the early 1990s in the Czech Lands, but between 12 and 14 percent in Slovakia, the more severe impact of the shift to a market economy was also reflected in greater economic hardship for larger groups of the Slovak population.

Thus, Czech leaders who wished to change social policy had to consider the different impact that the shift to a market economy had in the Czech Lands and Slovakia. They also had to take into account differing popular perceptions in the two regions concerning such important issues as the desirability of a rapid shift to a market economy, how much the economy should be privatized, and the willingness to see the costs of this shift, such as unemployment, as necessary and acceptable. Czechs and

Slovaks also differed in terms of their conceptions of democracy and their views concerning the responsibility of the state in shielding individuals from the impact of the shift to the market. There was much greater popular support for efforts to reduce the role of the state in the Czech Lands than in Slovakia immediately after the end of the communist system. (Boguszak and Rak 1990; Centrum 1990).

There were also important differences concerning social policy within the Czech leadership in the early 1990s. These divisions and the existence within the leadership of a group, with a strong concern for social justice, put limits on the extent and speed of change in social policies in the early years after the end of communism (see Castle-Kanerová 1992; Kabele and Potůček 1995; Potůček 1992; and Orenstein 1995).

While experts in the Ministry of Labor and Social Affairs and others struggled with how to reform social policy to eliminate the distortions of the communist era and deal with new needs created by the shift to a market economy, they also debated the relevance of Czechoslovakia's interwar system of social welfare provisions (see Castle-Kanerová 1992 for a brief overview of interwar and communist era social policies). The initial approach to social policy emphasized the role of the state in aiding those groups of the population most negatively affected by the economic transition, as reflected in the government's draft program for economic reform adopted in 1990.

With the breakup of the federation at the end of 1992, Czech leaders were freed from the need to account for the situation in Slovakia. However, despite more consensus among Czechs than among Slovaks about the need for individuals to assume more responsibility for their own lives, efforts to change social policy continued to encounter elite and popular opposition. This opposition became particularly evident in the mid-1990s, when the governing center-right coalition of Václav Klaus began its first serious effort to change social policy by reducing the role of the state in numerous areas and shifting to a needs-based, rather than universal system of benefits (Orenstein 1995; Vobruba 1993; Večerník 1993; see Musil 1995; Rys 1995; and Hartl 1995 for discussions of popular attitudes toward social policy reform). Left of center parties, including the social democrats, have been the main opponents of such a shift.

Political Developments and Left-Oriented Parties

It is against this background that the political landscape in the former GDR and the Czech Republic must be seen. In Germany as well as in Czechoslovakia, supporters of a more conservative policy appealed to citizens to support the market economy and accept more responsibility for their own personal futures in a free society. In both countries, parties opposing the Social Democrats also tried to stigmatize them by speaking of votes for either the Social Democrats or the communists as a "return to the left" (Rueschemeyer 1998a, Wolchik 1992). Yet in both countries, the Social Democrats gained significantly. In east Germany, where they were stronger to begin with, they had at the same time to contend with a significant competition from the reconstituted communist party. In the Czech Republic, the ČSSD had much less success initially but faced weaker competition from an unreformed communist party.

Developments in East Germany. The Social Democratic Party, which many had expected to win the largest percentage of the vote in the unified east, received only 24.3 percent of the vote in that part of the country in the first unified federal elections in 1990. The conservative Christian Democratic Union (CDU) and its neoliberal coalition partner, the Free Democratic Party (FDP), captured together more than double that share of the vote. The reformed communists (PDS) and the Alliance 90/Greens (a combination of predominantly left-leaning environmentalists and the remnants of the civic movements of 1989) followed with 11.1 and 6.3 percent, respectively. The Republikaner, an ultraright party, accounted for 3.3 percent. The first state elections had similar results; it was only in Brandenburg, one of the eastern states surrounding the city state of Berlin, that the SPD became the strongest party and ruled, though in a coalition government.

The SPD finds itself not only in competition with the CDU, the party under whose auspices unification took place, but also increasingly with the PDS. The SPD, governing in several states in coalition with the CDU, suffers from the perception that it is a party of the west, partly responsible for the problems of restructuring in the east after unification. Its connection with the trade unions is less close and more tentative in the east than in west Germany. And both the western-sponsored union structure and the SPD were seen as unable either to stem the massive unemployment or to prevent some of the unfair labor practices that continue to take place in a number of east German enterprises.

Equally important, the eastern SPD was the only party that was not allowed some continuing independent existence during the forty years from 1949–1989, when it was forced to merge with the Communist Party. Consequently, there was no established organization on which new political activities could rely. The western SPD helped, but that further made the eastern SPD look like a party of the west. This handicap contrasts with the situation of all other major parties, including the CDU, which has in the east a large membership of approximately 80,000 that was partly inherited from its satellite predecessor.

Another consequence of being outlawed for forty years is the disruption of local and regional traditions. In the east, much of the early leadership was provided by Protestant pastors who, though connected with

TABLE 4.1 Election Results in East and West Germany Federal Elections, 1990–1998 Percent

	CDU/CSU[a]		SPD		FDP		A90/G		PDS		EXR[b]	
	West	East[c]	West	East	West	East	West	East	West	East	West	East
1990	44.3	41.8	35.7	24.3	10.6	12.9	4.8	6.3	0.3	11.1	2.6	1.6
1994	42.1	38.5	37.5	31.5	7.7	3.5	7.9	4.3	1.0	19.8	2.0	1.2
1998[d]	37.1	27.3	42.3	35.1	7.0	3.3	7.3	4.1	1.2	21.6	2.8	5.0
1998–1990[e]	–7.2	14.5	+6.6	+10.8	–3.6	9.6	+2.5	–2.2	+0.9	+10.5	+0.2	+3.4
1998–1994[f]	–5.0	11.2	+4.8	+3.6	–0.7	–0.2	–0.6	–0.2	+0.2	+1.8	+0.8	+3.8

a. In East Germany only CDU.
b. Parties of the extreme right—1990: REP; 1994: REP; 1998: DVU, NPD, REP.
c. West Germany includes Berlin-West; East Germany includes Berlin-East
d. Preliminary official results.
e. Change in 1998 compared to 1990 in percentage points.
f. Change in 1998 compared to 1994 in percentage points.

SOURCE: Richard Stöss and Gero Neugebauer, "Die SPD und die Bundestagswahl 1998." Unpublished paper, Free University Berlin, Table 5, p. 19. (See: http://www.sowifo.fu-berlin.de/osi/start_frame.html).

numerous alternative groups in the former GDR, soon found themselves isolated from a secular population and colleagues more experienced in actual politics.

The SPD cannot easily respond to many of the problems that stem from the change of systems and from the dominance of west German concerns in national politics because the national party has its main base in the west. There are nearly 65 million people in west Germany and only somewhat over 15 million in the east. The membership in the party is approximately 750,000 in the west and 27,000 in the east, though the small membership in the east does not reflect voting patterns, which indicate considerable support for the party.

The PDS, which is essentially an eastern party with approximately 100,000 members and a tiny vote in the west, successfully articulates east-west issues, in addition to the issues experienced by those who were displaced out of more advantageous positions due to the transformation. It also seeks to express dissatisfactions arising out of the sheer pace and magnitude of change. It is effective locally, having maintained its organization and some of its resources even while reorienting the party to a considerable extent. Its role is more important at the local level than on the state and federal levels; and where it is in power, it frequently behaves differently than its public image may suggest, for instance, making cuts to avoid budget deficits.

After a poor showing in 1990, the party soon made gains nobody had expected. In the 1994 elections, the PDS received about a fifth of the votes in the former GDR (see Table 4.1) and became the strongest party in a number of cities such as Rostock, Schwerin, Neubrandenburg, Halle, and in the eastern districts of Berlin. The PDS appealed successfully to young people, 18–34 years old: 25 percent of them in eastern Germany voted PDS in the 1994 elections. Many of them see the PDS as a party with new faces, addressing their concerns, especially on the state and local levels. Federally, the PDS entered parliament in 1994, even though it did not quite make the obligatory 5 percent, because it won several seats in direct elections. In the 1998 elections, the party succeeded in passing the 5 percent threshold nationally. The PDS is able to be much more overtly oppositional than the SPD and can express east German interests more strongly, precisely because it does not have the possibility of governing on the federal level.

In the federal elections in 1994, the CDU lost votes in four out of five of the new German states, as well as in Berlin, where east and west are combined. But it remained the strongest party in all the eastern states except for Brandenburg, where the SPD became the strongest party. Its national coalition partner, the neoliberal FDP, lost three-quarters of its voting support in the east. The SPD gained in all the new states except Saxony, where the PDS and the CDU gained support (Rueschemeyer 1998b). Among the groups that supported the SPD, workers and white-collar employees represented a core constituency in both east and west, but their share among SPD voters was larger in the west. Even with the divisions in the left between the SPD and the PDS, it is interesting to note the strong appeal of both among younger east Germans aged 18–34—54.3 percent in the east compared to 44.3 percent in the west (Rueschemeyer 1998).

In 1998, the last federal election, the SPD became the strongest party nationally and formed a coalition government with the Greens. In the east, the SPD had increased its percentage in the east from 31.5 to 35.1, while the CDU vote declined dramatically from 38.5 percent to 27.3 percent. The parties of the far right increased their support in the east, but in the country as a whole did not pass the 5 percent hurdle (see Table 4.1).

The character and strength of the different parties in eastern Germany can be gauged from their relation to organized interests. Interesting research on the contact of the different parties in eastern Germany to associations and organizations on the county level gives some indication of the access they have to different constituencies as well as of their political inclinations. Not surprisingly, the left-oriented parties share a number of organizations with which they are all in contact.

Briefly, the CDU has the most frequent contact with employer associations. It also has close relations with professional (berufständische) associations. It maintains more contact with farmers' associations and the churches than the other parties, in addition to the organizations of war victims and for refugees (conservative associations that the other parties distance themselves from). The CDU has only moderate contact with youth organizations, women's associations and centers, and environmental groups, though there is some desire to strengthen these links. The CDU distances itself from the antifascist organizations, self-help and alternative projects, and associations for the unemployed, but at least some in the party expressed interest in having increased contact with the unemployed, as well as with the renters' association.

It is interesting to note that despite the powerful contacts to employers' associations, the reputation of the CDU for policy effectiveness increasingly diminished as the economic problems remained severe and as large numbers of east Germans began to lose hope that their situation would improve in the immediate future. The party has only weak links with those groups and organizations that developed to deal with problems in east Germany.

The SPD and the PDS both are socially oriented, representing among others the interests of the disadvantaged and weak. The SPD has frequent contact with welfare associations and unions, with renters' associations and unemployed workers' associations, and with women's associations, whereas the PDS has the most contact with the latter. Although there is a clear interest in the SPD in strengthening the contact with economic associations, these links are presently underdeveloped, as are those to the farmers' associations and professional associations. The SPD has less contact with the Protestant Church than the CDU and the Alliance 90/Greens, despite the fact that its early founders were active in the church. There is considerable interest in increasing links to the young and to environmental groups, and moderate interest in increasing contact with women's associations and art and cultural associations. Considering the small membership, the range of contacts is indeed considerable (Göthe, Kux, and Neugebauer 1996:88–98).

The PDS has close links with antifascist associations, renters' associations, unions, and welfare groups, though there is interest in increasing their contact, especially to the unions and the unemployed workers' associations. Overall in the east, there are differences within the PDS with respect to the unions. Just as the party is divided about its role in the political process, with reformers pushing for the PDS to evolve into a normal party on the political scene and more orthodox members and more western members rejecting the Federal Republic's parliamentary process, the relation to the unions is fraught with differences about accepting the compromises supported by the unions and the more moderate socialist parties. Members are divided on such issues as wage restraints and shorter hours in return for retaining jobs and maintaining advantages in the global economy.

Nearly half the county PDS organizations have contact with employer associations and are interested in increasing these as well (Göthe, Kux, and Neugebauer 1996:88–98). In its campaigns, the PDS attempted to appeal particularly to women and youth. We noted earlier that it had considerable success among young voters in the 1994 elections, even though two-thirds of the present party members are over sixty and only 10 percent are younger than forty.

As in the Czech case, Social Democrats elected to parliaments in the eastern part of Germany have had to decide whether or not to work with the growing party of reformed communists. There are deep divisions in the party on this issue due to a long history of competition between the two parties. The western leadership of the national party is extremely worried that any cooperation will offend its much larger western constituency. The CDU has used this cooperation between the parties in its campaigns to warn against support for the Social Democrats, even though the CDU itself cooperates with the PDS in many communities when things have to get done.

The SPD's national leadership took a strong position against cooperation with the PDS. This position has been challenged, however, by at least two SPD prime ministers of eastern states and by the party chair of another, Mecklenburg-Vorpommern. They insisted on regional independence with respect to this issue. Already since 1994, a SPD-led minority government has ruled with the toleration of the PDS in one eastern state, Saxony-Anhalt. In the spring of 1998, elections in Saxony-Anhalt strengthened the SPD and weakened the CDU.

A coalition of SPD and CDU was proposed by conservatives when the Alliance 90/Greens, the former coalition partner, failed to win seats in parliament, while the far right German People's Union (DVU) achieved dramatic success (see Table 4.2). Yet this coalition option was ruled out by the SPD because the CDU insisted on treating the PDS as equally unacceptable as the DVU. The SPD formed a minority government of its own, again relying on toleration by the PDS, and thus challenged once more the official stance of the party leadership. Finally, in state elections in Mecklenburg-Vorpommern later that year, the Social Democrats formed a coalition government with the reformed communists, the first such coalition in any German state. This development actually had the approval of the now nationally victorious SPD leadership. Thus, the PDS in eastern Germany has come to play a very different role than the Czech Communist Party. It has become a potential partner and at the same time competes more seriously with the eastern SPD than does the Czech Communist Party with the Social Democrats in the Czech Republic.[4]

A brief comment on the role of the unions. Before unification and the need to establish union structures in the east, the west German unions were preoccupied with their own difficulties. By 1991, the number of wage earners in Germany had decreased to 43 percent of the employed labor force, while the less easily organized salaried employees represented approximately 50 percent and civil servants, 7.4 percent. Complicating these issues at the workplace were the less established domains and boundaries of organization in the east (so that different unions competed with each other in enterprises), the reduced participation of employers in

TABLE 4.2   Seats in the State Parliament, Saxony-Anhalt

	1998	1994
SPD	47	36
CDU	28	37
Greens	—	5
PDS	25	21
DVU	16	—
Participation	54.8%	71.7%

SOURCE: *The Week in Germany* (May 1, 1998): 1.

their associations and their opting out of collective bargaining arrangements, and a preference among workers for using work councils to further their interests in a specific enterprise rather than viewing the councils' work in the context of union goals regionally and nationally (Rueschemeyer 1998b).

The work councils and enterprise boards tend to work with any party that supports their programs. However, in the 1994 elections, the CDU, which had been supported most strongly by the working class in the east and by the self-employed and Christian oriented citizens in the west, lost among blue-collar workers in both east and west, but especially in the east, while the SPD picked up more blue-collar votes. Eastern blue-collar workers are increasingly voting like their western colleagues. As in the Czech Republic, education in the union with respect to the parties' stance on social policy does have an impact on the party preferences of union members (Rueschemeyer, 1998a).

Developments in the Czech Republic.   As in eastern Germany, leaders of the Czechoslovak Social Democratic Party faced the need to rebuild the party from scratch after the end of communism. Party leaders trace the party's origins to 1878, when the Czecho-Slav section of the Austrian Social Democratic Party was established. In 1893, this body became the Czechoslovak Social Democratic Workers Party (dub 1998). Developments within the party paralleled those that occurred in other European countries. Before World War I, the party was divided over the place of Czech national issues within Austria and the role of Austria-Hungary. After the defeat of Austria in World War I, the party's main division centered around that between the more radical, far left and more centrist, rightist tendencies. This conflict was exacerbated by the Russian Revolution. Soviet efforts to create a more radical socialist party in Czechoslovakia led to a final split between the two currents in November 1921 and the formation of the Czechoslovak Communist Party.

The Social Democratic Party did quite well electorally in the interwar period. With 30.1 percent of the vote, the party was the strongest political force in the parliamentary elections held in 1919 (Suda 1980:34). It fell to fourth place in the 1925 elections with 8.9 percent, compared to the 13.2 percent the communist party won, but regained support by the 1929 elections, when it came in second (13.1 percent) to the Agrarian Party (15.0 percent). Party leaders participated in the coalition of five parties known as the "Pětka," or group of five, that formed the basis for most government coalitions during the interwar period.

The good fortunes of the party reflected the generally progressive character of political life in the interwar period. They also were influenced by the fact that, in contrast to the situation in the other new democracies created in Central and Eastern Europe in 1918, which quickly became authoritarian, democracy persisted in Czechoslovakia until outside forces ended it. This situation was favorable for the organizational development of the party, which created a network of auxiliary organizations for young people and women and became a dominant force within the trade union movement.

The Czechoslovak Social Democratic Party was suppressed along with other parties under German occupation during World War II. After the liberation of the country in 1945, the party was reestablished and competed in the 1946 elections. However, it did not benefit from some of the advantages that accrued to the Communist Party during this period of modified pluralism and came in last in the 1946 elections in which the Communist Party won 37.9 percent of the vote (Korbel 1959; Suda 1980:195–201).

After the establishment of a government clearly dominated by the communists in February 1948, the social democrats were forced to merge with the Communist Party. Right-wing leaders and activists were purged from the party or resigned, and the social democratic party, like almost all other parties in the country, was unable to operate. There was a brief attempt to resurrect the party in the context of the reform period of the late 1960s, but this, as well as other reforms, was ended by the August invasion (Skilling 1976).

Efforts to revive the Social Democratic Party began immediately after the end of communist rule in late 1989. The party held its first meeting since the 1940s on November 19, two days after the brutal police response to a peaceful demonstration that served as the catalyst for the downfall of communism. Activists who had taken part in the effort to recreate a social democratic party in 1968 and reform communists who had supported Dubček were involved in this process, as were Czech emigrés, including Jiří Hořák, who soon became chairman of the party. After the split of Civic Forum in early 1991 and the later demise of one of its successors, the Civic Democratic Movement, several prominent personalities who had been active in those movements joined the Social Democratic Party.

The social democrats fared very poorly in the 1990 elections, which many citizens viewed as a vote on the communist system. Hampered by its fledgling organization and by the general rejection of anything associated with the left at that time, the party did not pass the 5 percent threshold and was unable to seat any deputies in parliament. Civic Forum won the largest share of the vote in the Czech Lands. In Slovakia, Public Against Violence was the victor. The Communist Party's percentage vote was similar to its share in elections in the interwar period. The Czechoslovak Socialist Party, which drew on the historical traditions of the Czechoslovak National Social Party, also did not seat deputies in either the Czech or federal legislature (Obrman, 1990; see Table 4.3).

The fortunes of the social democrats improved somewhat by the 1992 elections. However, despite the increase in their proportion of the vote, particularly in the Czech Lands, the social democrats fell far short of the dominant coalitions. In the Czech Lands, support for the Communist Party in coalition with other left parties in the Left Bloc remained stable at approximately 14 percent. Several Socialist Party deputies ran on the ticket of the Liberal Social Union in the Czech Lands. In Slovakia, the successor of the Communist Party, the Party of the Democratic Left, received approximately 14 percent of votes to the federal and republic parliaments (Pehe 1992).

As Table 4.3 illustrates, the social democrats achieved significantly better results in the 1996 elections, when they came in second to the Civic

TABLE 4.3 Election Results in the Czech Republic, 1990–1998 Percent of the Votes

Party	1990	1992	1996	1998
Czech Social Democratic Party (ČSSD)	4.1	6.5	26.4	32.3
Civic Democratic Party (ODS)	—	29.7	29.6	27.7
Communist Party of Bohemia and Moravia (KSČM)	13.2	14.0	10.3	11.0
Christian and Democratic Union-Czechoslovak Peoples' Party (KDU-ČSL)	8.4	6.3	8.1	9.0
Freedom Union (US)	—	—	—	8.6
Association for the Republic-Republican Party of Czechoslovakia (SPR-RSČ)	1.0	6.0	8.0	3.9
Pensioners for Social Guarantees (DZJ)	—	3.8	3.1	3.1
Democratic Union (DEU)	—	—	2.8	1.5
Green Party (SZ)	4.1	—	—	1.1
Civic Democratic Alliance (ODA)	—	5.9	6.4	—
Free Democrats	1.0	4.6	2.0	—
Moravian Silesian Movement	10.0	5.9	0.4	—
Liberal Social Union (LSU)	—	6.5	—	—
Civic Forum	49.5	—	—	—
Czechoslovak Socialist Party	2.7	—	—	—

Several small parties that have not gained seats have been omitted.

SOURCE: Richard Rose, Neil Munro, and Tom Mackie, *Elections in Central and Eastern Europe Since 1990*. Studies in Public Policy 300, Center for the Study of Public Policy, Glasgow: University of Strathclyde, 1998, pp. 45–47 for 1990, 1992, 1996. 1998 data from http://www.volby.cz. Here taken from M. Orenstein (1998, 478).

Democratic Party. The social democrats won 25 seats in the newly created Senate, and party leader Miloš Zeman became speaker of Parliament.

The social democrats have appealed to those more likely to be hurt by the shift to the market. Thus, their main supporters have been found among industrial workers and those with lower skill and educational levels. The social democrats' electoral supporters are also older and include fewer entrepreneurs than center-right parties. (Hartl 1995; Tomáš Kostelecký 1995; Kunc 1995). The party's improved showing reflected the fact that there were losers in the economic transition in the Czech Republic. It also reflected growing popular dissatisfaction with the government's efforts to reform the social welfare system and with corruption. The party's leadership did a good job in capitalizing on the dissatisfaction of these groups. They also made inroads in 1996 into groups such as the police and the military that had continued to support the Communist Party after 1989 (Hartl 1996; Matějů 1997; and "Jak se proměňuje postavení politických stran?" 1998).

Analyses of the attitudes of supporters of various political parties in the Czech Republic found that supporters of the social democrats tended to be self-declared leftists on the left-right continuum; they also tended to hold values that placed them on the left side of the political spectrum. Social democrats' supporters also tended to have higher levels of anomie and lack of trust in the current political system (See Matějů and Vlachová 1997; and Matějů and Řeháková 1997 for discussions of the interaction of self-declared, left-right orientation and value-based determination of left-right orientation on voters' choices).

In the 1998 elections, the party emerged as the most popular party, winning 32.3 percent of the vote, compared to the 27.7 percent that went to the Civic Democratic Party (rep 1998). The social democrats maintained their support among the groups that had previously supported them. They also gained support from groups that had traditionally supported the center-right, but voted for the social democrats to protest the corruption and financial scandals that occurred during the last years of the Klaus government. In the 1998 elections, the Pensioners' Party, which campaigned on a platform of protecting the social welfare and other benefits of retirees, was a potential challenger for the votes of older voters. However, the small percentage of the vote the Pensioners' Party gained (3.1 percent) indicates that it was not successful in pulling many older voters away from the ČSSD.

Like most other parties in the Czech Republic, the Social Democratic Party is weak organizationally. With approximately 18,000 members, the party clearly does not possess the "organizational" advantage that socialist parties that grew out of the reformed communist parties did in countries such as Poland, Hungary, and Bulgaria in the early 1990s. Although, as already noted, it was not a new party, the Social Democratic Party faced the need to reconstruct itself and rebuild itself organizationally. It also faced the need to attract and train new leaders.

The party's success in the 1996 and 1998 elections reflected the growing disillusionment of voters with the policies and results of the center-right coalition. By 1998, the impact of growing economic difficulties of the financial and banking crises, charges of widespread corruption that led to Klaus's resignation as prime minister in December 1997, and the divisions among the center-right parties had alienated many voters from the center-right. The social democrats' success also reflects the impact of the leadership of Miloš Zeman, who joined the party and became chair of the Prague organization in 1992, and was elected head of the party at the 1993 party congress in Hradec Králové. A dynamic group of younger leaders in Parliament, including Petra Buzková who was then the vice-chair of the party and whom public opinion surveys have frequently identified as the most trusted politician in the country, also had a positive influence on popular perceptions of the party.

The party's main competition on the left has come from the various groups that grew out of the Communist Party of Bohemia and Moravia. In the early elections, the Communist Party was much stronger than the Social Democratic Party. Splits in the party reduced its strength, but it remains a significant political force. The social democrats have faced little competition from the Czechoslovak Socialist Party. Originally the Czechoslovak National Socialist Party, the party was allowed to exist as the Czechoslovak Socialist Party during the communist period. It went through a process of reform after 1989, and continues to exist, but has seated deputies in parliament only as part of larger electoral coalitions since 1990, when it was not represented in parliament.

Analysis of the results of the 1990 elections indicates that the Communist Party drew most support in those elections in regions where large numbers of voters voted for the Communist Party in the 1946 elections. In the 1992 elections, the party also did best in regions where significant portions of the population worked in heavy industry, and in Moravia, where levels of satisfaction with the government were very low (Kostelecký 1994:219). In the 1990 elections, the social democrats did the worst in Moravia, and in districts with large numbers of religious citizens. They also did poorly in districts where many people had university education, but did well in those with high levels of pollution. In the 1992 elections, the social democrats did well in regions where many voters had voted for the Communist Party in 1946. Support for the social democrats in the early elections bore less relationship to traditional indicators of the cleavage structure of society or previous political traditions than support for all other parties (Kostelecký 1994:221).

The leadership of the Social Democratic Party has consistently refused to cooperate with the Communist Party and its successors nationally, although cooperation has sometimes occurred locally. This policy reflects the fact that the Communist Party has not engaged in a thorough reform as has occurred in many other postcommunist countries. It also reflects the fact that many of the current leaders of the Social Democratic Party were former members of the Communist Party who supported the reforms of the 1968 era and either left the party or were purged after the end of those reforms. The impact of this policy regarding cooperation with the Communist Party was evident after the 1998 elections, when the social democrats continued to reject the option of forming a left coalition with it. After failing to persuade other political forces, including the Christian Democratic Union-People's Party, to enter into a coalition, party leader Miloš Zeman chose to form a government by entering into an agreement with his main center-right opponent, the Civic Democratic Party of Václav Klaus.

Social Policy Issues in Eastern Germany

The context in which social policy should be seen is largely the national one in both the German and Czech cases. In Germany, we find a somewhat stronger polarization of views between the major parties nationally than in the five new states. The CDU-led coalition in Bonn looks for a more drastic transformation of the German welfare state in response to the problems of increased international competition, the problems of unification, and an aging population. In conjunction, these have resulted in increased unemployment and government debt. The SPD agrees that some reconstruction of the German welfare state is necessary, but the CDU/FDP coalition wants to go much further in outright cutting of provisions. The SPD prefers to finance more provisions via general taxes rather than through wage-related taxes, and seeks to make the tax system more equitable. That would make for a more equal sharing of the burdens of unification because much of the welfare state expenditures on unemployment and training in the east are financed via wage-related taxes. Reducing wage-related taxes would also lower labor costs and, hopefully, reduce unemployment.

As prime minister of Lower Saxony (and now chancellor of the Federal Republic), Gerhard Schroeder, then the SPD's main spokesperson on economic policy, presented proposals that included a cut in non-wage labor costs. Payroll social welfare contributions, paid half by employers and half by employees, are presently 42 percent of gross wages. With this plan, payroll contributions would be scaled back and the differences made up by increasing the subsidy the federal government provides to the pension and unemployment insurance funds. To pay for that, the SPD advocated a raise in petroleum tax and in the value-added tax, a sales tax paid on most products at each level of production. After the CDU and SPD agreed on raising the value-added tax to 16 percent (a point higher than it was), the increase went into effect in April 1998.

Because of the possibility of governing in 1998, the SPD had to deal in its policy proposals with constraints that limit its ability to answer some popular needs in the east. The SPD presents itself as a progressive party, committed to pragmatic reform and an economic system of both public and private sectors. This stance is popular with the new constituencies the party tries to attract and keep. In its campaign, the party promised to rescind cuts in long-term sick pay and retirement pensions that the Kohl government implemented with its Bundestag majority in 1997. The 1998 coalition agreement includes an overhaul in the tax system that will reduce both the bottom and top income tax rates, while eliminating tax breaks. General tax revenues will be used to help support social welfare programs, which are presently funded by payroll contributions of employers and employees.

There are many other social policy issues that are of concern to east Germans. These include employment, education, housing, and women's integration into the labor force and related social supports, to mention only a few. It is impossible to adequately cover all of these in this chapter; some will only be briefly discussed.

Unemployment problems affect both eastern and western Germany, and the government, unions, and employers' associations see this as a major issue, if not *the* major issue that has to be addressed. Unemployment in the eastern part of Germany in 1998 was 19 percent, a figure that would have been greatly increased if those who were forced to retire early, those who still work short hours, and those in retraining programs were included in the calculation. The introduction of publicly supported jobs prevented the numbers from soaring, but these positions were created only for a limited period and they had been severely cut, although some were since restored again as the 1998 federal elections approached. The SPD, the PDS, and the eastern CDU representatives had asked the CDU-led government to fight against the reductions in publicly supported work positions. The CDU east has expressed frustration with the national party and its comparative lack of attention to the eastern constituency.

The policy of the SPD focuses on the need to develop an industrial base in the east and its research potential to stimulate the domestic market, to trim indirect labor costs, to encourage the service sector and the growth of small service companies, to develop self-employment and more part-time positions, especially for the elderly or for younger people entering the workforce. This policy would allow the creation of additional places for younger people (for different perspectives on this in the east, see Wolf-gang Thierse 1995) and back other programs to create jobs for the young, as well as expand apprenticeship programs.[5] In fact, as soon as the "red-green" coalition took office, it planned to launch a program to place 100,000 young people in jobs or vocational training. The German govern-ment is especially concerned with long-term unemployment among the young and will attempt to reduce the period of unemployment to six months or less.

While social policy issues are decided mostly at the federal level, the states, which have jurisdiction especially in education and culture, are important, too. The lack of enough apprenticeships is a source of great frustration in both the east and west. In the east, in the state of Branden-burg, where the social democrats are the strongest party and lead the government, there has been an early articulation of the problem and seri-ous efforts to address it. Reinhard Hoeppner, prime minister of Saxony-Anhalt, where the social democrats received the largest percentage of the vote in the April 1998 state election, noted in a talk at Forum Ost-deutschland that there was an apprenticeship available for every young person in the state.[6] In 1996–1997, the PDS supported the SPD in passing a law that kept teachers in their jobs, despite fewer students, by reducing their hours and salaries.

There are various models in Berlin to address unemployment and qualifications, developed by Christine Bergmann, former SPD Senator for Work, Occupational Education, and Women in Berlin and now a member of the federal cabinet. These models are funded by the state and in part by the European Union. The hope was to gain increased funding through support for federal legislation after the federal elections.[7]

Primary and secondary education in eastern Germany were restruc-tured along west German lines. In practice, this meant the replacement of the GDR's comprehensive polytechnical schools with a more differenti-ated selective system, capped by west German-style gymnasiums. But Brandenburg continued to emphasize comprehensive schools, while the other four states, led initially by conservative governments, instituted a two- or three-way partition of students into academic and general or vo-cational schools after their completion of primary school. These changes were carried out under the influence of administrators from west German partner states, some of whom remained in senior positions in the east.

With respect to housing, there is little states and communities can do about raising rents—which was done in stages—and increased privatiza-tion. The return of property to the original owners, victims of Nazism and east Germans who left the country during the communist period, is a complicated subject; the reaction to the east Germans living in west

Germany now reclaiming their homes was particularly intense among many east Germans. There have been efforts to retain land use for gardens that especially apartment dwellers use, and it has been the reformed communists, who have experience and knowledge in the community, who have been most successful in conserving that land.

States, cities, and communities that are strapped for funds have to take into account the market and their constituencies. Only a few years after unification, the city of Rostock was concerned with maintaining the residential areas, where approximately 60 percent of the population lives in apartment house complexes, as integrated, nonsegregated housing—even if the most affluent eventually leave. There was, and is, some effort to sell public housing in the residential areas that would relieve the city from having to make extensive repairs. Similarly, the city seeks to sell half-finished apartment complexes in the new residential areas because the city does not have the funds to complete the project. At the time, the cooperative associations, the Genossenschaften, which own 40 percent of the complexes, opposed privatization sales. Specifically, they opposed selling a building in which many older residents live for commercial purposes, or to marking an area for commerce that residents pressured the city to use for youth clubs. In the first case, the city backed down; in the second, the young people ended up meeting in cellars (Rueschemeyer 1993).

The SPD has committed itself to defend the social rental law and build more affordable housing in the Federal Republic, involving both housing associations and private investors. Interestingly, the SPD together with the CDU campaigned for an extension of the special support for rent so that the percentage of income paid for rent was somewhat lower in the east than in the west. In this way, pressure is put on the CDU in the east to respond to the needs of its constituency.[8]

In the large housing areas, the SPD program articulates a need to make young people feel that they belong to the community and to provide security. Housing developments in the east are less segregated than in the west but the dearth of activities for the young, combined with the difficulty of finding apprenticeships and work entry in many places, may further increase tensions.[9] Despite the efforts of the SPD to improve living conditions and protect housing in some areas, it is important to note that, because of its low membership in some neighborhoods in the east, the party is neither active as a local party organization nor indirectly through participation of its members in other associations.

Women's issues are an important part of the contested social policy agenda in eastern Germany. The GDR had a liberal abortion code that first became law in 1972, when it allowed abortion during the first three months of pregnancy. Over 85 percent of children between the ages of

1 and 3 were in day care centers, and nearly 90 percent of those between 3 and 6 were in kindergartens. Other supports for working parents included a guarantee of 40 days paid time off from work annually to care for sick children of 14 years or younger, and after childbirth a parental leave was granted until the child was a year old, at 75–90 percent of net pay, with a guarantee to return to the job at the same level of employment. In the last years of the GDR, this leave could also be taken by the spouse or the grandmother.

These supports were especially important for single parents, most of whom were mothers. These women had preferential access, before their married colleagues, to an apartment and to child care when they resumed their work outside the home. Naturally problems remained for many because the supports did not solve all the problems of the single parent. By the time unification occurred, about 50 percent of west German women were in the workforce, but only 3 percent of children under the age of 3 were in public day-care centers. Before unification, a mother in west Germany could take five paid days a year to care for a sick child of 8 years or younger.

The introduction of a quota system for women in public positions in the Green Party and the SPD in western Germany and in the PDS, Alliance 90/Greens, and, of course, in the SPD in the east opened up new opportunities for women in politics (Rueschemeyer 1998:89–115). In the most recent elections in 1998, about a third of the representatives elected to the federal parliament were women. The interests, if not the political activity of East German women after unification led to changes in social policies, especially with respect to abortion. West Germany's penal code outlawed abortion unless the woman met certain criteria. After enormous fights, reviews, and new changes in 1995, the new regulations allowed abortion without punishment during the first three months of pregnancy, preceded by mandatory counseling. There is still fighting about the kind of consultations women are required to undertake. Again, it is in the state of Brandenburg where the SPD holds government power that the fighting has recently become particularly intense. In Brandenburg, the Catholic charity association Caritas, which moved into the east after unification, rather than providing general counsel to women considering abortion, gives advice that is essentially oriented toward not having the abortion. The association has been warned that its financial support in Brandenburg will be at risk if it continues this policy. The state responds to the expectations of its east German constituency with respect to a social policy that most east German women consider less adequate than previous policies.

Other expectations of eastern women have been addressed by western politicians, especially when they coincide with political demands made in the west. Policy initiatives of this kind include an increase in the number of days from five to ten days allowed to care for a sick family member and for single mothers to 20, and raising the age of a sick child for whom such leave is granted to 12 years. Other goals include a kindergarten place for all children by 1999 and a 24-month parental leave. These changes were made in response to agitation in eastern Germany with the loss of benefits. However, there is little attention to the need for day care centers for children under the age of 3—even in the SPD. As already mentioned, the PDS addressed some of these issues in their 1998 campaign, but their constituency is essentially in the east.

East German women have been adversely affected by unemployment (two-thirds of the long-term unemployed are women) and the closing of day care centers by enterprises. Some of the issues involving discrimination at work are handled through equal opportunity and women's affairs offices set up in all communities with a population of 10,000 or more; however, these are not a substitute for political influence and coalition building to introduce legislation that would initiate regulations against discrimination. East German women see the parties on the left generally as potentially more supportive of them, and, in the 1994 elections, the Social Democrats and Reformed Communists together received proportionately more votes among east German women than they did among women in the west.

Social Policy Issues in the Czech Republic

Changes in social policy have occurred in several stages in the Czech Republic. Although the former Czechoslovak government moved aggressively to privatize state enterprises by voucher privatization and enact policies designed to stimulate the development of new private enterprises in the period immediately after 1989, it retained many of the social welfare provisions and social policies in place during the communist era. The end of government subsidies of basic foodstuffs and, eventually, energy, raised the cost of living dramatically in the first few years after 1989, despite government attempts to offset these increases by direct payments to citizens. The value of many social benefits, including children's and mothers' allowances, and payments to mothers to remain at home to care for their infant children (which were redefined as parental benefits and made available to fathers as well as mothers) decreased as the result of inflation and declining real wages (Musil 1995; Rys 1995; "Mateřská a 'otcovská' dovolena" 1993:7; Castle-Kanerová: 1992:113). Access to certain services, such as child care, also decreased noticeably, particularly for children under the age of 3, as municipalities found themselves unable to support the services they had previously provided and the management of privatized factories and other enterprises determined that it was unprofitable to provide child care for employees and workers.

The impact of this situation on the availability of child care is evident because the number of places in nurseries for children under 3 years old declined from 78,555 in 1989 to 17,210 in 1991 (Federální statistický úřad, Český statistický úřad, Slovenský statistický úřad 1992, 589; see also Wolchik, forthcoming; Kramer 1998; Illner 1998; "Školy nemají prost ředky na svoů další existenci" 1993; ria 1993a; kva 1993; ria 1993b).

However, although the Czechoslovak government's rhetoric promoted individual responsibility, it took a very cautious approach to changing benefits. Although poverty increased, an increase in the minimum living standard allowed groups that fell below the poverty line to receive social assistance payments (Orenstein 1995:184–85; Mareš and Rabušic 1997; Čermák 1998; Večerník 1993; see Kramer 1998). Rent control also continued and kept the cost of housing for much of the population very low, even after controls were reduced. Young people, who had to look for new housing on the market, often found the cost of apartments and houses prohibitive. The impact of the shift to market rates was compounded by the dramatic 73 percent decrease in new housing between 1990 and 1995 (Illner 1998:150; see also Orenstein 1995:182–83), but those who had housing did not face massive evictions or immediate dislocations. Similarly, those unfortunate enough to live in housing that was restored to previous owners through restitution faced pressure to find other places to live. But they were protected to some extent by laws that required new owners to find acceptable apartments for those whom they proposed to evict from their newly restituted properties.

The government also encouraged movement toward self-insurance, both in terms of health insurance and retirement (see Illner 1998; Orenstein 1995; Castle-Kanerová 1992; Kabele and Potůček 1995). However, before 1993, it took no action to reduce pensioners' benefits. Rather, pensions were increased to account for the increased cost of living and pension benefits were extended to groups of the population previously ineligible for them, such as nonworking wives who gained social security benefits as the result of their husbands' economic activity (Kabele and Potůček 1995:31–32; Vobruba 1993; and Večerník 1993).

After the June 1992 elections, the government adopted a more aggressive approach to social policy reform. This approach was evident in the areas of unemployment policies, social assistance, and health care (see Orenstein 1995; pech 1995a; pech 1995b). It was also evident in family and retirement policy.

In April 1993, children's allowances for families with one child whose incomes were two or more times greater than the minimum living standard were eliminated. The basis for payment of children's allowances also changed from the number of children in the family to the age of children in 1993 (s 1993; ika 1993; Navrátilová 1996b). In 1995, the number of families receiving children's allowances decreased again, as such allowances were limited to those families whose incomes were no greater than 1.8 times the minimum living standard (MS 1995).

The government also enacted changes in pensions, increased six times between 1990 and 1994 to offset the increase in the cost of living (DB 1994). Pensioners were protected somewhat from the impact of the shift to a market economy. However, a survey conducted by the trade unions indicated that over half of pensioners felt that they could not make ends meet in late 1994 ("Pension reform bill" 1995). State pensions, which amounted to 51 percent of the average salary in 1995, were expected to fall to 48 percent in 2006 and to 45 percent in 2020 ("Czech Seniors" 1995). According to the provisions of a law passed by parliament in June 1995, the minimum age for retirement was to increase to 61 for women, depending on the number of children, and 62 for men. Although the increase in retirement age was to be phased in gradually through 2007, this and other reforms, such as measures that tightened conditions for receiving disabilities pensions, were very controversial and were opposed by the trade unions (Kabele and Potůček 1995:31–32; Navrátilová 1996c; em 1995a). In 1995, the government also introduced a new system of supplementary pensions that relies on individual contributions, with no required matching funds from employers, to supplement pensions (em 1995b).

These measures provoked vigorous protest from trade unions. The Czech-Moravian Chamber of Labor Unions (ČMKOS), which includes unions with a total membership of 2.8 million, called for a 15-minute national warning strike to protest against the proposed reforms in December 1994 ("Czech Unionists" 1994). Union activists also organized other demonstrations to protest the proposed changes.

In the spring of 1997, the Klaus government introduced further cuts in social spending as well as other austerity measures as part of a plan to deal with the financial problems the country experienced after the failure of several state banks. These changes became evident in family policy in September 1997 when the threshold for receiving allowances was raised (Šimoník 1997). As in the past, the state continued to support single parent families, most of which are headed by women, through the social assistance system. However, many of these families found themselves below the poverty line (See Tošovský 1995; Čtk 1996). In early 1998, the caretaker government of Josef Tošovský proposed steep increases in the price of energy and rent. Thus, electricity was to increase by 30 percent, gas by 27 percent, and rents by 27 percent (Adamec 1998).

In the 1998 elections, the social democrats benefited from popular dissatisfaction with the government's efforts to reform social policy. A survey conducted in April 1997 found that over two-thirds of those surveyed felt that the government was not paying enough attention to the social side of the transformation. This dissatisfaction was most noticeable among voters who sympathized with the Social Democratic Party, whereby 85 percent were negative about social policy. Among those who sympathized with the Communist Party, 93 percent were negative. However, significant proportions of citizens who identified with center-right parties also were dissatisfied. Pensioners, workers, and residents with poor living standards were particularly critical (Rendlová 1997a).

A survey conducted in February 1997 found that the social democrats' proposal to lower the age for retirement received significantly more support (47 percent) than the government's proposals for pension reform (35 percent). Many respondents (56 percent) also felt that the government should pay more attention to current living standards, even at the price of slowing the economic reform, rather than concentrating more on economic reform, which would bring a better standard of living in the future (31 percent) (Rendlová 1997b).

The social democrats' campaign in the 1998 elections reflected these perspectives. Social considerations figured large in its motto: "To give equal conditions for development and fulfillment to all people is the basis of a socially just, free and democratic society and the precondition of the future prosperity of the whole country." They were also reflected in the party's platform, which argued that the governing coalition's "one-sided emphasis on economic reform and privatization . . . and neglect of the role of the state and civil sector allowed the undeserved enrichment of some individuals and insufficient reward for the labor of others." It also criticized the government for viewing social policy as a necessary evil and social expenditures as a nonproductive drain on investment and thus of the future economic prosperity of the country ("Sociální doktrina ČSSD" 1998). Departing from what it described as "the idea of a socially and ecologically oriented market economy," the party's social program called for an increase in the role of the tripartite council (the council that brings the government, employers, and unions together) in discussing social policy reform ("Sociální" 1998:1).

The party's platform promised to eliminate the planned increase in retirement age. It also proposed increasing the average pension to at least 50 percent of the average wage and linking pensions to prices and the development of real wages. In addition, it proposed the creation of a more adequate social insurance system separate from the state budget, with individual and state contributions to be funded in part from the National Property Fund.

In social assistance, the party's program was based on the principle that appropriate living conditions must be ensured for all, including minorities and Roma children. The party proposed a gradual increase in facilities for institutional care and social assistance. It also proposed giving local governments appropriate funds to carry out their responsibilities in this area and an increase in the minimum subsistence level, as well as a large increase in the minimum wage from 2,650 to 4,100 crowns per month.

In family policy, the party proposed new legislation to increase care for children, ease adoption, and improve conditions for maternal care of children. These included measures to assist families with handicapped children and single parents. The party's program also noted the need to limit the negative impact of pornography, rape, and the use of violence on children. One of the most notable aspects of the party's policies in this area is the proposal to return to a universal rather than needs-based system of children allowances. The program also envisioned a return to pronatalist policies to deal with the declining birthrate, including helping young families obtain housing and increased public services for children and families to allow mothers to combine their roles as mothers with their economic activities.

In the area of unemployment, the party emphasized the need for policies designed to ensure full employment and called for an increase in the role of the Office of Labor, with special attention to regions with increasing unemployment. It also proposed the creation of a wage scale in the private sector to protect workers without unions and measures to reduce the gap between management and employees.

Housing received the most attention in the social section of the party's platform. The party called for measures to resolve the housing crisis, including those that would reduce legal uncertainty concerning ownership and rights, steps to end speculation in housing, and measures to deal with the particular housing needs of the elderly and young people. It also called for tax breaks to increase new housing starts; an increase in the state role, especially at the local level, in making housing policy; the creation of funds for new housing in local budgets; as well as for steps to ensure housing for the weaker segments of society. One of the most controversial proposals was for a review of a 1994 law on privatization of housing, which the party's platform described as a particular threat to the elderly. The social democrats also pledged to enact legal measures to prevent speculation in housing and support housing cooperatives, as well as a slowdown of the proposed deregulation of rent and services connected with housing, such as energy and water ("Sociální" 1998; see also "Program bytové politiky" 1998).

In health reform, the party proposed to remedy problems with the 1990 reform in this sector. The party's platform stated that noncommercial health insurance would remain the basis of health care and pledged to optimize health care facilities and improve the financial cooperation of hospitals and clinics. It also called for closer regulation of the price of medicines, health care materials, and prosthetic devices, and for measures to address the insufficient wages of doctors and other health care personnel. It also proposed a merger of health and hospital insurance and an increase in the role of state organs in the organization and financing of health services.

The party also proposed changes in family policy. It called for a new concept of family policy and a new family law. In addition to restoring children's allowances to all families with children, it promised to devote special attention to single parent families and those with children with special needs. It also called for measures to address child care facilities and after school programs for children.

In education, the party emphasized the need for education to be accessible to all and for improvements to increase the quality of education at all levels. In addition to calling for the establishment of a national council for education, party leaders emphasized the need to increase teachers' salaries.

Since a social democratic government was just formed in July 1998, it is still too early to know what the party's leaders will do to enact these promises now that they are the governing party. The need to secure the agreement of leaders of the Civic Democratic Party for any major policy changes, as the agreement with that party requires, will clearly limit how much the social democrats can enact the changes they promised in the campaign. Soon after becoming premier, Miloš Zeman noted that he expected his government to have much difficulty in enacting its program in social policy (TAM 1998). It is too early to judge the overall impact of the social democrats on social policy reform, but party leaders already have taken numerous steps.

The social democratic government proposed measures in August to deal with the crisis in the pension system, which ran a deficit in 1997. Pensions accounted for most state social spending, which in turn accounted for 40 percent of the budget in 1997, and were expected to amount to 43 percent in 1998 and 46 percent in 1999 ("Pension System Getting Dearer" 1998). In September, Deputy Premier and Minister of Labor and Social Affairs Vladimír Špidla proposed a 2.4 percent increase in pension insurance payments, 1.8 percent of which was to come from employers and 0.6 percent from employees (rtj 1998). Špidla also called for additional steps to separate the pension fund from the state budget and for measures to increase the responsibility of individuals for making voluntary contributions to pension insurance and for establishing company pension funds

(VV 1998; vr 1998). The government also announced plans to index pensions twice in 1999 to maintain their real value. In October, Špidla threatened to cut pension payments by 540 crowns monthly if his proposed increase in payments was not approved by parliament (VV 1998).

The government also proposed an increase in sick pay benefits (PVR 1998) and a 17 percent increase in wages in the public sector after an agreement with public sector unions in September 1998 (RJC 1998). In November 1998, the government announced that it would ratify the European social charter, which the Czechoslovak government signed in 1992, but did not bring to a vote. The charter would require that minimum wages be increased from the current average of 2,650 crowns to between 4,500 and 5,000 crowns each month (TAM 1998).

Prime Minister Zeman provoked protest from labor groups in late September 1998, when he suggested that public works be used as a substitute for unemployment benefits in light of the expected increase in the number of unemployed to 500,000 in 1999 (VV 1998). The government announced a "National Plan for the Battle against Unemployment" that requested an additional two billion crowns for active employment policies. These were to include requalification programs and plans to assure employment for young people who have finished their educations.

Deputy Premier and Labor and Social Affairs Minister Špidla also pledged to take steps to eliminate the discrimination against women, older people, and Roma that results from unfair practices in job advertisements and at labor offices (VV 1998). The government announced its intention to propose a law to ensure that employees will receive their unpaid wages if companies go bankrupt (VV 1998). In early September, the government proposed a 17 percent wage increase in the public sector to counteract the 13 percent drop in real wages in this sector (TAM 1998).

Public opinion polls conducted in October 1998 indicated that approximately half of the population approved of the way the government was functioning, while the other half disagreed. Eighty percent of ČSSD supporters approved of the government, as did 51 percent of supporters of the Communist Party, and 49 percent of supporters of the Christian Democratic Union-Czech People's Party. Many Czechs (53 percent) also expected greater social justice from the social democrats than from the Klaus government. Citizens with elementary education and older people were particularly optimistic, although unemployed respondents did not expect greater social justice. Ninety-two percent of ČSSD supporters and 75 percent of Communist Party supporters approved of the government's social policy; 83 percent of the Civic Democratic Party, 76 percent of the Freedom Union's supporters, and 64 percent of the Christian Democrats disapproved (PK 1998).

This division of opinion has been reflected among the elite. Parliament's rejection of the government's first budget proposal, which proposed a 27 billion crown deficit, and of the proposed 2.4 percent increase in pension insurance contributions in October, illustrate the difficulties Zeman and his colleagues will have in getting their proposed changes enacted into law (Pitrová 1998).

Conclusion

In both Germany and the Czech Republic, social democratic leaders have articulated and defended a conception of social policy that has differed from that of their center-right opponents. During the early transition years, leaders of both parties criticized the governing coalition's approach to social policies and argued that the state should continue to provide for citizens in need and play a larger role in buffering the costs of the transition to a market economy. Hurt by the initial overall rejection of the left and the need to reestablish themselves as political organizations after the communist period, the social democrats fared poorly in elections in the early 1990s. This effect was more pronounced in the Czech Republic than in east Germany. The fortunes of both parties improved in the mid-1990s, and by 1998, both were the victors in parliamentary elections.

The successor organizations of the former ruling communist parties developed differently in the two countries. The Communist Party in the Czech Republic remained unreconstructed and had only limited voter appeal. The PDS took significant steps toward democratic reform, even though it did not sever all personal and ideological ties to the past. It soon succeeded in doubling its vote as it articulated specifically east German concerns in competition with the other parties, whose main organizational and constituency strength lies in West Germany. Now it is a partner in the government of two east German states.

Factors specific to each country's political situation contributed to the victories of the social democrats. However, in both cases, the social democrats were able to use growing popular dissatisfaction with the social policies of the center-right government to increase their support. The electoral programs of the two parties called for important changes in social policy as well as for paying greater attention to the social impact of the transition.

Since forming governments, social democratic leaders in both Germany and the Czech Republic have attempted to translate several aspects of their electoral programs' provisions concerning social policy into practice. As they have done so, they have encountered both political and economic obstacles. In the Czech Republic, the ability of the social democrats to push their agenda aggressively is limited both by the need to adhere to the agreement they signed with their main opposition, Vaclav Klaus's Civic Democratic Party, and by the serious economic problems evident in the recent downturn in the Czech economy. The impact that the social democrats' victories will have on the social policies of Germany and the Czech Republic is an open question. Yet, it is clear that the presence of these parties, and the support they have received from a large portion of the electorates in both countries, has been an important counterweight to efforts to reduce the role of the state in providing for individuals' welfare in these countries.

References

Adamec, Radek. 1998. "Pilip: Navrhujeme zdražit energie o 30 procent, plyn a nájmy o 27 procent." *Lidové noviny*. (February 17): 15.

Beneš, Václav L. 1973. "Czechoslovak Democracy and Its Problems." In *A History of the Czechoslovak Republic, 1918–1948*, edited by Victor S. Mamatey and Radomír Lůža. Princeton: Princeton University Press.

Boguszak, Marek, and Vladimír Rak. 1990. "Czechoslovakia—May 1990 Survey Report." Prague: Association for Independent Social Analysis.

Castle-Kanerová, Mita. 1992. "Social Policy in Czechoslovakia." In *The New Eastern Europe: Social Policy Past, Present and Future*, edited by Bob Deacon. London: Sage Publications.

Centrum pre výskum spoločenských problémov pri KC VPN. 1990. "Slovensko pred vol'bami." Bratislava. (April 11).

"Czech Seniors Watch Purchasing Power Disappear." *Information Access Company, Market Europe* 6:5 (October 26, 1995).

"Czech Unionists Stage Patchy Strike Over Pensions." *Reuters World Service*. (December 21, 1994).

Čermák, Martin. 1998. "Kdo je v České republice chudý?" *Lidové noviny*. (May 2).

Čtk. 1996. "Osamělé matky nejchudší." *Lidové noviny*. (June 22).

DB. 1994. "Old Age Pension Level Changes Since 1990." *ČTK*. (June 6).

dub. 1998. "ČSSD slavila sto dvacet let." *Lidové noviny*. (March 23): 3.

em. 1995a. "Bývalé letušky protestují, ostatní důchodci si polepší." *Lidové noviny*. (January 21): 3.

———. 1995b. "Vláda schválila návrh nového systému důchodového pojištění." *Lidové noviny*. (January 19): 7.

Federální statistický úřad, Český Statistický úřad, Slovenský štatistický úřad. 1992. *Statistická ročenka České a Slovenské Federativní Republiky 1992*. Prague: SEVT.

Göthe, Heiko, Ulla Kux, Gero Neugebauer, Oskar Niedermeyer, Guenter Pollack, Richard Stoess, Joerg Wischerman. 1996. *Organization, Politik und Vernetzung der Parteien auf Kreisebene in dem fünf neuen Bundesländern*. Freie Universität Berlin: Zentralinstitut Für sozialwissenschaftliche Forschung.

Hartl, Jan. 1995. "Social Policy: An Issue for Today and the Future." *Czech Sociological Review* III:2 (Fall): 209–20.

ika. 1993. "Rodinám s nízkymi příjmy." *Lidové noviny*. (April 10): 12.

Illner, Michael. 1998. "The Changing Quality of Life in a Post-Communist Country: The Case of Czech Republic." Prague: Institute of Sociology, Academy of Sciences of the Czech Republic.

Kabele, Jiří, and Martin Potůček. 1995. "The Formation and Implementation of Social Policy in the Czech Republic as a Political Process." Research Papers. Foundation for Research on Social Transformation. Prague.

Korbel, Josef. 1959. *The Communist Subversion of Czechoslovakia: 1938–1948: The Future of Coexistence*. Princeton: Princeton University Press.

Kostelecký, Tomáš. 1994. "Economic, Social and Historical determinants of Voting Patterns in the 1990 and 1992 Parliamentary Elections in the Czech Republic." *Czech Sociological Review* II:2 (Fall).

———. 1995. "The Party Systems in Poland, Czech Republic, Slovakia and Hungary." Manuscript. Prague: Institute of Sociology, Academy of Sciences of the Czech Republic.

Kramer, Mark. 1998. "Social Protection Policies and Safety Nets in East-Central Europe: Dilemmas of the Postcommunist Transformation." In *Sustaining the Transition: The Social Safety net in Postcommunist Europe*, edited by Ethan B. Kapstein and Michael Mandelbaum. New York: Council on Foreign Relations.

Kunc, Jiří. 1995. "The Party System in the Czech Republic." Manuscript. Prague: Institute for Fundamental Studies,

kva. 1993a. "Školy podraží, učitelky ale. nezbohatnoů." *Lidové noviny*. (September 7): 2.

———. 1993b. "Málo soukromy mateřských škol." *Lidové noviny*. (September 8): 2.

Leff, Carol Skalnik. 1988. *National Conflict in Czechoslovakia: The Making and Remaking of a State, 1918–1987*. Princeton: Princeton University Press.

Mareš, Petr, and Ladislav Rabušic. 1997. "Subjective Poverty and Its Structure in the Czech Republic." *Slovak Sociological Review* 29:3, 279–299.

Matějů, Petr. 1997. "Beliefs about Distributive Justice and Social Change." *Social Trends*. Prague: Institute of Sociology, Academy of Sciences of the Czech Republic.

Matějů, Petr, and Blanka Řeháková. 1997. "Obrat doleva nebo proměna vzorců volebního chování sociálních tříd?" *Sociální trendy*. Prague: Institute of Sociology, Academy of Sciences of the Czech Republic.

Matějů, Petr, and Klára Vlachová. 1997. "Krystalizace politického spektra a faktory působící na volební rozhodování v České republice." *Sociální trendy*. Prague: Institute of Sociology, Academy of Sciences of the Czech Republic.

"Mateřská a 'otcovská' dovolena." *Lidové noviny*. (October 4, 1993): 7.

MS. 1995. "Veřejnost u nás I v Evropě citlivě reaguje na změny přídavku na děti." *Lidové noviny*. (January 14): 2.

Musil, Libor. 1995. "Statusová solidarita a česká sociální politika." *Sociologický časopis*. 321, 423–434.

Navrátilová, Jana. 1996a. "Sociální dávky musejí motivovat." *Lidové noviny*. (June 17): 3.

———. 1996b. "Adresnost dávek je motivující." *Lidové noviny*. (July 20): 3.

———. 1996c. "Bude nutné zvýšit důchodový věk." *Lidové noviny*. (July 30): 1.

Obrman, Jan. 1990. "Civic Forum Surges to Impressive Victory in Elections." *Radio Free Europe Report on Eastern Europe.* (June 22): 13–16.

Orenstein, Mitchell A. 1995. "Transitional Social Policy in the Czech Republic and Poland." *Czech Sociological Review* III:2 (Fall): 179–180.

Palik, Ruth. 1998. "Social Policy in Germany: The Perspective of the DGB-Bundesvorstand." Paper presented for a conference on The Future of the German Welfare State. Watson Institute for International Studies, Brown University.

pech. 1995a. "Na připojištění pro pobyt v nemocnici mohou pacienti dokonce vydělat." *Lidové noviny.* (January 3): 2.

———. 1995b. "Rubáš: Zdravotnictví nepotřebuje sponzory." *Lidové noviny.* (January 19): 2.

"Pension Reform Bill Sparks Protest." *East European Banker.* (January 1995): 3.

"Pension System Getting Dearer, Must Be Changed—Pilip." *Business News.* (May 21, 1998).

Pitrová, Zuzana. 1998. "Sněmovna odmítla Zemanuv návrh rozpočtu." *Lidové noviny.* (October 15): 1.

PK. 1998. "Majority Expects More Social Justice From ČSSD Government." *ČTK.* (October 23).

Potůček, Martin. 1992. "Dilemmas of Social Policy in Post-November Czechoslovakia." Manuscript. Prague: Department of Sociology and Social Policy, Charles University.

"Program bytové politiky jednotlivých stran." *Lidové noviny.* (June 4, 1998): 5.

PVR. 1998. "Government Plans to Raise Sick Pay." *ČTK.* (October 19).

Rendlová, Eliška. 1997a. "Hodnocení současné sociální politiky." *Institut pro výzkum veřejného minení.* (April 5).

———. 1997b. "Aktuální sociální požadavky a ekonomický rozvoj." *Institut pro výzkum veřejného minení.* (February 17).

ria. 1993a. "Jesle k nezaplacení, a tedy ke srůžení." *Lidové noviny.* (August 4): 2.

———. 1993b. "Kolik zaplatíme za školy?" *Lidové noviny.* (September 3): 2.

RJC. 1998. "Government Approves Decrees on Public Sector Pay Rises." *ČTK.* (October 19).

Rueschemeyer, Marilyn. 1993. "East Germany's New Towns in Transition: A Grassroots View of the Impact of Unification." *Urban Studies* 30:3 (April): 495–506.

———. 1998a "Social Democrats after the End of Communist Rule: Eastern Germany and the Czech Republic." *Sociological Analysis* 1:3.

———. 1998b. "The Social Democratic Party in Eastern Germany." In *Participation and Democracy East and West: Comparison and Interpretations,* edited by Dietrich Rueschemeyer, Marilyn Rueschemeyer, and Björn Wittrock. New York: M.E. Sharpe.

Rueschemeyer, Marilyn. ed., 1998. *Women in the Politics of Post-Communist Eastern Europe,* revised and expanded edition. London; Armonk, New York: M.E. Sharpe.

Rys, Vladimír. 1995. "Social Security Developments in Central Europe: A Return to Reality." *Czech Sociological Review* III:2 (Fall): 197–208.

rtj. 1998. "ODS challenges Špidla's Promise to Raise Pay in Public Sector." *ČTK.* (September 4).

s. 1993. "Od dubna vyšší životní minimum." *Lidové noviny.* (January 6): 12.

Skilling, H. Gordon. 1976. *Czechoslovakai's Interrupted Revolution.* Princeton: Princeton University Press.

"Sociální doktrína ČSSD." 1998. http://www.cssd.cz/dokumenty/1998/socialni_doktrina.htm, (May).

Suda, Zdeněk L. 1980. *Zealots and Rebels: A History of the Ruling Communist Party of Czechoslovakia.* Stanford, Cali.: Hoover Institution Press.

Šimoník, David. 1997. "One out of Five Czech Families to Lose Child Care Supplements." *Carolina.* (September 12).

"Školy nemají prostředky na svou další existenci." *Lidové noviny.* (June 9, 1993): 2.

TAM. 1998. "Cabinet Expects Most Problems in Social Affairs Sector." *ČTK.* (August 16).

———. 1998. "Czech Government Going to Ratify European Social Charter." *ČTK.* (November 6).

Thierse, Wolfgang. 1995. "Fünf Jahre Deutsche Vereinigung: Wirtschaft-Gesellschaft-Mentalität." *Aus Politik und Zeitgeschicte.* (September 29): B40–41.

Večerník, Jiří. 1993. "Utáření nové sociální regulace v České republice." *Sociologický časopis* 29:2, 181–202.

Vobruba, George. 1993. "Nad národní sociální politika v procesu transformace." *Sociologický časopis* 29:2, 167–180.

vr. 1998. "Analysts Sceptical about Company Pension Funds." *ČTK.* (September 30).

VV. 1998. "Labour Ministry Preparing Increase in Pension Insurance." *ČTK.* (September 4).

———. 1998. "Špidla Threatens to Lower pensions by 500 Crowns." *ČTK.* (October 3).

Welsh, Helga. 1995. "Four Years and Several Elections Later: The Eastern German Political Landscape after Unification." In "Germany's New Politics," edited by David Conradt, Gerald Kleinfeld, George Romoser, and Christian Soe. *German Studies Review,* 35–50.

Wolchik, Sharon L. 1991. *Czechoslovakia in Transition: Politics, Economics and Society.* London; New York: Pinter Publishers.

———. 1992. "The Crisis of Socialism in Central and Eastern Europe and Socialism's Future." In *The Crisis of Socialism in Europe,* edited by Christiane Lemke and Gary Marks. Durham: Duke University Press.

Notes

*We are very grateful to Dietrich Rueschemeyer for comments on an earlier draft of this chapter and to Igor Prochazka for his research assistance.

1. Planungsgruppe der SPD Bundestagfraktion, "Deutschland erneuern—Damit es wieder aufwärts geht," n.d., p. 99.

2. Insurance programs are generally administered through semiprivate organizations representing, for example, occupational and territorial constituencies.

3. DM 6,300 in West Germany and DM 5,200 in East Germany.

4. For a more extensive discussion of the relationship between the PDS and other parties, see Thomas Baylis, "Political Adaptation in Postcommunism: The

PDS," paper presented at the American Association for the Advancement of Slavic Studies, Seattle Washington, November 1997, and Rueschemeyer (1998b).

5. The SPD noted the responsibility of employers in this latter area, proposed increased relief for those who take on apprenticeships and a subsidy for those who take on school graduates.

6. "Dokumentation der Tagung des Forum Ostdeutschland 1997," Forum Ostdeutschland der Sozialdemokratie, Berlin, p. 68.

7. Interview with Friedemann Walter, Senatsverwaltung für Arbeit, 1998.

8. *Berliner Zeitung*, Magazin, June 20/21 1998, p. IV.

9. Efforts to stabilize and improve housing in the large apartment house complexes have general political support according to Bernd Hunger, architect and urban planner in Berlin (interview 1998), though particular business interests, as mentioned above, may be heavily contested by residents. With unemployment, the residential areas generally have even more increased importance to many people than in the past and are more extensively occupied during the day.

5

Transitional Politics or Public Choice? Evaluating Stalled Pension Reforms in Poland

MICHAEL J. G. CAIN AND ALEKSANDER SURDEJ*

This chapter evaluates two approaches to transitional politics by looking at the development of social spending in Poland beginning in 1989. Increased social expenditures have emerged recently as a key issue in East European policy discussions because of the dangers this spending poses to continued economic development.[1]

In Poland, for example, spending on public pensions has increased dramatically throughout the 1990s and absorbed progressively larger portions of the gross domestic product. Despite widespread knowledge about the dangers posed by increased social spending and the threat of growing fiscal deficits, fundamental reforms in the social safety net were postponed by successive governments until 1999.

Why were reforms stalled for so long in Poland? Were failures to make fundamental improvements in social policy before 1999 mainly related to the special circumstances of transitional politics in Poland, or were they related to more general features associated with the structure of democratic competition? We answer these questions with seven propositions about pension growth and policy change, isolating the main factors associated with rising pension costs and stalled policy reforms. These factors not only provide the basis for a more complete specification of a multivariate model of pension spending but also allow researchers to understand the main economic and political influences on the development of Polish social policy.

This analysis of pension policy also provides researchers with the opportunity to assess the relative importance of different approaches to transitional politics. One approach, favored by political economists and policymakers, analyzes the determinants of regime change and the path of reforms by looking at the importance of the initial social and economic conditions within countries before regime changes. According to this approach, structural factors combined with historical and ideological influences are essential elements in explanations of transitional processes (Haggard and Kaufman 1995; Huntington 1991; Linz and Stepan 1996; Rustow 1970; White et al. 1993).

Another approach, favored by rational choice and public choice theorists, have used changes in voting rules, different patterns in political voting cycles, and different informational conditions to explain transitional processes and outcomes (Alesina 1994; Kaminski 1997; Olson 1995; Przeworski 1991). Although important points of agreement exist between these perspectives, the focus and goals of each set of research are often different. Public choice studies of transitional processes are generally less policy-oriented and more focused on adapting rational choice analyses of stable democracies to transitional politics.

In contrast to this focus, political economists tend to emphasize the special character of transitional processes when compared to political mechanisms in stable democracies. One group of researchers has investigated the applicability of general theories of democracy by adapting them to the special conditions of transition societies, while another group of researchers has illustrated how the unique character and histories of different societies limit our capacity to generalize about politics in transition societies.

We argue that these contrasting approaches should not be interpreted as competing theories of transitional processes, but rather treated as complementary approaches. When standard public choice analyses of politics are combined with the politics of decisionmaking during transitions and the inherited legacies of the communist welfare state, it is possible to develop a powerful account of why pension deficits grew throughout the 1990s and why many reform proposals failed.

Our analysis of pension policy not only illustrates the importance of history and ideas on policy developments in Poland but more precisely shows how the mechanisms of democratic functioning manipulate this history and these ideas. We therefore find both approaches to be essential for developing a full understanding of the politics of pension reform in Poland.

This chapter describes the economic problems facing Poland during the first stage of transition and the subsequent growth in pension benefits that occurred during this time. We then outline three general perspectives that can explain the growth of pension budgets throughout Central and Eastern Europe.

Two perspectives are associated with the special circumstances of transition in Eastern Europe, while another perspective explains growth, using standard public choice theories of democracy. These perspectives show that the demands for increases in state benefits were not strictly driven by transitional politics alone or by the special circumstances of transition in Eastern Europe. We conclude from the analysis that rational choice theories can be integrated with more traditional approaches of transitional politics to form more complete explanations of policy processes and outcomes in Eastern Europe (Bates et al. 1998).

The Organization of Pension Funds and Fiscal Crisis

Until a major reform in 1999, Poland's pension system was a publicly managed single-pillar, pay-as-you-go social insurance system, which means the contributions of current employees were used to finance the benefits of current retirees on a pay-as-you-go basis.[2] There are two main public pension funds in Poland; one is for the general population (Fundusz Ubezpieczen Spolecznych, FUS) and the other fund is for farmers (Kasa Rolniczego Ubezpieczenia Spolecznych, KRUS). FUS is managed and administered by the Social Insurance Office (Zaklad Ubezpieczen Spolecznego, ZUS) under the Ministry of Labor and Social Policy.[3] Retirees, disabled workers, families with dependent children, the handicapped and chronically ill receive payments from these funds.

Eligibility for most social insurance benefits in Poland depends upon a satisfactory work record, while retirement eligibility is based on a minimum age and minimum length of employment. Retirement benefits were generally granted when men reached 65 years of age with 25 years of full-time employment, while women were granted benefits at 60 years of age with 20 years of employment.[4] In practice, eligibility requirements and benefit levels varied greatly and were often changed or softened for particular groups. As we will see, soft eligibility requirements and special benefits to politically powerful groups became an important barrier to future restructuring and reform efforts.

The method of collecting and tracking social security contributions was based on rudimentary principles of financing, where employers supposedly paid the entire tax obligation of workers in the firm to public social security funds. Two features of this finance system were especially problematic. First, before 1989, state enterprises sometimes did not actually pay this tax because of soft budget constraints (Kornai 1986). This means social security payments were often made by the government and not by the enterprise.

Second, similar to pension financing in other countries in Eastern Europe, ZUS until 1999 did not track the accumulation of payments for individuals so it did not have individualized retirement accounts for workers. As a result, a weak relationship was established between individual contributions made by workers throughout their lifetimes and the retirement benefits they later accumulated. This latter property proved to be among the most problematic for revenue collection and became an important component in the new 1998 pension law.

Trends in Pension Growth

Pension funds in Poland are financed mainly through payroll taxes paid by employers on the gross wages of individual workers. This tax has grown considerably since the early 1980s.[5] In 1980, for example, payroll taxes were 15.5 percent on gross wages. This quickly increased to 33 percent in 1982 and, in 1992, increased to its present rate of 45 percent. Despite the rapid rise of payroll taxes, state budget subsidies have been required to make up deficit spending by each social security fund. As a percentage of total expenditures on pensions, subsidies to FUS and KRUS funds increased from 1 percent in 1991 to almost 10 percent in 1995 (Golinowska 1996; Hausner 1997).

To understand the growth of public pension spending in Poland, it is important to first describe the general economic environment at the time of transition. When Poland initiated stabilization and liberalization reform programs, designed to institute a free market economy in 1990, the reform programs resulted in inflationary pressures and a significant decrease in industrial production that affected national employment and GDP (see Table 5.1).

The downturn had actually begun before 1989, but became more widespread and deeper when links with COMECON (Council of Mutual Economic Assistance) were broken and trade barriers for Western exporters were removed (Mansur 1993; Poznanski 1996). Central planning and inefficient or misdirected capital investment left many industries unable to compete with firms in more mature market economies. Moreover, once the decision to drop the transferable ruble was made, trade within COMECON collapsed (see Table 5.2). Dramatic increases in unemployment were felt throughout the region as large sectors of manufacturing in Central and Eastern Europe (as well as Newly Independent States of the Former Soviet Union) were either forced to restrict or to end production.

To lessen the effects of unemployment caused by the transition to a market economy, many governments in Eastern Europe responded by encouraging older workers to retire. In Poland, for example, this was accomplished through statutory and regulatory changes in pension laws

TABLE 5.1   Poland: Macroeconomic Indicators

	1990	1991	1992	1993	1994	1995	1996	1997
Real GDP[a]	−11.6	−7.0	2.6	3.8	5.2	7.0	6.1	6.7
Inflation Rate†	585	70.3	44.3	37.2	29.5	21.6	18.5	13.5
Unemployment Rate†	6.3	11.8	13.6	15.7	16.0	14.9	13.6	10.8
Payroll Tax Rate[c]	43.0	43.0	45.0	37.0	[b]	[b]	45.0	45.0

[a] Annual Percentage Change.
[b] No data available.
[c] For social insurance (World Bank).
SOURCES: World Economic Outlook, IMF. †Central Office of Statistics (GUS).

TABLE 5.2   International Trade by Eastern Europe

	Exports		Imports	
Percentage Change[a]	1990	1991	1990	1991
The World	−3.3	−11	+2.9	+11.4
Other East Europe/CIS Countries	−18.6	−32.5	−18.2	−34.5
Industrial Countries	+11.6	+9.2	+24.2	+27.5
Developing Countries	−14.3	−24.6	na	−3.2

[a] From previous years
SOURCE: Economic Commission of Europe, *Financial Times*, March 20, 1992.

during the earliest stages of transition that relaxed eligibility requirements for workers while simultaneously increasing pension benefits to new retirees. These changes resulted in increases in both the number of pensioners and the average benefits pensioners received (see Table 5.3.).

The total number of pensioners in Poland increased from 17.9 percent of the population in 1989 to 23.1 percent, while average monthly pensions increased from 66zl in 1990 to 387zl in 1994. The ratio of the average pension to the average wage in the economy increased in 1994 from 55.8 percent in 1990 to 63.0 percent in 1994. These increases resulted in steadily increasing government expenditures on pensions, from 50 percent of all social expenditures to 54 percent in 1994 (Golinowska 1996).

As government obligations for social insurance increased, changes were occurring simultaneously in the labor market that influenced net tax receipts for social insurance. High levels of unemployment, early retirements, and changing demographic factors among the working population resulted in steadily decreasing numbers of workers paying into state insurance funds (see Figure 5.1).

In 1989, for example, 14.5 million Polish workers paid into the state social insurance fund, but by 1995 there were only 12.6 million workers

TABLE 5.3   Poland: Population, Retirement, and Employment Status

	1989	1990	1991	1992	1993	1994	1995
Population[a]	37,963	38,119	38,245	38,365	38,459	38,544	38,590
Employed[a]	17,002	16,280	15,326	14,677	14,330	14,591	14,740
Retirees[a]	6,827	7,104	7,944	8,495	8,730	8,919	–
Percentage of							
Retirees	17.9	18.6	20.0	22.1	22.7	23.1	–
System Dependency[b]	2.49	2.29	2.14	1.75	1.75	1.75	–
Pension Expenditures[cd]	–	4972	10,183	16,784	23,194	33,230	44,746
Pension Expenditures[c]							
% of GDP	–	8.6	12.6	14.6	14.9	15.8	15.6
Pension Deficit[c]							
% of GDP	–	0.5	3.1	6.1	6.0	6.1	3.9

[a] In thousands.
[b] Employed/Retirees.
[c] KRUS and FUS including rents.
[d] In million PLN
– No data available.
SOURCE: Central Statistical Office, Warsaw, 1995.

paying for social insurance. This resulted in an unfavorable dependency ratio of workers to retirees that placed increasing pressure on public budgets. In ZUS, the dependency ratio has decreased from roughly two and one-half workers supporting every pension beneficiary to considerably less than two workers supporting them. In KRUS, the dependency ratio is producing fiscal crisis: there are fewer than two workers for every two beneficiaries.

The economic factors leading to increased spending on social welfare in Poland are well known. Increasing state obligations to pensioners and an unfavorable ratio of workers to retirees left successive governments with very few realistic policy alternatives. Either total pension expenditures needed to be reduced, through cuts in average pension benefits, or additional taxes needed to be levied to make up increasing budget shortfalls.

Yet increasing taxes is probably not a viable policy option. The 45 percent social security tax is already burdensome on the economy and even substantial increases in social security taxes would probably be insufficient to eliminate budget shortfalls.[6] Government subsidies to make up the difference between contributions and payments have been alarmingly high. In 1996, for example, subsidies to all social insurance funds amounted to 3.9 percent of GDP. Policymakers were well aware that these subsidies posed serious macroeconomic risks to the economy and

FIGURE 5.1   Employed Workers and Pensioners in Poland, millions

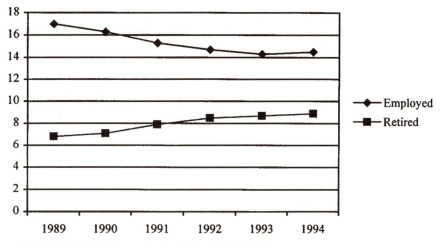

SOURCE: *Poland Quarterly Statistics*, GUS, 1995.

required fundamental changes in the structure of the social security system (Cain and Surdej 1996), yet reform was continuously delayed.

Transitional and Democratic Influences on Pension Policy

The economic problems associated with increased growth in social spending are well documented and understood. This led to an early consensus among economists and policymakers in Warsaw on the expected consequences of continued deficit spending and the importance of instituting fundamental changes in social security. Yet this consensus among policymakers presents a puzzle to political researchers. If the main economic factors associated with growing deficits were known, why have fundamental changes in the organization and delivery of social welfare taken so long to occur in Poland? What political factors fueled the growth in social security benefits and prevented fundamental changes from occurring in pension and other social welfare programs?

We answer these questions by contrasting several viewpoints on transitional politics with standard rational choice explanations of democratic functioning. Three viewpoints are proposed to explain the growth in social welfare spending in Poland and the inability of governments to institute social security reform successfully. The first is the legacy of state socialism. This viewpoint stresses the importance of initial conditions in transition states and suggests that increasing pension deficits are a natural consequence of failures to change inherited features of Soviet-type socialist organization.

The second viewpoint is the ideology and practice of transitional policy. According to this viewpoint, spending increases were directly related to the policy preferences of elites and their response to the worsening economic conditions associated with the transition to liberal market economies. Not only were policymakers influenced by arguments associated with shock therapy, but they also faced serious constraints during the transition to a market economy that prevented them from making significant changes in social welfare programs.

In contrast to the special conditions of socialism in Eastern Europe, or to the conditions associated with the transition to a market economy, it is possible that spending increases were due to the ordinary functioning of new democracies and adjustments by parties to changing political competition.

The third viewpoint is the rational democratic response, which suggests that policy changes in social welfare were brought about by political parties responding rationally to the demands of the electorate or to the demands of particular interest groups. This view argues that ordinary democratic factors associated with the organization of the polity, rather than the legacies of socialism or transition to a market economy, led to increases in social spending and prevented changes in policy from occurring.

These three viewpoints, and the propositions derived from them, shed much light on different features of East European politics and transitional theories of politics. Using Poland as a specific case, our analysis isolates the main factors associated with rising pension costs in East European democracies, providing the basis for a more complete specification of a multivariate model of pension spending. Our analysis also provides researchers with a greater understanding of the main political influences on the development of policy in Poland during the transitional period to a market economy. The analysis allows researchers to assess the relative merits of different theoretical approaches to transitional politics by comparing the main factors contributing to policy development.

Legacies of State Socialism

With minor variations, the Soviet model of social protection was the standard model of welfare in Poland and throughout other Eastern Europe countries during the 1980s (Standing 1996). This model of social protection provided cradle-to-grave security to all workers and their families. Pensions were an integral part of this system.

The central state administration managed all state pensions and delivered many state welfare benefits through state owned enterprises. Besides pension benefits, workers received liberal sickness and disability benefits, universal health care benefits, housing and consumer subsidies, as well as other in-kind benefits. Yet pensions are only one part of a life wage package provided to workers by the state under the Soviet model of social protection.

The organization of pension systems in Poland and other countries in Eastern Europe, the statutory formula for calculating benefits, the distributive properties of the system, the criteria for benefit eligibility, as well as the goals of pension systems were all directly inherited from state socialist economic systems. Naturally socialist pension systems were designed to serve policy goals that were much different from the goals of retirement systems in capitalist systems.

When compared with pension systems in market-based economies, East European pension systems were not designed to minimize public costs to the state, or to encourage individual savings, nor were they designed to protect specific groups from poverty or to alleviate poverty among the elderly. These organizational features and policy goals make sense only when understood from the perspective of decentralized market-based economies, not necessarily in centrally planned socialist economies.

Many organizational features inherited from socialist pension systems proved burdensome only after the transition to a market economy. Their negative influence became apparent when socialist welfare systems became exposed to new realities associated with decentralized market economies. For example, the inherited tax principles for contributing payments to social insurance funds remained the same when East European countries switched to market-based economies. These tax principles led to serious incentive problems for firms and individual workers.

With privatization and the introduction of hard budget constraints, firms no longer had the same incentives to contribute taxes to the central state administration. Workers had even less incentive to report wages. Since there was little relationship between individual contributions to ZUS funds and the retirement benefits they might receive later, there was little incentive for workers to report taxable income to ZUS. Workers could benefit by free riding on the tax contributions of others by either failing to report all wages or working in the shadow economy.

This gives us our first proposition on pension growth:

Unless fundamental restructuring in social welfare taxation systems occurs, pension deficits will naturally increase in East European transitional societies due to inherited methods of social insurance tax collection.

Evidence shows that these inherited features contributed to pension deficits in many East European countries, including Poland. The World Bank estimates that many East European countries that experienced pension deficits could have significantly reduced these deficits if full tax compliance was achieved (Andrews and Rashid 1996). In 1993, the actual

ZUS payroll tax in Poland was 45 percent, although the effective tax rate (the amount actually collected) was estimated at roughly 30 percent.[7]

Tax compliance by private firms has been an especially serious problem. Cichocka reports in 1993 that although slightly more than half the workforce was employed by the private sector, private firms accounted for only 15 percent of all ZUS contributions in 1992—despite the fact that private sector workers received higher wages than public sector workers. This suggests that small firms were underreporting wages and income. Of course there were also legal means to avoid ZUS taxes. Until February 1995, firms were not obliged to pay ZUS taxes on short-term contract work (Benio and Mlynarczyk-Misiuda 1997). Only recently have overtime pay to workers, weekend and holiday pay, and seasonal or yearly bonuses become subject to ZUS taxation.[8]

Tax compliance has been a significant problem in Poland, although not all of it can be attributed to tax evasion by private firms. Some compliance problems have been the result of state enterprises failing to pay ZUS taxes as well. Managers and workers of these enterprises have requested and received delays, subsidies, or outright cancellation of ZUS payments from government officials.

For example, at the of end 1996, state enterprises owed ZUS 4759.2 million PLN (new Polish zloty), or approximately 13 percent of all benefits paid by ZUS in that year. Of all money owed to ZUS, state enterprises owed 71.4 percent, while the private sector owed 28.6 percent. Large state enterprises have preferred to subvert the system more directly through their political connections, while small private firms often have bypassed it through the shadow economy. Regardless of their preferred methods of evasion, both state enterprises and private firms have played an important role in suppressing total tax receipts.

The redistributional properties of pension systems represent another inherited legacy from Soviet socialist economies and socialist welfare systems. Under Soviet socialist principles, state pension systems were not designed to redistribute benefits from better-off citizens to those who are worse off, since everyone theoretically had equal incomes. Instead, special pension benefits were used as a means to achieve specific economic or social objectives in socialist economies. Social planners could use pension eligibility rules or pension benefits to vary the attractiveness of jobs and to facilitate the allocation of labor across occupations. The ability of planners to vary these parameters was especially important when the wages of all workers were relatively equal. For example, farmers, miners, teachers, railroad workers, artists, journalists, customs officers, fisherman, and marine workers are covered by some type of early retirement conditions or favorable benefits rules (Hausner 1997).

In other cases, pension eligibility rules were relaxed or pension benefits increased as a political device to placate specific occupational groups, as in the case of shipyard workers or miners. If pension systems in Eastern Europe were originally designed on socialist distributional principles, then without changes they may be poor institutional means to protect groups from poverty. This gives us a second proposition on the legacy of state socialism:

Poor citizens in transitional societies of Eastern Europe will not be protected by existing pension benefits unless restructuring of socialist social welfare provision occurs.

There is strong evidence for this proposition. Poland, like many other pension systems in Eastern Europe, continues to have a regressive distribution of pension benefits that is an inherited legacy of the socialist model of social welfare. For example, ZUS taxes were levied on all wages, however low they were, while benefits were paid up to 250 percent of an average wage of the economy. More important was the distribution of poverty and pensioners. Higher percentages of nonpoor pensioners received pension benefits in Poland than poor pensioners. But the system was doubly regressive because the poor as a group received annual pensions benefits that were on average less than pensioners who were better-off. (Grootaert 1995). As reforms progressed, it appeared that protection of the poor had a lower priority than placating specific and powerful social interests.

Although many groups of poor pensioners in Poland were not adequately protected during the transition to a market economy, retirees have generally fared better than other segments of the population during this time period. Retirees in Poland enjoy one of the highest replacement rates in Eastern Europe.[9]

The elderly poor have also fared reasonably well as a result of changes instituted during the transition period. Despite this exception, pensions and unemployment benefits are not well-targeted to the poorest members of the society. Studies indicate the persistence of high poverty rates in Poland, even after pensions were indexed to the average wage. This suggests that pensions are having little effect at eliminating certain types of poverty (Golinowska 1996).

Outright abuse of social welfare programs has also misdirected state resources and otherwise eroded the intent of some social welfare programs. Perhaps the most notable and widespread abuse has been extremely lax disability requirements for workers. This has allowed many healthy workers to either retire early or qualify for additional social benefits (Golinowska 1997; Hausner 1997).

Between 1990 and 1994, the ratio of disability rents to pensions granted annually in Poland increased from 37.0 percent to 52.0 percent (see Table 5.4.). This abrupt increase strongly suggests that widespread abuse and poor administrative oversight was occurring. However, these results are even more striking when compared with member states in the European

Union (EU). In the EU, an average of 10 percent of all pension benefits are designated for individuals with disabilities. The 27 percent difference between Poland and the EU cannot be explained only by differences in health status between Poland and the EU. Although there have been general declines in health status throughout Eastern Europe during the transition, declines in health have not been especially dramatic in Poland (Goldstein et al. 1996). This suggests differences in the allocation of disability benefits can explain some of the observed disparities between Poland and the EU on disability compensation.

The Ideology and Practice of Transitional Policy

Inherited legacies associated with Soviet-type social welfare systems suggest that tax receipts for social security are likely to decrease during transitional periods. Pensions are also likely to be misdirected at nonpoor citizens rather than those who are truly disadvantaged. These legacies provide a rationale for governments to change social welfare institutions quickly to better fit new democratic and capitalist realities. However, Poland (like several other East European governments) failed to change its social security systems rapidly. In fact, Polish governments not only failed to institute fundamental changes to social welfare, they also passed laws throughout the 1990s that increased deficit spending on social welfare programs.

Below we investigate two sources of influence working against change. One influence derives primarily from the special conditions of governance during transitions, while another influence can be found in ordinary features of democratic politics. We focus here on several aspects of

TABLE 5.4 Poland: Number of persons who Received Pensions, Rents, or Disability Rents

Year/in thousands	1990	1991	1992	1993	1994	1995	1996
Pensioners[a]	2,353	2,775	2,982	3,081	3,155	3,230	3,313
Rents and Disability	2,187	2,318	2,435	2,497	2,567	2,629	2,672
Family Rents	1,015	1,032	1,064	1,091	1,121	1,150	1,187
Other Pensions	0,043	0,029	0,024	0,034	0,030	0,037	–
Pensioners[b]	1,506	1,790	1,990	2,027	2,046	2,049	2,028
Total	7,104	7,944	8,495	8,730	8,919	9,085	9,200

[a] Nonagricultural.
[b] Agricultural.
– No data available.
SOURCE: *Rocznik Statystyczny 1997*, pp. 166–167, Warsaw, 1998.

transitional politics that affected policymakers in Poland early in the transition process.

One aspect concerns how shock therapy and the ideology of market reforms influenced policymakers, leading them to postpone social welfare reforms in Poland. Another aspect of transition concerns the constraints policymakers faced during the dual transition period and how these constraints affected the introduction of new institutional changes in the society. As we will see, both features of transition provided ample reasons for policymakers to postpone change.

Shock Therapy and the Ideology of Market Reforms.   Dual transition to democratic capitalism resulted in an exceptionally wide scope of social changes in many East European societies.[10] This forced decisionmakers in Poland to prioritize different elements of reform during the dual transition. Since some reforms took longer than others to complete, prioritizing these reforms occurred almost naturally, which led to a sequence in the introduction of reform programs.

The first of these reforms was Balcerowicz's shock therapy plan that provided the foundations for the free market economy. Although there were important changes in social welfare policies at the start of this economic reform program (such as introducing unemployment benefits), there was no plan for instituting systemic changes in social welfare programs (Kemme 1991). Liberal policymakers generally believed that any fundamental reforms of social welfare should be postponed.

The reason social welfare reforms had a lower priority is partially related to the logic of shock therapy and the ideology of market reforms. Liberalization and stabilization of the economy were considered prerequisites for economic growth. Economic growth, according to this argument, would provide more jobs and increase tax revenues during the transition period. Applying this logic to social welfare spending, growth in the economy could help ease the demand for social welfare benefits and increase the supply of revenues to fund them. As we will see, this argument turned out to be wrong in the case of Poland. Moreover, Polish policymakers believed that the introduction of market reforms could result in spontaneous adjustments in providing social welfare benefits. This proved only partially correct in Poland.

The imposition of hard budget constraints and cuts in subsidies forced state enterprises to liquidate much of the social infrastructure they owned under the old socialist system. In an effort to avoid bankruptcies, state industries were forced to transfer, sell, or dismantle summer resorts, canteens, sport facilities, and kindergartens. These measures helped reduce pressure on the state budget and forced state enterprises to become more competitive, but they also led to fewer welfare provisions for workers when they were most needed. Such influences on the reasoning of policymakers provides another proposition on the structure of reforms in Eastern Europe during the early transition period:

The logic of shock therapy implies that social welfare reforms should be delayed until liberalization and stabilization reform policies are implemented.

The logic of shock therapy and the ideology of market reforms influenced the perceptions of many policymakers in Warsaw (Orenstein 1995). Sequencing arguments implied that fundamental reforms in social welfare should occur later during the transition, while the ideology of the free market suggested that spontaneous social welfare reforms could occur.[11] Both of these arguments provided a rationale for policymakers to postpone reforms in social welfare institutions.

Other theorists of market reforms suggested that policymakers should increase spending on social welfare programs. According to these theorist, transitional societies required a cushion to mitigate the negative affects of the transition to a market economy. They claimed that as economic conditions worsen and citizens become increasingly affected by negative economic changes, they are more likely to reject government reforms that enjoyed prior mass support (Haggard and Kaufman 1995; Przeworski 1991). Some liberal policymakers believed that to sustain liberalization and privatization in Eastern Europe, it was essential to introduce generous social welfare policies. This provides an important proposition on expected growth of social welfare:

Increasing expectations of economic hardships increases the probability that politicians will promise greater levels of welfare to greater numbers of people in transitional societies.

Evidence supports this proposition in Poland, especially at the start of the transition. Expecting that economic hardship would fall on broad strata of the Polish society, the Mazowiecki government attempted to provide from September 1989 until the end of 1990 a social welfare cushion. Early changes in social welfare policies were passed in conjunction with economic reforms just days before launching shock therapy. The early changes in policy included new and generous unemployment benefits and a new system of public food assistance.[12]

Many legislative initiatives focused on pensioners and retirees. First, there was the extension of early retirement rights to persons affected by large-scale layoffs and a new system of valorization. In addition, a quarterly indexation plan was introduced to protect pensions during the worst months of hyperinflation. By May 1990, the government increased the minimum pension to 35 percent of an average wage and indexed pensions to average wage growth.[13] The Parliament passed laws twice in 1990 to ensure the protection of the elderly in the face of increasing inflation. All these changes dramatically increased social welfare expenditures.

The introduction of new transitional policies affected government budgets in several ways. First, these policies increased the total number of people receiving social protection. Not only did increasing numbers of unemployed workers receive benefits, but new pensioners also began entering the system in record numbers, although many were not yet statutory pension age. This phenomenon increased current expenditures and virtually guaranteed that government pension expenditures would remain high well into the next century.[14]

Second, the introduction of these new policies also increased the average amount of benefits going to all pensioners. Especially privileged were pensioners who entered the system after 1989; these people received larger and more favorable benefits than those who retired before 1989 de Crombrugghe (1997). The combined influence of these factors, more pensioners receiving higher benefits, and increased pension expenditures dramatically and greatly pressured fiscal budgets. Such budget pressures could not be sustained, even under the most favorable economic conditions.

Constraints on Policy Implementation in Transitional Societies. The influence of shock therapy explains not only why policymakers preferred to postpone social welfare reforms but also why policymakers were willing to provide a costly safety net in Poland. Buying social peace may have been an important consideration for the liberal Mazowiecki government, but it was independent of the actual constraints decisionmakers faced during this period.

As political and economic reforms progressed in 1990 and 1991, it became increasingly apparent that the ability of leadership to plan and control the transition process was seriously constrained. The scope of change already occurring, coupled with the high degree of uncertainty about developments in the society, limited the range of responses available to top decisionmakers. In terms of policy responses, decisionmakers were constrained by the amount of change they could realistically manage or plan, the quality of information during the transition period, and the ability of state agencies to successfully implement social and economic policies.

Balcerowicz (1995) and others have argued that the dual transition to democratic capitalism made the scope of social change in many Eastern Europe transitional societies exceptionally large. According to Balcerowicz, changing the political and economic systems led to an extreme informational overload for top decisionmakers in Poland. This created an informational budget constraint[15] that required top decisionmakers to prioritize different elements of reform during the dual transition. This informational budget constraint on decisionmakers was a significant barrier to the development and introduction of systemic pension reforms early in the transitional process.

Managing systemic social welfare reform, even under normal circumstances is extremely difficult. Instituting fundamental changes in the goals, organization, and structure of ZUS required changing eligibility rules, developing new benefit formulae, training new administrative personnel, planning financing, and making budget projections, as well as educating citizens on their personal responsibility in saving for retirement. Not only would these kinds of changes demand enormous amounts of time for proper implementation, but they also needed to be instituted at a time when the scope of social change in Poland was already very large. This suggests an important constraint on the rate of social reform in transitional societies:

The greater the span and scope of social change in transitional societies, the less likely new reforms can be implemented successfully.

Another constraint on the early introduction of social welfare reforms was the quality of information needed to plan new policies. The poor quality of information during the first stage of transition made planning difficult, increased the probability of mistakes, and generated distrust among competing parties. For example, when Balcerowicz's radical reform package was first passed, temporary changes were implemented in social welfare policy that many believed adequate and relatively innocuous.

After receiving positive financial information on first quarter performance in 1990, policymakers believed that fundamental institutional reforms in social insurance could be postponed for several years, while changes in the economy were being implemented (Inglot 1995). This proved to be incorrect. The central government budget projections changed from a surplus of 0.4 percent of GDP in 1990 to a deficit of 3.8 percent of GDP in 1991 (Campbell 1993:26). In 1991 alone, the government had to adjust its budget revenue projections downward twice, and each time this led to severe disputes among parties in Parliament about the reliability and veracity of government fiscal projections.

Another important constraint on the ability of decisionmakers to implement new reforms was the nature of existing state bureaucracies. Balcerowicz pointed to this obstacle as an important impediment to change. First, there was an oversupply of bureaucrats who were both sympathetic to the old system and educated in detailed state intervention. This meant that top-down reform policies would likely encounter opposition from nomenklatura bureaucrats who staffed different ministries.

Second, there was a severe shortage of skilled bureaucrats needed to implement new market-based reforms (Balcerowicz 1995:157). Most bureaucrats were weak in areas that were important for managing new market reforms. Without sufficient analytical skills, training in macro management or tax administration, the implementation of new market-based social welfare reforms could be expected to proceed poorly.

Democratic Theory and Public Choice

Transitional theories of democracy explain why the legacies associated with Soviet social welfare systems were preserved and why transitional policies associated with shock therapy could be expected to increase spending on social welfare. But what about standard theories of democratic processes such as public choice theory; can models derived from this approach explain the persistence of inherited deficiencies in the Polish pension system? Can standard models of ordinary democratic processes show how additional growth in pension spending might occur?

To answer these questions, we first consider two general mechanisms proposed by public choice theorists (Gwartney and Wagner 1988). Public choice theory suggests that increases in pension benefits may be due to the influence of special interests on the legislature or the government. For example, rent-seeking behaviors by privileged groups can capture special benefits for which everyone will need to pay. Groups that have formed (and already solved the free rider problem) can be expected to block changes that threaten to cut their benefits (Congleton and Shughart 1990). This establishes our first proposition on the influence of democratic politics on policy outcomes:

Under normal democratic processes, well-organized minority interests can capture special benefits at the expense of the majority or block legislative changes that threaten to reduce their benefits.

Besides the influence of special interests or groups that are well organized with a desire to protect the status quo, increases in social security benefits could also result from demands by the median voter for greater social protection (Mueller 1989). For example, if the median citizen believes retirees require additional benefits to maintain adequate support or if the median citizen believes some groups deserve special treatment, rational politicians are likely to respond to such demands. This provides a second alternative proposition regarding the role of democratic politics on policy outcomes:

In mass democratic politics responsiveness to interest group pressure is only one part of the explanation of the functioning of political system. Rational politicians will also deliberately choose those policies that assure the level of welfare preferred by the median voter.

We can observe both kinds of democratic influences in the development of social welfare policy in Poland, but as seen in the following section, these influences had a small effect on pension growth.

Interest-Group Politics.   Because the introduction of pluralist political principles is relatively new in Eastern Europe, civil society has developed slowly from very modest roots (Szacki 1995). Groups that might normally lobby to block increases in social security taxes or pension benefits, such as business interests, were not yet organized. Instead, groups that were organized previously in the socialist system have continued to exert considerable influence. For example, the Catholic Church clergy, railway employees, coal miners, farmers, as well as former members of the communist nomenclature have retained disproportionate access to government officials. These groups often have used their influence to retain special privileges, such as special retirement privileges.

Several cases illustrate the importance of interest groups in gaining special pension benefits. One of the clearest cases is that of farmers and the special treatment they received from parties and governments after the transition to a market economy. Although farmers receive lower pension payments than other segments of the population, they also have considerably lower pension contribution rates. Farmers contribute only 10 percent of their gross income to KRUS compared to 45 percent contribution rates for industrial workers.

The liberal Mazowiecki government adopted new pension legislation in 1990 that relaxed eligibility requirements for farmers and exempted them from general pension contribution rules. After the SLD and Peasant Party (PSL) victory in September 1993, farmers again received special consideration for increases in pension payments under the more leftist Pawlak government.

Miners are another group that received additional and perhaps disproportionate social protection. Unlike farmers, miners received special consideration at different times, but mainly from the political left. In February 1993, left parties helped pass a special pension law for miners that consolidated their right to retire at the age of 55 or after having worked 25 years, regardless of age. In June 1994, again under Prime Minister Pawlak's government, miners received special pension provisions, increasing basic pension benefits by 50 percent for each year worked, while shortening eligibility requirements. In the spring of 1998, the coal mining restructuring plan introduced by the right-leaning Buzek government provided additional subsidies to coal miners.

The most important influence of interest groups on pension policy has not been their success in receiving new benefits, but rather their success in blocking reforms. This is easy to understand, given the large number of occupationally specific privileges inherited from the old socialist welfare system. In 1995, 24 percent of all retirees in Poland were covered by some type of special retirement benefits (Hausner 1997). Yet this figure does not include those who receive disability payments.

With so many groups receiving special benefits, achieving political consensus for pension reform is exceptionally difficult in majority rule legislatures. Winning coalitions supporting reforms are often unstable because they will need to contain coalitional actors, who are asked to relinquish special privileges for their preferred constituency when other coalitional actors are not asked to make any sacrifices.

The problem of cooperation in such coalitions is similar to the problem of cooperation in an "N-person prisoner's dilemma game," where coalitional actors who face cuts have strong incentives to vote against such reforms.[16] This suggests that forming a winning coalition to reform social security and cut pension spending is particularly problematic, when large numbers of groups retain occupationally specific privileges and must relinquish such benefits in order to pass a reform.[17]

There is ample evidence of many different kinds of failed reform proposals. For example, numerous comprehensive proposals for pension reform were discussed but never passed, such as the failed two-pillar reform proposal in 1991 by Wojciech Topinski and Marion Wisniewski. This was only the first of many failures.

The Ministry of Labor announced alternative reform plans at different times, but these were never passed. Another reform package was presented in May 1992 by the Senate Committee on the National Economy. Although this proposal was less comprehensive than the Topinski and Wisniewski proposal, it never advanced beyond preliminary stages of the legislative process. Comprehensive reform proposals were thwarted in the 1990s by successive governments at different stages and times.

In addition to failed comprehensive reform proposals, there were lesser proposals that failed. For example, many attempts throughout the 1990s to equalize special pension benefits to specific occupational groups never succeeded. In early 1990, the Ministry of Labor failed to persuade the Sejm to agree to eliminate bonuses for those groups in "special or dangerous conditions."

In December 1992, Prime Minister Suchocka, under severe budget pressures, urged the Sejm to approve reduced indexation of pensions to 91 percent of an average wage.[18] This proposal provoked an outbreak of protest both within and outside the parliament, and in early 1993 it was soundly defeated. In May 1993, the Sejm voted to increase the minimum pension from 35 to 40 percent of the average wage, but Prime Minister Suchocka managed to include the indexation provision. This bill was never signed into law. Although some early efforts to cut pension benefits to ex-communist state officials were successful, later proposals to cut special pension provisions for the ex-communist internal police force and military officials were unsuccessful.

Interest groups evidently influenced social welfare policy through standard political pressure. Some groups appeared to enjoy special access to particular political parties and governments, but together, these interests constrained the ability of decisionmakers to change either specific unwanted features of the existing pension system or the basic organization and delivery of pension benefits. However, the special place of the working class interests in Polish social welfare policy has been facilitated by the two largest trade unions in Poland: the right-based Solidarity trade union (NSZZ) and the left-based OPZZ trade union. These unions are not only interest groups that have influenced the political process, but also political actors that directly participate in electoral events.[19]

Mass Electoral Politics and the Median Voter. In addition to interest group pressures, public choice theory suggests that rational politicians will respond to the demands of the median voter. Although it is difficult to assess the validity of median voter claims in the context of welfare policy, there is evidence consistent with such policy influence models. To model this influence, we first illustrate the likely position of the median voter on social welfare policy, and then show the response of political left parties to median voter preferences.

Consider first the views of Polish citizens on social welfare. Evidence found in recent survey data shows that there are strong, residual sympathies for communist era cradle-to-grave welfare benefits (Mason 1995). These sentiments can be found throughout all segments of the society, although the strength of these attitudes are generally greater among older, rural respondents.

In 1992, for example, the Polish General Social Survey reported that 73 percent of their respondents agreed that government economic policies should reduce the financial disparities between high and low income families. In 1994, this increased to 78 percent. According to this same survey, Poles agreed almost unanimously that differences in income were too large (84 percent), that the government should provide a job for everyone who wanted one (90 percent), and that the government should provide everyone with a guaranteed basic income (86 percent) (Cichomski and Gawinski 1994:187–188).

Besides survey data on the general attitudes of Polish citizens, there is other evidence showing that some political parties responded to these attitudes. In the 1993 parliamentary elections, the SLD and Peasant (PSL) parties exploited this issue against parties of the political right. These elections returned a coalition of postcommunist parties (SLD and PSL) to power. Winning parties in the 1993 election each received higher support among older segments of the population. Almost immediately after the elections, the SLD reversed previous government policies that tried to rationalize pension spending. Minimum pensions were increased from 35 to 39 percent of an average wage in December 1993. The same month the Parliament increased the indexation of benefits from 91 percent of the average salary to 94 percent.

The importance of the median voter viewpoint on Polish social welfare policy can perhaps best be understood when considering reforms proposals. For example, the current statutory retirement age for women is 60, whereas the de facto retirement age is 55. This is among the lowest retirement ages in Europe, and it is an important source of deficit spending on pensions.

Proposals to change retirement ages were introduced by different governments between April 1997 and December 1998. However, these proposals were rejected. This is not surprising, given the views of most Poles on this issue. In March 1996, *Nowa Europa* reported that 86 percent of surveyed Poles accepted early retirement for women.[20] Whatever the political party in power, it is unlikely that such a reform will take place in the near future.

Evaluating the Contribution of Alternative Factors on Pension Policy

As Alesina (1994) has argued, there is probably no one model that can explain the production of policy in complex capitalist democracies. This chapter provides evidence for this conjecture by showing that no single theory of political economy or democratic functioning can fully explain the failure to reform the social welfare system in Poland or fully explain the reasons for growth in social welfare spending. Our analysis of pension growth suggests that several historically specific organizational factors and some more generic political factors independently contributed to increases in pension spending in Poland.

Some factors were associated with the socialist organization of the pension system in Poland, others were connected to the circumstances of the transition to market, while still other factors were related to normal democratic processes. The significance of all three factors shows that history, ideology, and democratic processes all contributed to the development of social welfare policy in Poland.

We assess in this section the importance of each factor in explaining both the growth in pension spending and the slow pace of change in pension policy. We then use this assessment to discuss the utility of traditional political economy approaches to transitions as compared with rational choice approaches to transitions. Instead of interpreting these contrasting approaches as competing theories of transitional politics, we argue that they should be linked together to form an alternative approach to policy development and change. This alternative approach admits that there are limitations associated with rational choice explanations and interpretive explanations of political change but shows that linking them provides a more realistic and complete picture of policy development in new democracies.

The Significance of Transitional and
Democratic Politics on Policy Outcomes

We argued that because firms and workers had few incentives to support state pension funds in the new free market, state tax receipts decreased as the black economy flourished. This specific organizational feature influenced the growth in deficit spending on pensions in Poland. Another organizational feature crucial to reform efforts concerned the initial distribution of pension benefits to different groups throughout the society. This legacy of the old socialist system not only provided a rationale for change in the system but also gave a large group of citizens a vested interest in defending the status quo.

The ideological viewpoints of liberal policymakers and the constraints they faced during the transitional period were also important factors in the development of social welfare policy in Poland. The initial policy responses to shock therapy combined with miscalculations about the extent of the recession contributed to large increases in government fiscal obligations. Ideology therefore must be considered in any explanation of growth in pension spending.

Our analysis of the politics of pension reform also illustrates the importance of standard features associated with democratic functioning in parliamentary democracies. Weak governing coalitions and political instabilities in many governments thwarted meaningful attempts to change the Polish social security system. Interest group pressures and coalitional actors in different governments successfully blocked both cosmetic changes and deeper structural reforms. Thus political instability, coalitional politics, and special interests conspired with transitional factors to block both short- and long-term improvements in social welfare policy.

The Relative Importance of Each Factor on Social Policy

We can say with reasonable certainty that these general factors explain most changes that occurred in Polish social welfare policy from 1989–1995. However, desegregating the influence of each factor in a multivariate model assumes we can determine the independent effect of each factor on the policy process. This is a much more difficult methodological endeavor because policy outcomes resulting from transitional factors are not independent of policy outcomes resulting from democratic factors. Another reason it is difficult to reach conclusions about the relative importance of each factor concerns the role of hypothetical or counterfactual analysis.

Much of our discussion of social welfare policy focused not only on what factors contributed to the growth of deficits in Poland but also on how these factors prevented change. This was especially important when attempting to assess the influence of the legacies of socialism on the growth of deficits. Can researchers say with certainty that if fundamental changes had been made in the Polish social welfare system, the significance of these legacies on pension growth would have approached zero? It is difficult to infer this validly, even with a fully specified model of deficit spending.[21]

Despite the uncertainty associated with such inferences, some general tendencies seem apparent. Transitional politics appear to have had the greatest impact on pension growth and rising government deficits when compared to other factors. Many policies introduced during the earliest phase of transition (1990–1992) had a significant and sustained impact on the growth of pension benefits. This does not mean that inherited factors associated with the socialist organization and delivery of pensions did not contribute to pension deficit spending:

Even if transitional politics did not change pension policies, deficit spending would have appeared because of the failure to change inherited systems of taxation for pensions.

Therefore, transitional policies had the greatest impact on government deficit spending on social welfare, but these were aggravated by the interaction of earlier legacies. This means the legacy of socialism and transitional politics explain the greatest proportion of spending growth and public deficits during the 1990s.

Interest group politics played a very limited role in contributing to increased growth in pension spending. When interpreted from this perspective, public choice explanations of pension growth explain only a fraction of all policy outcomes. Several groups, particularly coal miners and farmers, were successful at reaping greater pension benefits. When these benefits are interpreted as a proportion of all new growth in pension benefits from 1990, the contribution of this factor is minimal.

Electoral politics modeled by the median voter also played a role in pension increases, but this too was very limited. Parties on the political left used this issue in the 1993 parliamentary elections to achieve power and then responded by rewarding their supporters with increases in pension benefits. The small influence of these democratic factors suggests that public choice models only capture a very limited amount of all growth in pension benefits.

Another effect of democratic politics that is important, but difficult to assess precisely, concerns the influence different groups had in blocking social welfare reforms. Groups that received special privileges had a vested interest in the status quo and used their political position to help block institutional reforms. Many pension privileges were established before the transitional period, but could not be easily reversed in the new democratic system because of the strong incentives legislators had to protect these groups. Democratic politics therefore played an essential role in slowing the pace of change. When understood from this perspective, democratic politics must be considered an essential element of any explanation for why change in social welfare policy did not occur rapidly.

Although fundamental changes in the pension system were not initiated by parliament until 1997, there were a long series of changes in the rules governing pension benefit formulae and the distribution of tax burdens.

Neither the legacy of socialism in Poland nor specific features associated with the initial conditions of transition can explain this frequent political tinkering. Many changes in rules to the pension benefit and tax regime can be explained, not by transitional politics, but by standard processes associated with democratic rule and political election cycles.

Therefore, any conclusions by policymakers about the most important effects of these different variables on policy outcomes must specify carefully the nature of the dependent variable. When explaining growth in deficits, legacies and transitional factors were more important than democratic factors. When explaining why the scope and pace of change in social policy was so slow, democratic factors were more important than transitional factors. Finally, when explaining changes in rules, democratic factors were probably the most important influence on policy outcomes.

Conclusions on Transitional Politics
and Public Choice Theory

Analyses of transitional politics in political economy are often contrasted with rational choice explanation of politics, but these approaches provide separate and significant components for understanding of the development of social welfare policy in Poland. Several historical features associated with the organization of the socialist state influenced the development of Poland's pension system and helped define the subsequent politics of social welfare in the 1990s.[22]

Public choice theories of democracy explain why special privileges were never eliminated and why fundamental reforms were stalled. Yet the initial contribution of history to these processes is also essential for understanding the full picture of Polish social welfare policy. Rational choice explanations can help us understand the importance of this history to the development of policy, but the initial contribution of this history to instrumental explanations of politics is partially exogenous to the rational choice models discussed in this chapter.

The explanation for why groups received special benefits relates mainly to inherited properties associated with the socialist welfare state. Special pension benefits were used as a means to allocate labor in socialist societies. This is a crucial mechanism for the allocation of labor when the wages of workers are relatively equal. In this sense, the legacy of communism provides a rationale for understanding why pension benefits were distributed unequally.

Political economists who emphasize the importance of initial conditions for understanding transitional politics and the path of change are correct. However, once government officials created such benefits, it is easy to understand why pension reforms were frequently derailed using standard explanations of democratic politics.

According to the logic of collective action and because the benefits of the status quo are concentrated and their costs are disbursed throughout the larger society, no group had an incentive to protect the general interests of the society. By contrast, once rents were established for particular interest groups, these groups had a continuing interest in protecting the rents they already received. In this sense, public choice theory provides a compelling general argument for the maintenance of the status quo in Poland and explains why reforms to reduce pension spending were rarely achieved.

Our explanation for why deficit social spending increased sharply throughout the 1990s mainly related to the initial transition to a market economy and to key decisions by policymakers during that period. In the language of rational choice theory, the ideology of shock therapy, coupled with the logic of market functioning, influenced the preferences and expectations of liberal decisionmakers in Warsaw. This ideology led decisionmakers to increase pension expenditures and postpone needed social welfare reforms. Although rational choice theory can easily explain the effects of such decisions, it cannot explain why this ideology or logic had such an important influence on decisionmakers. If ideology was a crucial factor in understanding the growth of pension deficits, rational choice analyses of this factor provides no explanation of why it was so significant. Why decisionmakers possessed such preferences and why they expected markets to solve problems in social welfare provision must be taken as a given in rational choice.

Our analysis of the politics of pension reform in Poland provides strong evidence for the importance of linking rational choice analyses of politics with what some have called "interpretivist explanations of transitions" (Bates et al. 1998). We argued that when inherited legacies associated with communist rule are combined with an understanding of the ideological influences on decisionmakers and standard public choice analyses of politics, it is possible to develop very powerful accounts of transitional politics. Such accounts not only explain the importance of history and ideas on policy development but also show more precisely how the mechanisms of democratic functioning manipulate this history and these ideas.

We therefore share the sentiment of our colleagues (Bates et al. 1998) that rational choice explanations and other accounts of transitional politics need not be seen as competing theories but rather as complementary approaches. When these approaches are combined, they provide robust explanations of democratic transitional processes.

References

Alesina, Alberto. 1994. "Political Models of Macroeconomic Policy and Fiscal Reforms." In *Voting for Reform Democracy, Political Liberalization, and Economic Adjustment,* Stephan Haggard and Steven B. Webb, eds. Oxford: University Press.

Andrews, Emily S., and Mansorra Rashid. 1996. "The Financing of Pension Systems in Central and Eastern Europe." The World Bank Technical Paper No. 339. Washington, D.C.: The World Bank.

Balcerowicz, Leszek. 1995. *Socialism, Capitalism, Transformation.* New York: Central European Press.

Bates, Robert H., Rui J. P. de Figueiredo Jr., and Barry R. Weingast. 1998. "The Politics of Interpretation: Rationality, Culture and Transition," *Politics & Society* 26:2 (June).

Benio, Marek, and Jolanta Mlynarczyk-Misiuda. 1997. "Country Reports: Poland," *Emergo: Journal of Transforming Economies and Societies* 3:2 (Spring).

Campbell, J. L. 1993. *Transformations of Postcommunist Fiscal Systems,* Friedrich Ebert Stiftung, Cracow Academy of Economics.

Cain, Michael J.G., and Aleksander Surdej. 1996. "At the Cross-Road of Change: Current Problems and Future Perils in the Polish Pension System," *Emergo: Journal of Transforming Economies and Societies* 3:4 (Autumn). Centrum Badania Opinii Spolecznej (CBOS). September 1995. "Spoleczne Reakcje na Propozycje Reformy Emerytalno-Rentowej." Warsaw: Centrum Badania Opinii Spolecznej.

Cichocka, Hanna. 1993. "Powyzej mozliwosci ponizej potrzeb." *Gazeta Wyborcza,* No. 70A.

Cichomski, Bogdan and Zbigniew Sawinski. 1994. *Polish General Social Survey: 1992–1994.* Warsaw: Institute for Social Studies, University of Warsaw.

Congleton, Roger D., and William F. Shughart. 1990. "The Growth of Social Security: Electoral Push or Political Pull?" *Economic Inquiry* XXVIII (January).

de Crombrugghe, Alain. 1997. "Wage and Pension Pressure on the Polish Budget." World Bank Policy Research Working Paper, No. 1793. Washington, D.C.: World Bank.

Goldstein, Ellen, Alexander S. Preker, Olusoji Adeyi, and Gnanaraj Chellaraj. 1996. "Trends in Health Status, Services and World Bank.

Golinowska, Stanislawa. 1996. *State Social Policy and Social Expenditure in Central and Eastern Europe.* Warsaw: Center for Social and Economic Research.

————. 1997. "Delayed Reforms of the Social Policy." In *Economic Scenarios for Poland.* Conference Papers No. 5. Warsaw: Center for Social and Economic Research.

Grootaert, Christiann. 1995. "Poverty and Social Transfers in Poland," World Bank Policy Research Working Paper, No. 1440. Washington, D.C.: World Bank (March).

Haggard, Stephan and Robert Kaufman. 1995. *The Political Economy of Democratic Transitions.* Princeton: Princeton University Press.

Hausner, Jerzy. 1997. "Security Through Diversity—Conditions for the Successful Reform of the Pension System in Poland." Paper presented at the Fifth Central European Forum Vienna. (October 24–26).

Herk, Leonard, M. Socha, and U. Sztanderska. 1996. "Wplyw zasilkow dla bezrobotnych na funkcjonowanie rynku pracy." In *Studia nad Reformowana Gospodarka*, Okolski and Sztanderska, eds. Warsaw: Panstwowe Wydawnictwo Naukowe.

Huntingdon, Samuel, 1991. *The Third Wave: Democratisation in the Late 20th Century.* Tulsa: University of Oklahoma Press.

Inglot, Tomasz. 1995. "The Politics of Social Policy Reform in Post Communist Poland." *Communist and Post-Communist Studies* 28:3.

James, Estelle. 1997. "New Systems for Old Age Security: Theory, Practice and Empirical Evidence," Policy Research Working Paper, No. 1766. The World Bank, (May).

Kaminski, Marek, Grzegorz Lissowski, and Piotr Swistak. 1997. "The 'Revival of Communism' or the Effect of Institutions? The 1993 Polish Parliamentary Elections." (March). (Forthcoming in *Public Choice*).

Kemme, David. 1991. *Economic Transition in Eastern Europe and The Soviet Union: Issues and Strategies.* New York: Institute for East-West Security Studies.

Kornai, Janos. 1986. *Contradictions and Dilemmas: Studies on the Socialist Economy and Society.* Cambridge: MIT Press.

Linz, Juan J., and Alfred Stepan. 1996. *Problems of Democratic Transition and Consolidation: South America, and Post-Communist Europe.* Baltimore: Johns Hopkins University Press

Mason, David S. 1995. "Attitudes toward the Market and Political Participation in the Postcommunist States." *Slavic Review* 54:2 (Summer).

Nowa Europa. 1996. "Spoleczenstwo o reformie." (March 1).

Olson, Mancur. 1995. "The Devolution of Power in Post-Communist Societies: Therapies for Corruption, Fragmentation and Economic Retardation." In *Russia's Stormy Path to Reform*, Robert Skidelsky, editor. London: Social Market Foundation.

Ordeshook, Peter C. 1986. *Game Theory and Political Theory.* Cambridge: University Press.

Orenstein, Mitchell. 1995. "Transitional Social Policy in the Czech Republic and Poland." *Czech Sociological Review* III (February).

Przeworski, Adam. 1991. *Democracy and the Market.* Cambridge, U.K.: Cambridge University Press.

Rada Strategii Spoleczno-Gospodarczej (RSSG). 1997. "Reforma Systemu Emery-
talnego w Polsce. Bezpieczenstwo dzieki Ronorodosci." Report 24. Warsaw:
Rada Strategii Spoleczno-Gospadarczej (October).

Rustow, Dankwart. 1970. "Transitions to Democracy: Toward a Dynamic Model."
Comparative Politics 2.

Standing, Guy. 1996. "Social Protection in Central and Eastern Europe: a Tale of
Slipping Anchors and Torn Safety Nets." In *Welfare State in Transition: National
Adaptations in Global Economies.* London: Sage Publications, 225–255.

Szacki, Jerzy. 1995. *Liberalism after Communism.* Budapest: Central European
Press.

White, Stephen, Judy Batt, and Paul Lewis, eds. 1993. *Developments in East European Politics.* New York: Macmillan and Co.

World Bank. 1994. *Averting the Old Age Crisis.* World Bank Research Report. Oxford: University Press.

Zubek, Voytek. 1997. "The End of Liberalism?" *Communist and Post-Communist
Studies* 30:2, 181–203.

Notes

*We would like to thank Dr. V. R. Panchamukhi, Dr. Ramgopal Agarwala, Dr.
Sanjaya Baru, and Dr. Raj Sharma from the Research and Information System for
the Non-Aligned and Other Developing Countries, New Dehli, India, for their
comments on an earlier draft of this paper. We also benefitted from discussions
with Ilean Cashu and Mitchell Orenstein. William Shugart provided useful comments and editorial suggestions. Michael Cain wishes to acknowledge the Croft
Institute at the University of Mississippi for travel and research support.

1. In Poland, Hungary, Moldova, and the Ukraine increases in social spending
have been directly linked to increasing obligations in pension expenditures (Andrews and Rashid 1996). Romania also expects deficits in the near future unless
reforms of its pension system succeed. Unlike Poland, Hungary, and Romania, in
Moldova and the Ukraine price subsidies have contributed to increases in social
spending. In Poland and Hungary, unemployment compensation has also been
an important, though relatively small factor in deficit spending (de Crombrugge
1997).

2. By contrast a multi-pillar capitalized social insurance system reserves some
proportion of employee contributions for market investments that are later used
for retirement. Therefore pay-as-you-go social insurance need not accumulate
capital assets.

3. Since 1995, separate offices for the so-called uniformed sector (veterans, police, and judges) were established outside the administration of ZUS under the
Ministries of National Defense and Labor.

4. In Poland retirement benefits were generally based on the time worked. See
Dziennik Ustaw Nr. 40, pos. 267.

5. See de Crombrugghe, 1996; p. 32, table 9.

6. Current forecasts predict that the Polish pension system can survive with minor adjustments to the year 2010. Policymakers will then face the dilemma of increasing tax contributions to approximately 60 percent of gross wages in order to maintain the current replacement rate or to reduce the replacement rate to less than 50 percent, while maintaining the current level of contributions (RSSG 1997).

7. See Andrews and Rashid 1996, figure 15, p. 14.

8. The Sejm passed legislation in February 1997 to close this loophole that was effective in July. See *Rzeczpospolita*, July 2, 1997. See also Dz. U. Nr. 20, pos. 107, March 4, 1997.

9. See Cain and Surdej 1996, table 2, p. 25.

10. In other transitions, it was possible for the leadership to focus on reforming the political system while the economic system remained intact, or on reforming the economic system while the political system remained the same. However in Eastern Europe both systems were changed almost simultaneously.

11. Postponing radical reforms in social welfare could not be attributed to the lack of knowledge about restructuring plans. In January 1991, Wojciech Topinski and Marion Wisniewski of the Ministry of Labor proposed a radical reform package that would have transformed the PAY-GO system into a capitalized, two-pillar system. Although this reform was well received in the press, it encountered strong opposition in the government and was rejected (Inglot 1995).

12. This law introduced a system of unemployment benefits that had strong welfare structure rather than social insurance features. This law had soft eligibility criteria and an overly generous and relatively long benefit period. There was little in the way of job training or monitoring job searches. See Herk et al. 1996, pp. 175–179.

13. Dz. U. Nr. 36, pos. 206, art. 67, 74.

14. This was not always the result of legislative initiatives. The Polish constitutional court also blocked several attempts to reduce entitlements to pensioners.

15. An informational budget is the total amount of information a person or organization can realistically use to choose among policy options.

16. The exact structure is similar to a threshold game with a provision point. See Ordeshook 1986, p. 214.

17. The former plenipotentiary of pension reform, Professor Jerzy Hausner, acknowledged this problem when formulating new reform proposals in 1996–1997. Hungary's former minister of finance, Professor Tomasz, also found this to be a serious impediment for Hungarian reform proposals.

18. At the end of 1997, a pension was calculated according to the following formula: P = 24 percent*QB + (1.3*YC + 0.7 percent*YNC)*PB, where P = pension, QB = the basic quota set as equal to 97 percent of the average monthly wage in the economy. (This was used for indexation); YC = the number of contribution years; YNC = the number of noncontribution years (for instance, maternal leave); PB = an individual pension basis calculated as the average wage of an employee from 9 out of the last 18 years of his working life.

19. In 1993, for example, the OPZZ was a part of electoral coalition of the postcommunist SLD and after the victory of SLD the OPZZ deputies became the

largest homogenous part of SLD. In 1997 the OPZZ was still a part of the SLD coalition, which came second in the election. When the political right regained power in 1997 under the AWS coalition, the NSZZ trade union retained a very influential position in the new government. Their deputies held 56 of the 201 seats held by AWS and controlled several ministries, including the Ministry of Public Administration and Ministry of Social Policy.

20. See *Nowa Europa*, March 1, 1996.

21. de Crombrugghe (1997) provides a specified model that provides some evidence for this conjecture, however.

22. In 1998, the Parliament adopted a set of bills that allowed for a new pension system starting in January 1999. (See chapter by Cook and Orenstein for a basic outline of the reform.)

6

The Role of the Hungarian Nonprofit Sector in Postcommunist Social Policy[1]

ROBERT M. JENKINS

Much has been written in recent years on social welfare and social policy in the transition period in Central and Eastern Europe. Some authors have noticed the lack of attention to the social safety net and expressed concern about the potential political backlash that may emerge (Mandelbaum 1997). Others have suggested that the lack of strong public protest to the costs of transition has resulted from the generous social protection policies in place (Kramer 1997). Typically, the slow pace of reform of the social policy system is noted (Elster et al. 1998; Nelson 1998). Most authors uniformly recognize the growing burden of social welfare expenses and the potential negative impact that they can have on future economic growth.

Generally lacking in these analyses is a systematic attempt to address the role that the private, nonprofit sector has come to play in social policy.[2] Kramer (1997:54) briefly notes that it is unlikely that nonstate charity organizations will have the financial capacity to take over a major share of responsibility for state funded programs. Elster and his colleagues (Elster et al. 1998:242–244) note that the initial hope that the state could withdraw quickly from social policy commitments because of the growth of the nonprofit sector was unrealistic. Whereas these authors are correct, they do not offer systematic evidence about the contributions of the nonprofit sector. Moreover, their analyses are limited by the view that the major contribution of the nonprofit sector to social policy is to reduce the financial requirements on the state.

It is important to consider the role of the nonprofit sector in social policy, not because it might lessen the financial obligations of the state but rather because it offers an alternative to the state in the provision of social services. The emergence of the nonprofit sector as an alternative service provider has been an important development of the welfare state in Western Europe and North America (Gidron et al. 1992; Kuhnle and Selle 1992; Salamon and Anheier 1994). This development has occurred even though the state remains the central financier of social welfare. Providing social services in the Netherlands has been left almost entirely to the nonprofit sector, while in Germany the nonprofit sector plays a significant role in social policy. Even in France, the nonprofit sector has become an important provider of welfare services. And in the United States, nonprofit expenditures on social welfare were more than three-quarters of federal and state expenditures, excluding pension and veterans' benefits and spending on primary and secondary education (Salamon 1992:37).

Moreover, the role of the nonprofit sector in social policy is not simply as a service provider. At the same time it plays a role as an advocate in the formulation and implementation of social policy (Kramer 1981). Ferge (1998:301–302) has emphasized the advocacy, or "voice," role of civil society and the nongovernmental movement in promoting democratization of state welfare policy. Noting the dual role of civil society as social service provider and advocate, she argues that it is as advocate that civil society plays its paramount role in democratization.

This chapter systematically addresses the role of the Hungarian nonprofit sector in social policy. After initial comments on the social policy context, the chapter offers an overview of the nonprofit sector in Hungary in the middle of the 1990s. An overview and evaluation of both the service provision and advocacy roles of the Hungarian nonprofit sector follows.

The Social Policy Context in Hungary

Social policy in Hungary is shaped by the institutional structure of postcommunist politics and by the policy legacies of the communist era. The policy process in Hungary remains highly centralized, with basic decisions made by the government (the prime minister and ministries), which is the primary initiator of legislation. Due to the strength of the prime minister's position, the independence of ministries from parliamentary control, and party centralization, Parliament exercises only limited influence in the development of policy. The yearly budget is the main source of parliamentary influence, but its preparation is made by the government, with the Finance Ministry playing a decisive role. The government and the individual ministries have broad powers to use decrees as administrative tools.

Formal interest representation institutions, like the Interest Reconciliation Council, which brings together employer groups, labor unions, and government representatives, are in place but are not sites of important decisionmaking.[3] Instead, interest groups work to lobby ministries and the prime minister's Office (and Parliament, when necessary). Professional and economic interest groups, employers, and trade unions, are experienced at such lobbying techniques, with influence changing in relation to their closeness to the parties in government. Much of this access is informal and occurs behind closed doors. Hungary is a small country and long years of working together in professional situations has led to the building of dense networks of personal ties. These networks help perpetuate the informal bargaining that characterized the communist era.

As one expert in education told me,

> It is my professional opinion that one of the most important obstacles today to social democracy is that built into the depth of this resulting system, and consequently within the deep processes of society, is this informal bargaining situation. And it is very hard to transform these into public negotiations. For example, it means that in public education the professional interest lobby is very strong. It makes background negotiations with the government rather than with teachers, parents, children, or the operators of the schools.

Of course, such a system of informal bargaining reinforces the fragmentation of social interests and potentially increases competition between them, with the result that political authorities are further strengthened.

The policy legacy of the communist era has also significantly shaped Hungarian social policy since the change in regimes. This legacy included a broad range of benefits—pensions, sick pay, maternity and child care allowances—which were nearly universal by virtue of their link to employment. As Szalai and Orosz (1992:153) note, social welfare was a part of the income policy of the regime, allowing a convenient manner for disposable income to be increased. As a result, social expenditures increased in the 1980s at a far more rapid rate than economic growth, adding tremendous pressure on an already strained state budget (Okolicsányi 1990; 1993).

Another element of the communist era social welfare system was the paternalistic provision of benefits, with little room for articulation of interests from below (Deacon 1993). Services were typically undercapitalized and lacking in basic equipment, while economic inefficiencies further reduced resources available to fund social measures.

The first post-transition government led by the Hungarian Democratic Forum (HDF) sought to pursue a "social market economy," which would combine elements of social guarantees with targeting and means-testing of benefits (Gedeon 1995). The conservative HDF also wished to increase the fundamental role of churches in value-formation and provision of social services (Ferge 1992). It was able to meet this latter goal by providing state support for church schools and social services.

The HDF-led government also expanded the decentralization of social welfare. As early as 1989, the former regime had moved to decentralize social assistance to local governments, but the financial basis for activities was inadequate. The Act on Social Administration and Social Provision, or The Social Act (Law 1993/III), reformed the system of social assistance by obliging local governments to offer specified benefits and services by providing financing from subsidies and block grants. As a result, local governments became responsible for most social services, except social insurance (pensions and health care) and family benefits. The Social Act also provided a systematic opportunity for nonprofit organizations to participate in provision of social services through contracts with local governments.

Another major reform undertaken by the HDF government was the separation of the Social Insurance Fund into separate pension and health funds in 1993. These new funds had boards composed of equal numbers of representatives from trade unions and employer organizations. In competitive elections, the National Federation of Hungarian Trade Unions (NFHTU), the successor to the former party-controlled National Council of Trade Unions, won decisive majorities among trade union positions on both new boards and became a major voice in social policy (Pataki 1993).

The HDF-led government had a mixed record on social policy. The decentralization of social assistance was an important move away from the traditional patterns of central control of social services, although local governments still remained in a dependent position in terms of financing. The reform of the social insurance system, however, lessened accountability for pension and health care expenditures. Both funds ran deficits, increasing the stress on the state budget, and despite exploding costs associated with pensions and the large commitment to family benefits, the government did not undertake significant reforms of these benefits. Analysts suggested that the HDF feared the consequences of such politically unpopular moves (Gedeon 1995; Bartlett 1997).

In the 1994 parliamentary elections the Hungarian Socialist Party (HSP), successor to the former ruling party, scored a major victory and later formed a coalition government with the second-place finisher, the Alliance of Free Democrats (AFD). The HSP had run on an electoral platform that promised benefits to many constituencies and had concluded an electoral agreement with the NFHTU (Bárányi 1995). The new government inherited a deteriorating economic situation, with the government budget deficit over 7 percent of GDP and the current account deficit more than 9 percent of GDP (World Bank 1995).

After more than six months of unsuccessful negotiations with labor and business leaders, the government was forced to abandon attempts to establish a social pact to face the economic crisis and instead introduced unilateral measures to stabilize the economy. The measures, quickly dubbed the "Bokros package" after Finance Minister Lajos Bokros, included currency devaluations, an import surcharge, public sector wage ceilings, and cuts in state spending, including social welfare benefits (Szilágyi 1995; EIU 1995). Despite protests and opposition from within the government and the HSP, the Bokros package passed Parliament in May 1995. Some of the social welfare changes were later modified by the Constitutional Court, which ruled that cuts in maternity and child care allowances had to be delayed to allow time for adjustment and also altered the means-testing formula for family benefits.

The results of the stabilization measures were significant improvements in the government and current account deficits. The HSP-led government also attempted other reforms in the area of social policy. It was able to pass a major reform of the pension system that added a mandatory private pension plan for those entering the labor force in 1998 to the existing pay-as-you-go system.[4] Workers 47 years of age and under were given the option of participating in the new private system. The government also reorganized representation on the two social security boards in 1997. However, these reforms were not able to stem the deficits in the pension and health care funds.

It is ironic that the HSP came to power in 1994, in alliance with the NFHTU and promising an expansion of benefits, but the government it led introduced significant cuts in some social benefits and attempted to lessen the influence of labor and other interest groups in the running of the social security funds. The HSP-led government was forced to respond to economic crisis and the combined pressure of international financial organizations and the domestic liberal economic lobby, which was well represented both within the HSP and the junior coalition partner AFD. However, the government was not able to tackle the problematic issue of health care reform.

As a result of the 1998 parliamentary elections, a new, conservative government headed by the Federation of Young Democrats—Hungarian Civic Party (Fidesz-HCP) came to power. Fidesz-HCP had criticized the cuts in social benefits of the HSP-AFD government and promised to restore family benefits and free tuition in universities. The party had also pledged to cut taxes and stimulate economic growth. The new government has split the welfare ministry, creating separate ministries for health and for family and social affairs. The future of social policy remains uncertain in the face of campaign promises and ministerial reorganization, but problems associated with social policy will likely continue to present challenges.

The Nonprofit Sector in Hungary

There are two major types of nonprofit organizations in Hungary, associations and foundations. As defined in the Hungarian Civil Code, associations are membership organizations (Sections 61–64) and foundations are property-based organizations (Section 74). Associations were permitted to exist during the communist era but were under tight administrative control. Foundations were eliminated as a legal entity when the Civil Code was formulated in 1959 but were reintroduced in 1987, though they too were kept under the administrative control of authorities. In January 1989, Parliament passed the Law on Association (Law 1990/II), which removed regime controls on the organization of associations. And in January 1990, the Civil Code was amended to give foundations rights independent from government supervision (Law 1990/I).[5]

Beginning in 1993, new legal distinctions were introduced into the nonprofit sphere. A separate category of foundations—public foundations—was created for which the founder is a governmental entity. By 1995, public foundations numbered 458, or 2.9 percent of all foundations. Also introduced in 1993 were new legal distinctions among associations: public associations, public interest companies, and mutual insurance funds.[6] In 1995, there were 250 public associations, 184 public interest companies, and 211 mutual insurance funds. In total, these amounted to 2.3 percent of all associations in 1995. Except where otherwise noted, this paper uses the terms foundation and association to refer to the broader categories of organizations and not the narrower legal forms.

The growth of the Hungarian nonprofit sector since 1989 has been dramatic. From just under 8,800 organizations in 1989, the sector grew to more than 43,000 registered organizations in 1995, an almost five-fold increase (see Table 6.1). Of the two dominant legal forms for the nonprofit sector, foundations and associations, the growth has been most dramatic for foundations, which have increased almost forty-fold. From less than 5 percent of all nonprofit organizations in 1989, foundations made up more than one-third in 1995. Still, the growth in associations has also been impressive, more than tripling in six years.

Origins of the Nonprofit Sector

Despite the growth of nonprofit organizations since 1989, it is important to note that the origins of the sector can be best located during the

Table 6.1   Growth of the Hungarian Nonprofit Sector, 1989–1995

Year	Foundations		Associations		Total	
	Number	% Yearly Change	Number	% Yearly Change	Number	% Yearly Change
1989	400	—	8396	—	8796	—
1990	1865	366.3	14080	67.7	15945	81.3
1991	6182	231.5	17869	26.9	24051	50.8
1992	9703	57.0	21528	20.5	31231	29.9
1993	11884	22.5	22926	6.5	34810	11.5
1994	14216	19.6	26107	13.9	40323	15.8
1995	15650	10.1	27685	6.0	43335	7.5

SOURCE: Központi Statisztikai Hivatal (1997:13).

communist regime.[7] The communist era was characterized by a party and state monopoly of social, political, and economic organization. Some relaxation of this monopoly occurred in Hungary in the late 1960s, in the economy and certain areas of social life. Relaxation of political monopoly happened only in the late 1980s, in response to the pressures of social self-organization and internal reformers in the regime. Before relaxing the political monopoly, areas of social life that were deemed sensitive to political power were under the control of the regime.

There were three basic types of organization active during the former regime that still have a strong impact on the nonprofit sector in the 1990s: (1) so-called social organizations, which functioned as supports of the ruling party; (2) formal (voluntary) associations, which existed in fields of activity that the regime did not wish to control directly; and (3) informal associations, which developed from the growth of civil society in the late 1980s. These organizations have continued their existence in the new environment and are an important component of the nonprofit sector. Of those nonprofit organizations registered in 1995, almost one-quarter (23.5 percent) were founded before 1990 (KSH 1997:21).

The Hungarian Civil Code of 1959 gave explicit recognition to "social organizations," which included political organizations, trade unions, and women's, youth, and other organizations (Ministry of Justice 1982). Among the social organizations were the Communist Youth Federation (CYF), the Pioneers youth organization, the Association of Hungarian Women, the Hungarian-Soviet Friendship Society, the National Peace Council, and the Patriotic Peoples Front (PPF). The latter was an umbrella organization that included both national and local organizations that coordinated the nomination process for elected positions.

From 1989 onward, these social organizations began to transform into new legal forms, primarily associations. In many cases, this transformation involved changing the name of the organization and making new declarations of goals. The new organizations made every effort to keep the property belonging to the old organizations. The PPF transformed in 1990 into the Alliance of Social Associations, one of several large associations of nonprofit organizations that have used their connections to the former regime to lobby Parliament. Among the goals of these associations has been the creation of a second chamber of Parliament in which civil associations would have representation. So far, this effort has received little support from Parliament.

An enduring legacy of the social organizations of the communist era has been the activists they have produced. Many leaders of nonprofit organizations that developed after 1989 began their organizational careers as members, and oftentimes leaders, in the social organizations of the former regime. Particularly valuable as an organizational experience was the Communist Youth Federation (CYF). Former CYF members and leaders have moved on to hold positions ranging from executive directors of nonprofit organizations to government ministers. During the early 1990s, the Leftist Youth Alliance provided an organizational home for many former CYF members and the Alliance claims many members among the parliamentary deputies of the Hungarian Socialist Party (HSP). This network of activists has been successful in obtaining state resources for the nonprofit sector and helped shape legislation affecting the nonprofit sector during the socialist-liberal government of 1994–1998.

From a numerical standpoint, the voluntary associations that were permitted to exist during the former regime have provided great continuity to the nonprofit sector. In 1970, there were almost 8,900 associations in Hungary. Of these, 98 percent were active in three areas: sports, leisure and hobby activities, and volunteer fire brigades (KSH 1994:12). Although the number of associations active in these three areas had expanded to more than 13,800 in 1995, this growth had not kept pace with overall growth of associations, and the percentage of total association activities taken by these three categories had dropped to just under 50 percent (see Table 6.2).[8] Still, there was strong continuity of organizations in these categories: in 1995, the percentages of nonprofit organizations founded before 1990 was 44.4 among sports organizations, 42.7 in leisure and hobby organizations, and 73.6 in civil defense and fire brigades (KSH 1997:21).

Another pre-transition source of the nonprofit sector is the informal associations that developed during the rebirth of civil society in the late 1980s. While the political organizations that later transformed into political parties are the most visible representatives of these organizations,[9] far more numerous are associations active in culture, religion, education and research, health affairs, social welfare provision, professional and economic interest associations, and other areas. In 1989, almost 2,200 of the 8,400 associations (26 percent) were active in these areas and only 74 percent were active in the traditional areas of sports, leisure and hobby, and fire brigades (KSH 1994:12). In 1995, almost one-quarter (23.1 percent) of the nonprofit organizations involved in education, one-fifth (19.7 percent) of the politically oriented nonprofit organizations, and 17.1 percent of the professional and economic interest organizations had been founded before 1990 (KSH 1997:21). In other activities, the percentage of nonprofit organizations founded before 1990 was much smaller.

An Overview of the Hungarian Nonprofit Sector

Table 6.2 provides a snapshot of the activities of associations and foundations in 1995. Despite the great growth in the number of associations after 1989, the traditional areas of leisure and hobby activities (23.9 percent) and sports (22 percent) were still the largest categories among associations in 1995. The third largest category was professional and economic interest associations at 19.4 percent. Organizations active in culture were a distant fourth, accounting for 6.7 percent of associations.

The distribution of foundation activities differed substantially from that of associations. The area of greatest activity among foundations in 1995 was education, with over 27 percent of all foundations in this group.[10] The second largest category of activity was culture (15.8 percent), with foundations active in social service provision closely following as the third largest category (15.1 percent).[11] At just over 9 percent, health was the fourth largest category among foundations.[12] The distribution of foundation activities reflected the important role that foundations play in raising funding for social policy and culture. The vast majority of Hungarian foundations are operating foundations, designed to raise funds for the fulfillment of activities.

Table 6.3 presents data on the economic profile of the Hungarian nonprofit sector in 1995. The first column shows the average income of organizations in each activity category. A few categories of nonprofit organizations—the pension and health insurance funds, economic development organizations, and grant-making organizations and nonprofit associations—operate with disproportionately large budgets compared to the majority of organizations in the sector. These three categories of organizations represent less than 4 percent of all nonprofit organizations. The vast majority of organizations appear to be much closer to average of Ft 4.5 million ($32,600) in income in 1995.

The second and third columns in the table address the contribution of each activity category to overall income of the nonprofit sector in 1995. This share distribution of nonprofit sector income more closely

Table 6.2 Activities of the Hungarian Nonprofit Sector, 1995

Activity Group	Percent of Foundations	Percent of Associations	Percent of Total
Sport	6.4	22.0	16.4
Leisure, hobby	2.7	23.9	16.3
Professional, economic interest	0.3	19.4	12.5
Education	27.3	1.3	10.6
Culture	15.8	6.7	10.0
Social provision	15.1	2.8	7.2
Health	9.1	1.2	4.0
Community development, housing	4.6	2.8	3.5
Civil protection, fire brigades	0.4	4.0	2.7
Religion	5.3	1.0	2.6
Public security protection	2.0	2.8	2.5
Research	3.4	1.4	2.1
Environmental protection	2.4	2.0	2.1
Grantmaking, nonprofit associations	0.2	2.3	1.6
Political	0.6	1.9	1.4
Economic development	2.2	0.8	1.3
International relations	1.6	1.2	1.3
Legal defense	0.5	1.5	1.2
Pension, health insurance funds	0.1	1.0	0.7
Total	100.0	100.0	100.0

SOURCE: Központi Statisztikai Hivatal (1997:17).

reflected the number of organizations than average income. The three categories with the largest average incomes accounted for less than a quarter (22.7 percent) of the total income of the nonprofit sector. The categories of activity with the largest share of total nonprofit income in 1995 were professional and economic interest organizations (15.9 percent of total income), sport organizations (12.1 percent), and social services provision organizations (11.4 percent). These three activities were also the third, first, and sixth largest categories, respectively, in terms of the number of organizations. The category of cultural activities was fourth in share of nonprofit sector income (9.4 percent) and fifth in the number of organizations.

The picture that emerges from these data is that the nonprofit sector has expanded upon its traditional base in sports and leisure, but that these activities remain important both in terms of the number of organizations and in their contribution to the nonprofit economy. In addition, professional and economic interest representation is another major activity within the sector, both in terms of number of organizations and economic

Table 6.3   Incomes of the Nonprofit Sector, 1995

Activity group	Ave. Income (Ft Millions)	Total Income (Ft Billions)	Percent of Sector Total
Professional, economic interest	5.7	31.1	15.9
Sport	3.3	23.6	12.1
Social provision	7.1	22.3	11.4
Culture	4.3	18.4	9.4
Economic development	32.4	18.3	9.4
Education	3.2	14.9	7.6
Pension, health insurance funds	46.6	13.7	7.0
Grantmaking, nonprofit associations	18.0	12.3	6.3
Leisure, hobby	1.7	11.8	6.0
Research	7.7	7.0	3.6
Community development, housing	3.3	4.9	2.5
Health	2.7	4.6	2.4
International relations	7.1	4.1	2.1
Environmental protection	3.1	2.8	1.4
Legal defense	3.7	1.9	1.0
Religion	1.8	1.8	0.9
Political	1.7	0.8	0.4
Civil protection, fire brigades	0.4	0.5	0.3
Public security protection	0.6	0.7	0.3
Total	4.5	195.6	100.0

SOURCE: Központi Statisztikai Hivatal (1997:57).

contribution. Other important activities within the Hungarian nonprofit sector are culture, social service provision, and education.

The Social Policy Share of the Nonprofit Sector

If we focus on the social policy categories of the data just presented, it becomes clear that these categories—education, social service provision, and health—are important activities within the nonprofit sector, suggesting that nonprofit organizations do play an active role in social policy implementation. These three categories have the largest number of foundations (first, third, and fourth, respectively). Additionally, the social service provision and education categories are third and sixth in their share of nonprofit income. Social policy-oriented nonprofit organizations primarily raise funds for the implementation of social policy.

To put this picture in more dynamic relief, Table 6.4 shows the social policy share of the Hungarian nonprofit sector between 1992 and 1995. In 1992, 17.3 percent of all nonprofit organizations were involved in the

Table 6.4   Social Policy Share of Nonprofit Sector, 1992–1995

Percent share of organizations	1992	1993	1994	1995
Education	7.5	9.5	10.2	10.6
Social provision	6.9	7.9	7.5	7.9
Health	2.8	3.7	3.9	4.0
All social policy	17.3	21.1	21.6	22.6
Total	100.0	100.0	100.0	100.0
Percent share of sector income		1993	1994	1995
Social provision		13.4	13.6	11.4
Education		6.4	7.4	7.6
Health		2.6	3.5	2.4
All social policy		22.4	24.5	21.4
Total		100.0	100.0	100.0
Nonprofit sector income (Ft billions)		121.7	144.1	195.6
Nonprofit share of GDP (percent)		3.4	3.3	3.5

SOURCE: Központi Statisztikai Hivatal (1997:17, 57; 1996:10, 77; 1995:13, 18).

three social policy categories. The percentage jumped in 1993 and gradually increased to 22.6 percent in 1995. More than one out of every five nonprofit organizations is primarily involved in social policy activities.

The share of nonprofit sector income accounted for by social policy organizations is consistent with the share of organizations. In 1995, the social policy categories accounted for 21.4 percent of the sector's income, down about 3 percentage points from the previous year. This decline did not hold for education-oriented nonprofit organizations, which consistently increased their share of sector income between 1993 and 1995.[13] Since the income of the nonprofit sector was equal to about 3.5 percent of GDP in 1995, the social policy nonprofit organizations contributed about three-quarters of 1 percent of GDP in that year.

The vast majority of these social policy-oriented nonprofit organizations are foundations. In 1995, foundations constituted 92.4 percent of all education nonprofit organizations, 81.1 percent of all health nonprofit organizations, and 69.2 percent of all nonprofit social service provision organizations. Social policy organizations are a central component of the foundation type. The three categories of social policy accounted for 51.5 percent of foundations but only 6.3 percent of associations in 1995.

The sources of income for social policy-oriented nonprofit differed slightly. Government sources were far more important for nonprofit social service provision organizations (46.3 percent) than for either education (26.3 percent) or health (27.2 percent) organizations. Correspondingly, social service provision organizations received less income from private support (23.3 percent) than did education (30.3 percent) and health (44.5 percent) nonprofit organizations.[14] The remaining sources of income included basic activities (membership fees, service fees, sales related to primary activity), economic activities (interest income, financial investments, business income), and other miscellaneous sources.

These data suggest that the nonprofit social service provision organizations played a more important role in the implementation of social policy than did either education or health nonprofit organizations. Nonprofit social service provision organizations had larger average incomes and a greater share of nonprofit sector income. They also received Ft 10.3 billion ($74 million) in income from state sources in 1995, over 25 percent of all state support to the nonprofit sector. Education organizations received Ft 3.9 billion ($28.2 million) and health nonprofit organizations less than Ft 1.3 billion ($9.1 million) from state sources in the same year (KSH 1997:64–65).

The Nonprofit Sector and Social Policy[15]

Whereas the majority of the activities of the Hungarian nonprofit sector take place outside of social policy, the data just presented suggest that social policy activities constitute a sizeable percentage of the sector. Both the number of organizations involved in social policy and the share of nonprofit sector income they hold exceed 20 percent. But what share does the nonprofit sector hold in social services?

Systematic data measuring the share of the nonprofit sector in social policy provision are hard to obtain. However there is some limited evidence. The Central Statistical Office (1997:139) has published data on institutions offering both short-term and long-term residential care. Clients in such care facilities include the elderly, psychiatric patients, disabled, and homeless. In 1996, local governments provided the vast majority (82 percent) of care for this institutionalized population. However, church institutions were responsible for the care of 7.2 percent and nonprofit organizations provided for 4.3 percent of the institutionalized. Church and nonprofit organizations had increased their share from 6.7 and 3.2 percent, respectively, in 1993.

These data indicate a move away from the state monopoly of implementing social policy. Church institutions were most significantly involved in care for the aged, serving 10.2 percent of the population, and care for the disabled (6.6 percent). In particular, church institutions provide care for 22.4 percent of the institutionalized disabled children. Nonprofit organizations were most responsible for care of the homeless, serving 20.8 percent of that population. They also served 3.3 percent of the disabled children.

There is also data available on the role of churches and nonprofit organizations in education. In 1996, church and nonprofit organizations each maintained 2.9 percent of all schools.[16] In that same year, church schools had 3.0 percent of all students and 3.4 percent of teachers, while nonprofit schools had 1.7 percent of students and 2.3 percent of teachers. The church school share of students was largest in gymnasia—the general academic secondary schools (11 percent), while the nonprofit share of students was largest among specialized secondary schools (5.2 percent) and vocational secondary schools (4.6 percent). There were also large nonprofit shares of students in higher education: church schools with 5.3 percent and nonprofit schools with 4.7 percent of all full-time students (Central Statistical Office 1997:185–202).

Churches and nonprofit organizations have not only increased their share in institutionalized care, but they also increased their share in education. In 1994, churches operated 2.3 percent of all schools, with 2.3 percent of students and 2.4 percent of teachers. Nonprofit organizations operated 1.4 percent of schools in that year, with 0.9 percent of students and 1.2 percent of teachers.

These limited data show that the nonprofit sector plays a small but important role in social policy implementation in Hungary in the mid-1990s. Churches and the nonprofit sector have increased their roles in both institutionalized care and education in recent years. The nonprofit sector in these activities accounted for only a small percentage of the population served (4.3 percent of institutionalized persons and 1.7 percent of all students), but in some specialized activities its contribution was much greater. Importantly, the trend of the past four years has shown increasing shares for the nonprofit sector.

A brief synopsis of two organizations providing services for the disabled offers an idea of the kind of nonprofit organizations that are involved in social service provision. The first organization, Motivation, is a small foundation that has evolved in a few short years to offer a number of services. It began as an information office designed to gather data on the needs of the disabled in everyday life; then it expanded by offering information on employment possibilities for the disabled and helping employers integrate the disabled on the job. In the process, Motivation developed a strong relation with the labor center in the local government and expanded from the mobility disabled to other groups of disabled. Subsequently, the foundation also began to offer care of the disabled living at home. This program then developed to involve a rehabilitation component. The evolution of the foundation grew out of a very personal experience and desire to meet needs: the director's child had been left mobility-impaired by an accident.

A second organization is the National Federation of Associations of Disabled Persons (NFADP), a large association. One of the oldest organizations representing the interests of the disabled in Hungary, the NFADP combines advocacy and service roles. The executive director, Csaba Csikán, who is himself mobility-impaired, says that he regularly writes his opinions to ministers about issues of concern. He also is a leading member of the Social Council of the Ministry of Welfare (see below). Other organization leaders view Mr. Csikán as having very close relations with officials at the ministry. Aiding him in his advocacy activities is the lengthy relationship of the NFADP with political powers.

Founded in 1981, the organization received support from Judit Csehák, a doctor who was a trade union official and later a member of the politburo of the former ruling party and a deputy prime minister. In addition to representing the interests of the disabled, NFADP also provides services to the disabled population, including transportation and housing rehabilitation, both financed primarily by the state. Mr. Csikán reports that the 1996 budget for the organization was Ft 102 million ($668,000), of which about Ft 72 million came from state sources.

Motivation is typical of the many small foundations that are active in social policy provision in Hungary. They work with small budgets, are involved in numerous programs, and receive financing from a variety of sources. Their activities bring them in close contact with local governments, with whom they must have good relations to be successful. The NFADP represents a much smaller group of organizations, the large associations, which combine advocacy and service activities. These organizations have very large budgets, with the majority of funding coming from the state. Their history and size enable them to gain access to government policymakers, and they use this access to represent the interests of their members and to gain opportunities for service provision.

Nonprofit Organizations and the Making of Social Policy

Despite evidence that social policy activities are a significant component of the Hungarian nonprofit sector and that this sector provides a small but important share of service delivery, the role of the sector in social policy remains ambiguous. There is hardly a formal, institutionalized role for the nonprofit sector. Consistent with the broader policy process, the involvement of nonprofit leaders and nonprofit organizations in social policy remains ad hoc and to a great extent dependent upon the informal connections that exist with political leaders and organizations.

There is one formal social policy institution in which the nonprofit sector participates. The Social Council, a formal institutional structure at the

Ministry of Welfare, brings together representatives of central and local government, employers, employees, and various types of social policy organizations. The council was created by Government Decree (1990/ 1060) to be a harmonizing body designed to prevent and alleviate social tensions and monitor social issues. The Social Council is divided into self-governing sections that determine their own organizational structure and membership.[17] According to a Ministry of Welfare official, there are more than 200 member organizations.

There are two bodies of the Social Council, the Executive Board and the Social Forum. The former is composed of two representatives from each of the sections of the Social Council. There are two co-presidents of this board, one elected from the board and the other a deputy state secretary from the Ministry. The Executive Board meets at least four times a year and addresses topics of its choice. Additionally, the Executive Board also convokes the Social Forum at least once each year. Each member organization sends one representative to the Social Forum, which reviews the activity of the Social Council and gathers opinions on social policy concepts and legislation.

Members of the Executive Board typically are representatives of the more influential organizations active in each section. For example, a representative of the NFHTU represented the employees section; the president of the National Association of Large Families, a very influential lobby, represented the section on social work and education; Mr. Csikán, the president of the NFADP, represented the disabled section; and the deputy state secretary for social affairs in the ministry and a senior adviser from the Prime Minister's Office represented the central government section.

Despite this formal structure of interest representation, the Social Council does not play a central role in social policy formulation. As one association leader commented about the Social Council,

> There isn't so much happening, [though] there are preliminary discussions and debates on proposals. In principle, the Social Council should be the supporting institution or opinion-giving institution for the Ministry. In fact, the Ministry often issues decisions without conferring.

Another association leader echoed this view, saying that not much resulted from the Social Council. This leader went on to say that the Social Council would have liked to have been a partner of the government but it was not. Other nonprofit activists confirmed this assessment. One said that it was good for the government to say that it had the Social Council, but it never used the opinions of the people on the council.

The first leader went on to explain that he spent much time lobbying and in other informal meetings at the Ministry of Welfare. So despite the absence of a central role in formal policymaking, leaders of the social policy-oriented nonprofit organizations can make their opinions known to ministry officials. This access seems particularly true for the leaders of large associations representing populations served by the ministry. Whether these opinions result in social policy outcomes depends on the broader mix of influences placed on the ministry and the government. Associations representing disabled populations were cited by a number of nonprofit leaders as being very important in the informal social policy process. There are four large federations representing the visually impaired, hearing impaired, mentally disabled, and physically disabled.

Individual leaders from nonprofit organizations also have opportunities to be involved in policymaking by participating in the preparation of legislative proposals and reviewing state-sponsored competitions for funding. One nonprofit leader in education told me he participated in the preparation of education legislation. A group of nonprofit leaders drafted a document intended to improve the relationship between nonprofit organizations and the Ministry of Welfare in 1995, but the proposal received little attention from the ministry after a deputy state secretary with strong links to the nonprofit sector resigned his position. Other leaders from nonprofit organizations participated as experts for the parliament and ministries in the allocation of subsidies to nonprofit organizations (see below). As one association leader noted, all the big organizations are involved in the review process as experts.

Sources of State Finance

Much of social policymaking occurs through the state budget process. As such, the distribution of state finance is central to understanding social policy outcomes. There are several channels by which nonprofit organizations can obtain state funds: (1) a special parliamentary committee distributes limited funds to social organizations (associations); (2) ministries have budget support for social (nonprofit) organizations; (3) certain named organizations receive direct support from the state budget; (4) nonprofit organizations receive compensation for the provision of special tasks; (5) organizations active in education and certain social services may obtain normative financing for the provision of services, and (6) from 1997, qualifying organizations were eligible to receive contributions of 1 percent from the personal income tax.

The distribution of state funds to social organizations is rooted in the communist regime. Only in 1990 was the process made public, with the specific amounts published. The HDF-led parliament created a special parliamentary committee in 1991 to distribute state budget funds to social organizations. Only associations working on the national level could submit applications to the committee requesting support; foundations were not eligible for the competition. Proposals were ranked by subcommittees in five areas: health and social policy, youth and children, nature and environmental protection, culture, and other public interest activities. In addition to members of Parliament, nonprofit leaders and other experts worked on the subcommittees. According to committee members, health and social policy organizations were given priority in the allocation. Based upon the subcommittee rankings, the special committee made a recommendation for spending to the full Parliament, which then had power to amend the distribution. According to both deputies and nonprofit leaders, political considerations usually played a role in the decisions of the full Parliament. The total amount of this subsidy peaked in 1992 at Ft 420 million ($5 million) and declined slightly in current spending terms in succeeding years, stabilizing at Ft 390 million ($2.4 million in 1996). In 1997, the amount appropriated by the committee fell to Ft 225 million ($1.1 million).

Ministries in the social policy area also have moneys for distribution to social organizations. Each ministry organizes its own procedures and utilizes its own experts in the distribution of funds. For example, in 1996 the Ministry of Welfare opened a Ft 120 million ($728,000) competition for programs in three areas: (1) health, (2) youth and family protection, and (3) adult, poverty, and elderly assistance. Though the amount was small compared to total amounts available to the nonprofit sector, the competition for the funds was intense.[18] The ministry used five-member expert committees to review the applications for these funds. Five of these experts were drawn from the Executive Board of the Social Council, along with four from the ministry itself. The more active associations, like the National Association of Large Families and the National Federation of Associations of Disabled Persons, were represented on the review committees.

A policy of support for specific social organizations began during the former regime and continued into the post-transition period. Not all of these organizations were involved in social policy, but many were. In addition to the associations for persons mentioned above, sizeable state support went to the Hungarian Red Cross and the Maltese Charity Service (Knights of Malta).[19] Nonprofit and for-profit organizations are also eligible to contract with ministries for specific task financing. Such financing can include running specific programs and preparing research studies for ministerial use.

Another important source of state financing for nonprofit organizations active in social policy provision is normative assistance or financing. The yearly budget designates per capita payments for the provision of education and certain social services, such as nursing and rehabilitative care, institutional and day care for the handicapped, chemical dependency therapy, and care for the homeless. These payments govern budget distributions to state organizations (primarily local governments) and have been expanded to include nonprofit organizations as well. Depending on which party has held power, the government has used this normative financing system to help their allies, either professional groups or churches.

Politics and the History of Normative Financing in Education

The evolution of normative financing for primary and secondary education illustrates the importance of political relations in the financing of social policy. In the 1990 budget, the former regime allowed nonstate institutions to be eligible for normative financing, but permission from the Ministry of Education and Culture was necessary to receive such funding. Revisions of the Law on Education (Law 1990/XXII) in February 1990 gave explicit right to nonstate actors (organizations and private persons) to establish and maintain educational institutions and to receive state budgetary assistance. These changes were tied to initiatives by professional educators to establish new schools and to ruling party attempts to improve relations with churches. At the primary level, experimental schools were created using Waldorf, Montessori, and Rogers methods. At the secondary level, an alternative school emphasizing economics and administrative skills was formed. A new Jewish school was also in the process of being organized. The government also had made an informal agreement with the traditional churches about restoring religious schooling.[20]

After the HDF government took power in 1990, normative financing became one of the key elements for the government's goal of restoring the historical role of churches in Hungarian life. The National Renewal Program of the HDF government emphasized the need for the "moral and material rehabilitation" of the churches and promised financial help to overcome the "deep wounds" of 40 years of communist rule (Oltay 1991). Direct financial commitments from the state budget to churches increased from Ft 308 million ($4.9 million) in 1990 to Ft 1.1 billion ($14.5 million) in 1991. The Parliament passed legislation in June 1991 creating a framework for the restitution of church properties. By 1993 direct support for church operations had increased to Ft 2.8 billion ($27.8 million) and an additional Ft 2 billion was designated as the yearly sum for restitutions (Oltay 1993).

One of the difficulties with the system of normative financing for schooling was that the subsidy covered only 50–60 percent of the total costs of operation. Local governments covered the remaining costs of state schools, but nonstate schools were forced to find additional financing to cover their costs. In 1993, the law on public education was again modified (Law 1993/LXXIX), providing sector neutrality with respect to the funding of primary and secondary education. The law required local governments to supplement the operating costs of nonstate schools as part of 10-year agreements providing authorization for the nonstate schools. However, local governments were not obliged to sign such agreements and, in fact, had strong disincentives to sign them. Not only did nonstate schools compete with state schools, but the length of the contract also committed local government subsidies for an extended period. Many local governments refused to enter into the contracts. Private schools also had a disincentive to sign: if they made such agreements, they could not charge tuition from students. At the same time, private schools had a strong incentive to make such agreements: without them, they did not receive the supplementary assistance, nor were they eligible for normative financing.[21] Church schools were able to avoid these disadvantages because the Ministry of Education and Culture signed a 20-year agreement with the churches to provide supplementary financing.

With the formation of the HSP-AFD government in 1994, the situation of the nonprofit schools improved. Activists of the nonprofit schools had good relations with both governing parties. One of the first measures of the Ministry of Education and Culture under the new government was to conclude an agreement with nonprofit schools that provided them with normative financing. In 1996, the law on public education was again modified (Law 1996/LXII). Agreements with local governments were eliminated and eligibility for normative financing became automatic with the registration of any primary or secondary school.

One family, the Horn family, has been particularly instrumental in advocacy for education and nonprofit organizations, and illustrates the good relations between nonprofit educators and the HSP and AFD. Miklós Horn has been a secondary school teacher, college teacher, and college administrator. Additionally, he held a leading position in the HSP after 1989. One of his sons, György, is the director of a nonprofit secondary school and very active in professional education circles. Another son, Gábor, is also director of a nonprofit secondary school and was a leading official in the Democratic Trade Union of Teachers and the Democratic League of Independent Trade Unions. Gábor Horn is also a member of Parliament and national board member of the AFD. The various political connections of this family and their commitment to the non-profit sector have been very helpful in shaping education policy toward the sector.

Expansion of Funding for the Nonprofit Sector

It was in the historical context of this politicization of normative financing that the Parliament acted in December 1996 to approve taxpayer support for organizations meeting public purposes, including certain nonprofit organizations (Law 1996/CXXVI). With the filing of individual income tax returns in March 1997, citizens were allowed to designate 1 percent of their tax payment to qualified organizations. Among the qualified organizations were associations and foundations that had been registered for at least three years and operating in certain listed activities for at least one year.[22] Also included as qualified organizations were religious organizations and religious instruction organizations that had been registered for at least three years, public foundations, and certain named state institutions, including museums, the Hungarian Academy of Sciences, and other special funds.

This legislation was strongly promoted by parliamentary deputies from both the HSP and AFD. Among the parliamentary sponsors were HSP deputies who had close ties with the nonprofit sector, particularly children and youth organizations, and AFD deputies who had close ties to nonprofit schools, like Gábor Horn, and, more generally, the nonprofit sector. The parliament was able to overcome opposition from the Ministry of Finance, which resisted the reduction in state revenues that would result. The final bill was full of compromises. The inclusion of churches was opposed by the churches themselves, who viewed the move as a threat to their special financing, but was designed to please deputies who wished to see direct budget line support to churches eliminated. Public foundations and the selected state institutions were included in the measure to satisfy their supervising ministries. The Finance Ministry was ultimately able to obtain wording that allowed it to delay verification of organization eligibility from the March filing until September, and not have to make payment until October 31, thus allowing the state treasury to hold the funds for more than six months.

For the 1996 tax year, 1.3 million taxpayers supported the 1 percent contributions. As a result, more than 12,000 associations and foundations received Ft 1.7 billion ($8.4 million) in contributions. Another Ft 140 million went to public institutions and religious organizations, while Ft 250 million was lost through mistakes in filling out forms or failure to meet the minimum contribution of Ft 100 (Szilágyi 1998). The combined contributions represented about one-half of 1 percent of the total personal income taxes of Ft 389.4 billion ($2.4 billion) for 1996 (NBH 1998).[23] The new contribution system was clearly successful in channeling financial support to the nonprofit sector.

The Future of the Nonprofit Sector in Social Policy

As its position on the 1-percent personal income tax contribution proposal indicated, the Finance Ministry has not been a major supporter of the nonprofit sector in Hungary. The yearly tax legislation and accompanying budget estimates have always provided the ministry and its tax office an opportunity to restrict both the direct subsidies granted to nonprofit organizations and the tax benefits they accrue.[24] Many nonprofit leaders say that throughout the 1990s they have had to wage strong lobbying to maintain their tax and other state financial benefits in the face of the increasing pressures to limit the state budget.

There is some indication that the view toward the nonprofit sector may be changing in state financial circles. In January 1997, the Prime Minister's Office held a meeting of representatives from the Finance Ministry, the Welfare Ministry, and the Ministry of Education and Culture, as well as a handful of nonprofit experts. The meeting focused on the reform of the social welfare system in the context of state budget reform. In the materials prepared for the meeting, the growing role of the nonprofit sector in provision of social services was recognized (MEH 1997). This recognition suggests that state policy is shifting to view the nonprofit sector not just as a political but also as an economic ally.

Some of the data provided for this meeting (see Table 6.5) hint at the role of the nonprofit sector in future social expenditures, showing national income results for 1992–1995, projections for 1996–1997, and estimates for 1998–1999. These data illustrate the growing importance of the nonprofit sector throughout the 1990s. The role of the sector in health provision has increased slightly, but it continues to remain small and is projected to reach only about 3 percent of total health care expenditure in 1999. The nonprofit sector also will play a small but increasingly important role in education, growing from just over 1 percent in 1992 to an anticipated 7.3 percent in 1999. Within social policy, the greatest growth and role of the nonprofit sector is in social service provision activities. From 2.7 percent of expenditures in 1992, the nonprofit sector is expected to account for over 21 percent of social provision in 1999.[25]

There is also evidence in this table of one of the forces leading to the increased role of the nonprofit sector. The data clearly show a projected decline in total social expenditure as a percentage of GDP in the late 1990s. It seems reasonable to conclude that state authorities hope to shift service provision to the nonprofit sector to lower costs. While systematic cost

Table 6.5   Social Expenditures in Hungary, 1992–1999

Social expenditure as % of GDP

	1992	1993	1994	1995	1996	1997	1998	1999
Education	6.3	6.4	5.2	5.9	5.6	5.6	5.6	5.3
Health	5.1	5.0	4.1	4.8	4.7	4.6	4.4	4.2
Social provision	1.3	1.5	1.2	1.5	1.5	1.5	1.5	1.5
Culture and sport	1.3	1.7	1.4	1.4	1.2	1.1	1.1	1.0
Total social expenditure	13.9	14.7	11.9	13.5	13.1	12.8	12.6	12.0
Social allowances	n/a	18.5	15.1	16.0	15.5	15.0	14.9	14.4
Total social expenditure plus social allowances	n/a	33.2	27.0	29.5	28.5	27.8	27.5	26.3
GDP (Ft billions)	2943	3548	4365	5494	6595	7890	9175	10825

Nonprofit organization expenditure as % of total social expenditure

	1992	1993	1994	1995	1996	1997	1998	1999
Culture and sport	29.7	50.8	62.9	60.5	63.4	80.0	78.8	82.2
Social provision	2.7	14.8	19.7	18.8	20.0	19.7	20.6	21.4
Education	1.1	3.9	4.3	4.3	5.4	6.8	7.1	7.3
Health	0.7	1.1	1.8	1.5	2.6	2.8	3.0	3.1
Total	3.7	9.6	10.8	10.7	11.6	13.1	13.4	13.7

SOURCE: Miniszterelnöki Hivatal (1997).

data are not available by sector, the Central Statistical Office (1997:139) data cited earlier show that operational costs per institutionalized client are lower in the nonprofit sector (Ft 160,200) than in the state sector (Ft 333,600).[26]

Social service provision is one area of social policy where a shift of services to the nonprofit sector is unlikely to encounter strong resistance from state employees. Both the health sector and education have strong and vocal unions that are likely to protest changes. State social services provision is a newer phenomenon so employees are not as well organized, and they are also more apt to work for local governments. Thus, there is likely to be less resistance to shifting expenditures toward the nonprofit sector.

Underlying all these projections are the problems of the state budget. The Hungarian state is under pressure to reduce expenditures and improve the efficiency of its operations. These pressures were behind the stabilization measures of the Bokros package and continue to shape the environment for state policy. With reduction in social expenditures a central element of state budget reform, the future role of the nonprofit sector in social policy will be affected by budgetary policy. To the extent that the nonprofit sector is viewed as a less expensive alternative for service delivery, its role in implementing social policy is likely to further increase. However, counter-balancing any shift of service delivery to the nonprofit sector could be increased pressure to reduce budget costs by cutting subsidies to nonprofit organizations and by reducing the outlays for programs that finance nonprofit service provision.

Conclusion

This chapter attempts to rectify a lack of Western attention to the role of the nonprofit sector in the social policy process in the transition countries of Central and Eastern Europe. It focuses on the social policy activities of the nonprofit sector in Hungary. This sector has undergone dramatic growth since the transition in 1989, with the number of organizations growing five-fold between 1989 and 1995. At the same time, the social policy role of the nonprofit sector has increased significantly. From almost no presence in social policy activity during the early 1980s, organizations engaged in education, health, and social service provision had grown to constitute between one-fifth and one-quarter of the organizations and the income of the nonprofit sector in 1995.

The data presented in the chapter show that the Hungarian nonprofit sector is diverse. The historical origins of the nonprofit sector in the former regime remain strong, with activities that were allowed during the communist period—in sports, leisure and hobbies, and volunteer fire protection—still constituting a sizeable share of the sector. At the same time, new areas have developed. The most significant of the new activities is the growth of professional and economic interest representation. In addition, activities in culture and social policy—education, health, and social service provision—now constitute an increasingly large share of organizations and income in the sector.

While the role of the nonprofit sector in social policy has clearly grown, it remained relatively small in the mid-1990s. Broad, systematic data are lacking, but the largest share of nonprofit organizations in social policy appears to have been in social service provision, where evidence indicates that nonprofit organizations accounted for between 15 and 20 percent of expenditures in the middle of the decade. In education, the nonprofit sector had the next largest share, at over 4 percent of expenditures. Finally, health sees the smallest nonprofit participation, with only about 1.5 percent of expenditures.

Despite these small shares of expenditures, it is important to note several points about the nonprofit sector role in social policy. First, that role is increasing and is projected to continue at a faster rate of growth than social policy expenditure as a whole. How far this trend will continue is hard to predict, but the relative cost efficiency of the nonprofit sector in the delivery of services will attract policymakers as they seek to reduce state budget commitments. In the care of institutionalized populations, the nonprofit sector averaged only about half of the per client operating costs of the state sector in 1996.

Second, in some selected areas, like care of the homeless, the nonprofit sector makes disproportionate contributions and may be taking the lead in the development of standards of care. Nonprofit organizations have a freedom to innovate and try new service delivery strategies that state bureaucracies are either unable or are slow to adopt.

Third, and very important, the nonprofit sector offers pluralism in the delivery of services. When compared to the centralized and bureaucratized system of service delivery that characterized social policy under communism, the nonprofit sector offers an important alternative for service delivery. In addition, the small size and closeness to clients give nonprofit organizations an advantage over state organizations in responding to grassroots needs. The growth of nonprofit organizations in social service activities is partly a response to the increased freedom to create organizations to fill unmet needs.

Motivation, the aforementioned foundation serving the disabled, provides a good example of this pluralism at work. The organization was formed and has evolved to meet the unfulfilled needs of special populations. To meet these needs it has sought out a variety of sources to finance its programs. It is such grassroots identification of needs and the attempt to meet them that displays the advantages of pluralism in service delivery. Small organizations with highly motivated individuals can make a real difference in the lives of people.

At the same time, it is important to be realistic about the limits to relying on the nonprofit sector for social service provision. The nonprofit sector does not generally operate on the principles of universalism and equity that underlie access to state service delivery (Smith and Lipsky 1993). As a result, the sector cannot easily replace the state as the primary deliverer of social services. Nevertheless, in the context of societies in transition, there is a central issue about the problems of monopolization of social service delivery that must equally be taken into consideration. The nonprofit sector can be an important complement to the state in service delivery.

This chapter suggests that even though the service provision share of the nonprofit sector is growing, the role it plays in advocacy and interest representation appears to be limited. No doubt the small weight of the sector is important in explaining this limited voice. But a crucial part of the explanation lies in the institutional structure of politics and policymaking in postcommunist Hungary. While the monopoly of the party-state has been eliminated, the government still remains the dominant institution. Decisionmaking within the government remains centralized, with centralized political parties reinforcing this character. Access to decisionmakers generally depends upon informal ties that have developed through years of close professional and personal contact. In most cases, the new organizations of the nonprofit sector stand at a disadvantage in this regard.

Some nonprofit organizations and leaders do enter the policymaking process by virtue of their history and the interests they represent. On this basis, the large associations representing client populations, like the National Federation of Associations of Disabled Persons (NFADP) discussed above, have good access to social policy decisionmakers. In many ways, these associations function as quasi-governmental organizations. Large proportions of their budgets come from the state and their leaders are closely involved in discussions with ministry officials. This closeness can make these groups less advocates of member interests than agents of state policy.

There is also a danger inherent in the service role that these large associations play. Their reliance on state funding for social service provision may make them less critical in the policy process. Moreover, these organizations that should advocate for populations end up competing with other organizations providing services. To some leaders of smaller organizations, the relationship between the large associations and the government is too cozy. One leader of a small organization criticized the mixing of advocacy and service roles in the NFADP, saying that it made sense that the organization had better access to decisionmakers since it represented many organizations. On the other hand, this same leader was critical of the fact that the NFADP competed with smaller organizations in the provision of service, saying that its size and closeness to government gave it an unfair advantage.

The vast majority of smaller nonprofit organizations do not share this closeness to the state that characterizes the large associations. Although these smaller organizations may depend on state financing for particular programs, they tend to draw resources from a variety of state sources (ministries, parliament, local government, special funds), which lessens their closeness to any single set of state actors. They also rely on diverse nonstate sources (grantmaking foundations, international donors, program fees) for their incomes. Compared to the large associations, the smaller organizations—which are primarily foundations—have a much greater diversity in their funding sources.

Closeness and informality in interest representation are not limited to the nonprofit sector but are characteristic of policymaking in Hungary. In this regard, the experience of nonprofit organizations in education confirms the observations about the large associations providing social welfare services. Generally speaking, the lobbying activities of the education nonprofit organizations have been more successful than those of social service provision nonprofit organizations. At times they have been disadvantaged relative to church schools, but the nonprofit education organizations were able to gain a voice in policy earlier in their development and have been better able to shape administrative outcomes in their favor. Professional educators have used their experience and connections to receive coverage from financing programs that were largely designed for state schools and later expanded to cover church schools. Much of this success has to do with the connections of leaders of nonprofit schools with political parties, connections that were developed in professional and political circles during the previous regime. In this way, the experience of the education professionals and the large associations mirror one another.

The dependence of nonprofit organizations on broad political trends and state policy is not unique to the Hungarian nonprofit sector. Nonprofit organizations throughout the developed world depend upon indirect government subsidies through the tax advantages that they and their donors obtain. Decisions about these indirect subsidies, as well as direct state subsidies and other payments, are critical to the nonprofit economy. As such, the nonprofit sector must be always be examined in its relationship with the state, for public policy sets the parameters for the development of the sector.

While the Hungarian nonprofit sector received early support in its legal foundation, it has had to fight to maintain, let alone expand, state commitment to its role. In its fight, the nonprofit sector has been helped by broader policy preferences among political elites. Conservative party preferences for the redevelopment of church institutions have been used by the nonprofit sector to expand state support in education. The same pressures to increase the role of churches combined with informal ties and pressure from nonprofit organizations to lead the government to expand the role of the nonprofit sector in providing social services. Despite a history of lobbying and pressure from the nonprofit sector, the role of the sector in social policy remains limited.

In the face of a continuing tradition of centralized state decisionmaking and social service provision, the role of the nonprofit sector is likely to remain limited. The one policy issue that may lead to an increase in the social policy role of the nonprofit sector is the pressure to reduce the growth of the state budget. To the extent that the nonprofit sector comes to be viewed as a cost-efficient alternative to state services, there is a real possibility to increase its share and role in social policy. To the extent that the social policy role of the nonprofit sector increases, its voice in Hungarian politics will also increase. Past experience shows that those organizations that play important roles in Hungarian society develop relationships with political and government leaders and gain access to policymaking, albeit informal and dependent upon personal networks. In the future, nonprofit organizations, may then gain a greater voice, but access will be Hungarian style.

References

Bárányi, Zoltán. 1995. "Socialist-Liberal Government Stumbles Through Its First Year." *Transition* 1 (July 28): 64–69.

Bartlett, David L. 1997. *The Political Economy of Dual Transformations: Market Reform and Democratization in Hungary.* Ann Arbor: The University of Michigan Press.

Central Statistical Office. 1996. *Statistical Yearbook of Hungary 1995.* Budapest: Hungarian Central Statistical Office.

———. 1997. *Statistical Yearbook of Hungary 1996.* Budapest: Hungarian Central Statistical Office.

Deacon, Bob. 1993. "Developments in East European Social Policy." In Catherine Jones, ed., *New Perspectives on the Welfare State in Europe.* London and New York: Routledge.

Economist Intelligence Unit (EIU). 1995. *Hungary: Country Report,* 2nd quarter 1995. London: The Economist Intelligence Unit.

Elster, Jon, et al. 1998. *Institutional Design in Post-communist Societies: Rebuilding the Ship at Sea.* Cambridge and New York: Cambridge University Press.

Ferge, Zsuzsa. 1992. "Social Policy Regimes and Social Structure: Hypotheses about the Prospects of Social Policy in Central and Eastern Europe." In Zsuzsa Ferge and Jon Eivind Kolberg, eds., *Social Policy in a Changing Europe.* Boulder, Colo.: Westview Press.

———. 1998. "Social Policy Challenges and Dilemmas in Ex-Socialist Systems." In Joan M. Nelson, Charles Tilly, and Lee Walker, eds., *Transforming Post-communist Political Economies.* Washington, D.C.: National Academy Press.

Gedeon, Péter. 1995. "Hungary: Social Policy in Transition." *Eastern European Politics and Societies* 9 (Fall): 433–458.

Gidron, Benjamin, Ralph M. Kramer, and Lester M. Salamon. 1992. "Government and the Third Sector in Comparative Perspective: Allies or Adversaries?" In Benjamin Gidron, Ralph M. Kramer, and Lester M. Salamon, eds., *Government and the Third Sector: Emerging Relationships in Welfare States.* San Francisco: Jossey-Bass.

Jenkins, Robert M. 1992. "Movements into Parties: The Historical Transformation of the Hungarian Opposition." *East Central Europe Working Papers Series,* No. 25. Cambridge, Mass.: Minda de Gunzburg Center for European Studies, Harvard University.

———. 1995. "Politics and the Development of the Hungarian Nonprofit Sector." *Voluntas* 6 (August): 183–201.

———. 1998. "Hungarian Nonprofit Organizations and the Politics of the Post-Communist State: Report to the Aspen Institute Nonprofit Sector Research Fund." Manuscript.

Központi Statisztikai Hivatal (KSH, Central Statistical Office). 1994. *Alapítványok és Egyesületek. A Nonprofit Szektor Statisztikája* (Foundations and Associations. Statistics of the Nonprofit Sector). Budapest: Központi Statisztikai Hivatal.

———. 1995. *Nonprofit Szervezetek Magyarországon 1993* (Nonprofit Organizations in Hungary 1993). Budapest: Központi Statisztikai Hivatal.

———. 1996. *Nonprofit Szervezetek Magyarországon 1994* (Nonprofit Organizations in Hungary 1994). Budapest: Központi Statisztikai Hivatal.

————. 1997. *Nonprofit Szervezetek Magyarországon 1995* (Nonprofit Organizations in Hungary 1995). Budapest: Központi Statisztikai Hivatal.

Kramer, Mark. 1997. "Social Protection Policies and Safety Nets in East-Central Europe: Dilemmas of the Postcommunist Transformation." In Ethan B. Kapstein and Michael Mandelbaum, eds., *Sustaining the Transition: The Social Safety Net in Postcommunist Europe.* New York: Council on Foreign Relations.

Kramer, Ralph M. 1981. *Voluntary Agencies in the Welfare State.* Berkeley, Los Angeles, and London: University California Press.

Kuhnle, Stein, and Per Selle. 1992. "Government and Voluntary Organizations: A Relational Perspective." In Stein Kuhnle and Per Selle, eds., *Government and Voluntary Organizations: A Relational Perspective.* Aldershot: Avebury.

Kuti, Éva. 1996. *The Nonprofit Sector in Hungary.* Manchester and New York: Manchester University Press.

Mandelbaum, Michael. 1997. "Introduction." In Ethan B. Kapstein and Michael Mandelbaum, eds., *Sustaining the Transition: The Social Safety Net in Postcommunist Europe.* New York: Council on Foreign Relations.

Ministry of Justice of the Hungarian People's Republic. 1982. *Civil Code of the Hungarian People's Republic.* Budapest: Corvina.

Miniszterelnöki Hivatal (MEH, Prime Minister's Office). 1997. "A Jóléti Elosztó Rendszerek Reformjának Hatása Az Államháztartásra (Effects of the Reform of Welfare Distributing Systems on the State Budget)." Manuscript.

National Bank of Hungary (NBH). 1998. *Annual Report 1997.* Budapest: National Bank of Hungary.

Nelson, Joan M. 1998. "Social Costs, Social-Sector Reforms, and Politics in Postcommunist Transformations." In Joan M. Nelson, Charles Tilly, and Lee Walker, eds., *Transforming Post-communist Political Economies.* Washington, D.C.: National Academy Press.

Okolicsányi, Károly. 1990. "Social Security System in Need of Reform." *Report on Eastern Europe* 1 (November 30): 9–11.

————. 1993. "Hungary's Misused and Costly Social Security System." *Radio Free Europe/Radio Liberty Research Report* 2 (April 23): 12–16.

Oltay, Edith. 1991. "Church-State Relations in the Postcommunist Era." *Report on Eastern Europe* 2 (July 21): 10–13.

————. 1993. "Controversy over Restitution of Church Property in Hungary." *Radio Free Europe/Radio Liberty Research* 2 (February 5): 54–57.

Organization for Economic Co-operation and Development (OECD). 1995. *Social and Labour Market Policies in Hungary.* Paris: OECD.

Pataki, Judith. 1993. "A New Era in Hungary's Social Security Administration." *Radio Free Europe/Radio Liberty Research Report* 2 (July 2): 57–60.

Salamon, Lester M. 1992. *America's Nonprofit Sector: A Primer.* New York: The Foundation Center.

Salamon, Lester M., and Helmut K. Anheier. 1994. *The Emerging Sector: An Overview.* Baltimore: The Johns Hopkins University, Institute for Policy Studies.

Smith, Steven Rathgeb, and Michael Lipsky. 1993. *Nonprofits for Hire: The Welfare State in the Age of Contracting.* Cambridge and London: Harvard University Press.

Szalai, Julia, and Eva Orosz. 1992. "Social Policy in Hungary." In Bob Deacon, et al., eds., *The New Eastern Europe: Social Policy Past, Present and Future*. London: Sage.

Szilágyi, Zsófia. 1995. "A Year of Economic Controversy." *Transition* 1 (November 17): 62–66.

————. 1998. "Media Supporting 1% Donation Campaign, Except for Public TV." *Budapest Business Journal* (March 9–15): 18.

Várhegyi, György. 1996. *Independent Schools in Hungary*. Budapest: Association of Foundation and Private Schools.

World Bank. 1995. *Hungary: Structural Reforms for Sustainable Growth*. Washington, D.C.: The World Bank.

Notes

1. This paper is a substantially revised version of a paper originally presented at the Second International Research Symposium on Public Services Management, Aston University, Birmingham, England, September 1997, and subsequently presented at the conference, Left Parties and Social Policy in Post-Communist Europe and Russia, Watson Institute, Brown University, Providence, Rhode Island, October 1997. The author gratefully acknowledges the Nonprofit Sector Research Fund at the Aspen Institute for support of the research that led to these results. Useful comments were provided by Mitchell Orenstein and John L. Campbell.

2. In this chapter the term "nonprofit organization" refers to private (i.e., non-state) organizations that have legal recognition of their public purpose, are constrained from the distribution of profits to members or owners, and receive tax advantages as a result of their special status. The fact that public purposes are recognized and tax advantages granted by the state makes these organizations closely tied to the political sphere. I argue that the nonprofit sector, the set of organizations that satisfy this definitional requirement, is a product of public policy and should be analyzed as such.

3. For a differing interpretation, see Cook and Orenstein in this volume on the importance of the Interest Reconciliation Council in the debate on pension reform.

4. Voluntary private pension funds had been legalized in 1993, along with voluntary private health care funds.

5. For more detail on the legal changes in 1989 and 1990 and the legacy of the political transition for the nonprofit sector, see Jenkins (1995).

6. Public associations are the legal category covering business and professional chambers and the Hungarian Academy of Science; public interest companies conduct economic activities, but do not distribute profit to members; and the mutual insurance funds provide a voluntary supplement to the state funds in such areas as pension and health care.

7. Of course there were nonprofit organizations before the Communist era. For a discussion of this history see Kuti (1996).

8. Actually the number of fire brigades dropped from 2,701 in 1970 to 1,090 in 1995. The growth among these types of associations was in sports clubs and leisure and hobby associations.

9. For more details about the process by which these political organizations transformed into parties, see Jenkins (1992).

10. The vast majority (70.2 percent) of these foundations were involved with kindergartens, primary schools, and secondary schools.

11. Among those activities classified as social (welfare) provision are children and youth services, large family organizations, family therapy organizations, organizations for the physically and mentally disabled and the chronically ill, kidney and diabetes organizations, sight- and hearing-impaired organizations, elderly services and institutions, and organizations serving the homeless, refugees, and the poor and needy. Also included are multiple-goal humanitarian organizations and other organizations concerned with general social life.

12. The largest group (28.7 percent) of foundations in health supported hospitals and sanatoria, with sizable numbers involved with public health (23 percent) and multiple goal and general health (23.7 percent).

13. Data on incomes of the nonprofit sector were not available for 1992. The income share held by education nonprofit organizations in 1993 is estimated from a broader category of education and research using the average of the proportion of education in 1994 and 1995.

14. For the nonprofit sector as a whole, state sources of income were 20.9 percent and private sources were 22.2 percent in 1995 (KSH 1997:65).

15. This section draws heavily from interviews made during field research in 1996 and 1997. For details of this research, see Jenkins (1998).

16. Categories of schools include kindergartens, primary schools, schools for the disabled, apprentice schools, specialized secondary schools, vocational secondary schools, gymnasia (general academic secondary schools), and universities and colleges. In 1996 there were 10,347 such schools in Hungary, with 2.065 million full-time students and 177,272 teachers.

17. In 1994, the sections were government, local government, employers and entrepreneurs, employees, social work and education, children, youth, elderly and pensioners, disabled, women, ethnic and nationality, and disadvantaged situations.

18. Total state assistance obtained by all nonprofit organizations in social provision and health activities in 1995 was Ft 11.6 billion, about 100 times the amount available in the Welfare Ministry competition the following year. A Ministry official said that total requests in the competition in 1996 came to Ft 25 billion.

19. In 1994, the Red Cross received Ft 240 million ($2.2 million) and the Maltese Charity Service received Ft 320 million ($2.9 million) from the central state budget, an amount equal to 13.8 percent of all state assistance to social provision-oriented nonprofit organizations.

20. Religious schooling was never completely eliminated. Four Catholic orders—Benedictine, Franciscan, Piarist, and Poor School Sisters—were each allowed to maintain two schools, plus the Reformed (Calvinist) Church and the Jewish community had been each allowed one school (Várhegyi 1996).

21. There were a handful of profit-oriented primary and secondary schools among the nonchurch private schools, but the vast majority were nonprofit, i.e., organized as foundations.

22. Among the listed activities that qualified for support were health, social, cultural, educational, scientific, and research activities; assistance to children,

youth, elderly, disabled and disadvantaged; support to national and ethnic minorities in Hungary and ethnic Hungarians abroad; environmental protection, national heritage protection, child and youth protection, traffic safety, civic rights protection, public order and security activities; and amateur sports and sports for children, youth, and the disabled.

23. In 1995, total private contributions to the nonprofit sector, both corporate and individual, totaled Ft 43.4 billion ($311 million). The Ft 1.7 billion in individual contribution in 1996 is likely to represent a large increase in private source income for the nonprofit sector.

24. Scrutiny was justified to an important extent by the fact that in 1990 and 1991 many for-profit activities were using nonprofit forms to gain tax advantages. Regulatory changes in January 1992 largely eliminated this problem (see Kuti 1996).

25. The largest role for the nonprofit sector was held by culture and sport. The MEH data projected that by 1999 the nonprofit sector will account for over four-fifths of spending in these areas.

26. Per client costs were much higher for foundations (Ft 194,400) than for associations (Ft 74,200), no doubt reflecting the greater use of volunteers by the membership organizations. Interestingly, per client costs for church institutions (Ft 304,300) were quite close to those of state institutions.

7

The Political Economy of
Social Policy Reform in Russia:
Ideas, Institutions, and Interests

MICHAEL MCFAUL

Since becoming an independent state after the collapse of the Soviet Union, the Russian state has had no social policy reform. Practices from the past have continued and proposals for radical change have been scripted, but no post-Soviet Russian government has pursued a strategic plan for dealing with social welfare issues.[1] This is an amazing fact, considering both the Soviet legacy of providing for all and the tremendous hardships faced by workers and pensioners since market reform began in January 1992.

More dramatically than in any other postcommunist transformation except the Kyrgyz Republic, Russia's poor have become much poorer since the beginning of market reform and Russia's rich have become much richer (Milanovic 1998:41). Yet, little has been done to redress these disparities. Why have no new social policies been adopted and why has society not responded more vigorously to the absence of a policy?

Ideas, institutions, and the balance of power among Russia's key interest groups combine to provide insights into both the absence of reform regarding social policy and the lack of social unrest in response to this absence.[2] Ideas were most salient in the beginning of the market reform. The individuals charged with reforming Russia's economy in the fall of 1991 had very specific ideas about the role of social policy in transition.

Russia's changing institutional context and changing balance of power altered fundamentally how deeply these ideas were pursued. The political institutions and balance of power that have organized Russian politics since 1992 have been more effective at preserving the status quo than in providing the environment for reform of social policy in any direction.

This chapter aims to document the inertia. Section one begins with a brief analytical discussion of the politics of economic reform, demonstrating why "non" policies can persist longer than we once believed. Section two then turns to the original ideas about social policy reform first sketched by the Russian government in 1992. Section three traces how these ideas were amended and undermined by the political realities of the first Russian Republic. Section four discusses the implementation and lack of social policy in the new institutional and political context of the second Russian Republic. Section five concludes with a discussion about the future of social policy reform.

Unraveling the Paradox of Simultaneous Transformations

In the early years of debate about postcommunist transformations, scholars identified a paradox about the simultaneous transitions to the market and to democracy (Przeworski 1991). In the short run, analysts rightly observed that command economies would have to endure declines in economic output before they could begin to grow again as market economies. During this economically depressed period, the majority would suffer. If these countries were democracies, this suffering majority would vote against economic reform.[3] Simultaneous market and democratic reforms were doomed to fail.

Two responses emerged as a solution to this dilemma. One proposal was to sequence reforms—markets first and democracy second. Advocates of this approach recommended that postcommunist states must insulate reformers from societal pressures until economic growth created a new majority coalition in support of reform. The greater the autonomy of the state from society, the more efficient the state will be in making and executing tough economic policies (Haggard and Kaufman 1996).

Proponents of this relationship between state design and economic growth have argued that authoritarian regimes have proven to be better equipped to carry out radical economic reforms than democracies (Migranyan and Klyamkin 1990; Huntington and Nelson 1976; Huntington 1968).[4] Among democratic systems, advocates of this sequencing approach argued that presidential systems would be more capable of implementing the policies that spur growth than parliamentary systems (Haggard and Kaufman 1996).

A second response articulated by those sensitive to this paradox was a "go slow" approach (Murrell 1991; Pereira, Maravall, and Przeworski 1993; and Roland 1995). If the shock of economic reform was lessened, then the number of people suffering would be smaller and the degree of suffering by the majority would be milder. This majority might be willing to endure minor, finite hardship and still support the general course of market reform. To be successful, the "go slow" strategy had to devote considerable resources to developing social policies that eased the pain of transition. The strategy of resolving the simultaneity paradox also called for more representative institutions—not less—as a way to create a voice and a stake in the new system for a wider segment of society.[5]

These two solutions to the paradox of simultaneous political and economic transition have stood the test of time in several postcommunist transitions, and especially in East Central Europe. The simultaneity paradox and the solutions to it have been less illuminating the farther east one travels within the postcommunist world. Autonomous states—including many authoritarian states—have pursued "go slow" economic reform strategies, which produced very negative results. Several variables intervened to distort the translation process between economic downturn and regime persistence.

Most important, the preferences of the majority do not always dictate the actions of the state. In almost all kinds of regimes, small, well-organized interest groups can act more effectively in the pursuit of their interests than large, mass-based groups. This is true in democracies as well as authoritarian regimes, though centralized states and presidential systems are more susceptible to lobby groups than decentralized states or parliamentary systems. From the vantage point of the state leaders, well-organized lobbies may be more critical to their chances for survival than larger mass-based groups (Weingast 1994). State leaders seek allies that preserve their political power first and worry about reforms second.

Another intervening variable that influences the translation process between societal preferences and state action is the quality of representation. Some groups—parties, trade unions, or business associations—may claim to but do not represent the interest of their constituents. Other representative groups may genuinely pursue the interests of their supporters, but be incapable or too incompetent to provide effective representation.

Third, coalition politics, especially during elections, can play a key role in determining what interests are represented within the state and what interests are marginalized. Minority groups that cannot forge winning coalitions during elections run the risk of a permanent lack of representation. Failure to forge winning electoral coalitions can result from the size of the minority group, the militancy of the group, or the rules governing the election in question. Minority groups too small to influence coalition politics and militant groups too strident to ally with centrists can be both marginalized and ignored. Likewise, majoritarian electoral systems—be they single mandate parliamentary systems or presidential runoffs systems—discriminate against minority groups and allow the majority to rule without offering a voice to electoral losers (Shugart and Carey 1992).

Finally, during transition periods, it is often assumed that reforms are both necessary and inevitable. In fact, the costs of continuity are usually lower than the costs of policy change (North 1991). Even during revolutionary periods of change, inefficient institutions of the past persist because powerful beneficiaries of inefficient practices have an interest in preserving them (Hellman 1996) and because an alternative way of organizing business—a new focal point—does not emerge. Inertia is especially probable when those most adversely affected by inertia are too weak to challenge and/or to overthrow those in power.

This set of qualifications to the paradox of simultaneous transitions provides an analytic framework for understanding policy reform and policy inertia. To test these assumptions, we now turn to an analysis of social policy reform—or the lack thereof—in post-Soviet Russia.

The Gaidar Blueprint

When the Soviet Union collapsed in 1991, the economy was in total shambles. Soviet gold and hard currency reserves were depleted, the budget deficit had ballooned to 20 percent of GDP, money was abundant but goods were scarce, production had stopped, and trade had all but collapsed (Aslund 1995). During the winter of 1991, experts predicted starvation throughout the Soviet Union, prompting Western government to ship in emergency food supplies. This was the economy for which Yeltsin and his government also assumed responsibility when they created the independent state of Russia in the fall of 1991.

Given these conditions, a consensus quickly crystallized regarding the necessity of economic reform. Within the Russian government, no one in the fall of 1991 cautioned against going "too fast" (Gaidar 1997). At the time, leaders in the Russian Congress also advocated rapid and comprehensive economic reform measures. Even Ruslan Khasbulatov, the new chairman of the Russian Congress, confirmed his belief in market reforms, warning that it was too early for euphoria as radical economic reforms had yet to be implemented (Khasbulatov 1991).

All recognized the urgency of the moment regarding the economy. How to respond to the economic crisis engendered more debate.[6] After reviewing several candidates and their programs for reform, Yeltsin selected a young economist, Yegor Gaidar, to design and execute Russia's transition to a market economy. Gaidar was an unexpected choice. Before this position, Gaidar had never held a serious political office. Nor did Yeltsin know Gaidar personally. The Russian president met Gaidar through Gennady Burbulis, who subsequently served as the intermediary between Yeltsin and his young reform government (Pringle 1992).

Yeltsin admired Gaidar's confidence, candor, his unwavering style, and his ability to speak plainly (Yeltsin 1994b:164). Gaidar's plan to move swiftly also coincided with Yeltsin's approach to economic reform. Though uneducated in the ways of economic policymaking, Yeltsin firmly believed at the time that a radical change was necessary, and Gaidar promised radical and swift change (Aslund 1995:64–65). Yeltsin also recognized that Gaidar had a coherent and unified team that could execute a reform agenda more effectively than one individual (Yeltsin 1991).

Though never published as a written document or elaborated in a single speech, Gaidar's program for economic reform called for immediate liberalization of prices and trade, simultaneously achieving macroeconomic stabilization through strict control of the money supply and government spending (Bush 1991). Gaidar and his advisors believed that the emergence of real prices and a stable currency would stimulate the formation of markets, which in turn would foster the formation of other market institutions. In this period of market emergence, the state's principal responsibility was to balance the budget and control the printing of money so that stabilization could be achieved.

Once stabilization had been accomplished, massive privatization was to follow. Whereas economic transformation was recognized by Russian government officials and Western advisors alike as a "seamless web," requiring a comprehensive program to undertake several parallel economic reform measures (Lipton and Sachs 1990; Gates, Milgrom, and Roberts 1993), privatization was highlighted as the cornerstone of a successful market economy (Brzeski 1992:195–200; Grigoriev 1992:196–197).

Above all, privatization aimed to "rationalize" the use of resources and thereby maximize the overall productive capacity of the economy (von Brabant 1992). Eventually, Gaidar's government anticipated that privatization would rationalize the size of enterprises, meaning that large conglomerates would dissolve into several entities, while the size of each of these newly privatized enterprises would be scaled down dramatically. This process would take place through bankruptcies—an essential mechanism for reorganizing property and capital. To achieve these benefits associated with private property in large enterprises, the process of privatization was designed to produce a separation of management from ownership, a canon of modern capitalist economies (Berle and Means 1991).

In the initial proposals for privatization issued by Yeltsin's government, this separation was to be achieved by mandating the creation of open joint stock companies for former large state enterprises (Boycko, Shleifer, and Vishny 1995). First, closed joint stock companies were decreed illegal. Yeltsin's team wanted to force enterprises to accept out-side ownership. Second, ownership was to be dispersed. Twenty-five percent of the shares at each enterprise were to be distributed to the worker's collective at no cost. These shares, however, were to be nonvot-ing. Another 5 percent were offered to the management at full price, but voting. The remaining shares were to be distributed through a mass voucher program. This distribution aimed to create dispersed ownership of large enterprises so that millions of Russian citizens would have a stake in the process. By outlawing closed joint stock companies and cre-ating a voucher market to serve as a transitional substitute for capital markets, the GKI program planned to expose entrenched directors to the discipline of financial markets as well as product markets. Toward this end, boards of directors were decreed into existence and conferred, on paper, with the same fiduciary responsibilities found in American and European corporate law. Ultimately, this privatization program was to create Western-style corporations out of former state-owned enterprises.

The policies and sequence of reform regarding liberalization, stabiliza-tion, and privatization were consistent with Gaidar's neoliberal ap-proach to markets and market development; the less the state intervened in the market the better. But the plan also conformed with the realm of the possible for Russian reformers. The Russian state—an entity that did not exist when Gaidar assumed responsibility for economic reform—did not have the capacity to implement economic policies administratively. Policies that needed a strong state to implement them, such as gradual price liberalization or state-run competitive auctions of enterprises, were untenable at the time.

As Vladimir Mau, an advisor to Gaidar at the time, wrote, "The weak state was an objective reality, which had to be taken into account when selecting an economic-political strategy" (Mau 1995:42).

At the early stages of conceptualization, Gaidar and his government also planned to maintain a minimum level of social support for those hit hardest by the shock of price liberalization (Aslund 1995:69). Speaking at the Fifth Russian Congress, Yeltsin promised that "the liberalization of prices will be accompanied by acts of social defense of the population" ("Vystuplenie B. N. Yeltsina" 1991).

Meanwhile, control of inflation was considered the overwhelming pri-ority of Gaidar's "social policy." Gaidar, for instance, resisted the idea of wage indexation and agreed to implement such a state policy only if Western financing for the program was secured (Aslund 1995:68).

Deputy Prime Minister and Labor Minister Aleksandr Shokhin also re-jected inflationary policies such as savings compensations. As he stated bluntly in November 1991, "I consider indexation [of Sberbank accounts] from the budget to be nonsense. Sberbank is a commercial structure" (Shokhin 1991). For these neoliberals, conquering inflation was their most important "welfare" policy as inflation hit hardest the poorest in society.

Over the long run, Gaidar and his associates firmly believed that economic growth was the best social policy for Russia. Until growth occurred, they believed that the state could not afford comprehensive social assistance programs. The economy had to produce a surplus before the state intervened to redistribute the surplus. Insofar as they articulated a new role of the state in providing social support, the Gaidar team pushed local governments to assume a greater role for providing social services (Wallich 1994).

Institutional Legacies:
Neoliberal Ideas Clash with Soviet Realities

Drafted in a political vacuum and informed by Western models of macroeconomic management and industrial organization, the Gaidar strategy for more generally reforming social policy and the economy did not take into account the institutional context left over from the Soviet era, which still structured economic life when the Gaidar team assumed responsibility for economic policymaking. Because Russia's revolutionaries who assumed power in 1991 refrained from using force to destroy the Soviet old regime, they retained many Soviet institutions and the organizations and actors empowered by them (McFaul 1996a; McFaul 1993).

Eventually, those threatened by Gaidar's ideas about reform regrouped and rebelled to protect the institutional arrangements that benefited them. During the first Russian republic (from January 1992 until October 1993), these actors acted collectively to amend, if not undermine altogether Gaidar's original ideas for reform. A poorer version of past Soviet social policy practices lingered, while radical attempts at reform failed.

The Organization of the Soviet Enterprise

No Soviet institutional arrangement was more consequential to diluting, challenging, and transforming neoliberal ideas about social policy than the Soviet enterprise. Long before Anatoly Chubais or Yegor Gaidar had ever begun to pen their proposals for privatization, Soviet enterprise directors had seized de facto many of the rights associated with ownership (McFaul 1995). When the Chubais/Gaidar privatization program threatened to "take back" these property rights from the factory directors, the directors mobilized to protect their ownership claims. The battles over ownership claims resulted in serious consequences for the organization and distribution of social welfare.

Acting allegedly on behalf of the workers, the Soviet state owned all enterprises, and Soviet enterprise directors acted as the state's agents in managing the assets. Over time, the state's ability to oversee the activities of the enterprise directors became increasingly weaker as the number of transactions, prices, quotas, and production targets to be monitored grew. Meanwhile, the organizations mandated to supervise the directors (KGB, CPSU, Soviet ministries) weakened.

Individual apparatchiks within the huge centralized bureaucracies of the massive Soviet party state had no personal incentive to closely monitor agents at the enterprise level other than to receive bribes.[7] Profits of individual enterprises were determined by bureaucrats rather than markets. Therefore, the loss of profits to agents had no direct adverse effect on any individual owner. The Soviet state was the loser (Kornai 1992:73). Moreover, production measurements in the Soviet economy were quantitative, not qualitative, creating easy opportunities for shirking.

The acuteness of this problem of principal control over agents already had begun to undermine the Soviet command economy well before the appearance of Gorbachev. (Naishul 1992). Directors, through their control of information about their enterprises, began to acquire de facto the bundle of rights typically associated with ownership (Barzel 1989). Most important, directors increasingly assumed control over the operation and use of their enterprises. At the same time that directors' control over state enterprises increased, these same directors retained responsibility for the welfare of their firms' employees and pensioners.

Soviet enterprises under Stalin assumed responsibility for several social services typically not associated with the workplace in capitalist economies. Especially in small, one-company towns reconstructed after World War II, enterprises provided housing, schools, and medical facilities to their employees, while large conglomerates often ran their own farms and stores. Some enterprises even provided local electricity and transportation services. Because all enterprises were "owned" by the state anyway, distinctions between private and public were not important. The enterprise director served as both the provider of work and the provider of welfare (Puffer 1992). This institutionalized arrangement at the enterprise meant that directors assumed a very paternalistic relationship toward their workers, especially as labor was scarce and could be held at the firm at no real cost to the personal fortunes of the factory director.

At the same time, workers had few opportunities to organize and represent their interests to oppose the directors. Communist Party trade unions and later workers' collectives provided several services to workers as well, but these "aristocratic workers" colluded with the directors rather than defend worker interests against management.[8] With no other representative body to turn to, workers relied on their directors to represent their interests to the state planners, the local bureaucratic authorities, and the central party bosses (Berliner 1957; Willerton 1992; Cook 1997).

Soviet Interest Groups Fight Back

Soviet enterprise directors had acquired de facto control over their enterprises well before market reforms began and then further consolidated these property rights claims under the rubric of enterprise reform initiated by Soviet Prime Minister Nikolai Ryzhkov during the Gorbachev era (Nellis 1991b). They were therefore prepared to fight to maintain their "ownership" when Gaidar and his associates introduced their plan to privatize Russian enterprises. Given the organization of social welfare during the Soviet period, these directors enjoyed the support of trade unions in this battle against neoliberal reform.

At the time, the Civic Union constituted the most successful political organization to represent the enterprise directors and the trade unions in rebuffing neoliberalism. Arkady Volsky was the intellectual and organizational catalyst for the Civic Union. Volsky, a former CPSU Central Committee member with close and long-standing ties to enterprise directors, and his organizations represented the interests of that portion of the Soviet *nomenklatura* that wanted to preserve their previous economic privileges, but in new market conditions.

The Civic Union claimed to be "centrist" and consciously tried to carve out a middle road between Gaidar and the communists. Different from militant communist groups, the Civic Union declared its support for the market, private property, and the general objectives of reform outlined by Yeltsin's first postcommunist government. The Civic Union, however, strongly rejected the strategy of shock therapy originally promoted by Gaidar (Volsky 1992).

In the cases of liberalization, macroeconomic policy, and integration into the international capitalist system, Civic Union leaders claimed that the Gaidar government was duped by the IMF, the World Bank, and other Western institutions into destroying Russia's industrial base and welfare system (*Izvestiya* August 5, 1992:2). Civic Union leaders argued that falling production rates were due to weak consumer purchasing power, exacerbated by the "artificial" ruble-dollar course, and was not caused by the inability of Russian firms to produce marketable goods. The Civic Union leaders maintained that the Russian government allowed unrestricted dumping of imports into the Russian market with which local manufacturing plants could not compete. To correct this situation, the Civic Union proposed a carefully calibrated wage and price indexing, subsidies and credits to strategic industries, and greater restrictions on both imports and foreign investment, in effect assigning the state a greater role in managing liberalization (*Grazhdansky Soyuz* 1992).

In the case of privatization, the Civic Union supported the general goal of transferring property to individual hands, but pushed to give property rights to managers and directors of enterprises and not outside owners. Civic Union leaders criticized the government's mass privatization program through the voucher system, asserting that the scheme would not redistribute property but simply concentrate ownership into the hands of those who had money at the time—former black marketeers, the mafia, and foreigners (*Financial Times* October 23, 1992:3). Above all else, the Civic Union's privatization formula promised little unemployment and few bankruptcies. As Volsky explained,

> Why do I talk about the Chinese experience so much? Because there, reforms have been carried through without a fall in the population's living standards. While in our country, they have been elevated to the formula: Reforms demand sacrifices. . . . Who said so? Why is it that the sacrifices must be borne by the population and not the theoreticians who, through their incompetence, have in practice brought the economy to collapse? (*Rossiiskaya Gazeta*, October 31, 1992:2, in *FBIS-SOV-92-215*, November 5, 1992:46).

The Civic Union's promises of an easier way to reform won widespread support, especially in those sectors of the economy such as the military-industrial complex and agriculture, which feared full-scale marketization. The Civic Union also won the favor of the Federation of Independent Trade Unions of Russia (FNPR), which claimed that only the Civic Union defended the interests of workers during the transition to a market economy (Rutland 1992). The Civic Union's advocacy of greater social protection for workers, as well as greater ownership rights for workers' collectives during the process of privatization, strengthened the image of the Civic Union as the voice of a pro-labor social policy, in contrast to the harsh proposals advocated by the radical liberals in the Yeltsin government.

During 1992, Yeltsin increasingly believed that he needed Civic Union's support to maintain social harmony and political power. Communist militants opposed to capitalism had little leverage against the government as they were beyond mollification. At the same time, ardent supporters of capitalism also could be ignored as they neither represented important social groups at the time nor had an exit option. In contrast, Yeltsin feared the power of enterprise directors and the workers at their plants as serious threats to his hold on power and market reforms. Consequently, he sought compromise with the Civic Union (*Nezavisimaya Gazeta*, November 5, 1992:1).

In addition to the perception that the Civic Union represented key interest groups, the organization's influence in policy debates about economic policy and social policy was enhanced by the institutional ambiguity that haunted Russian politics during the first Russian republic. First, the balance of power between the executive and legislative branches of government remained ambiguous throughout the first Russian republic because Russian leaders could not agree upon a new constitution. Given this ambiguity, the Russian Congress increasingly reasserted its policymaking role during this period. This situation boded well for antiliberal political forces like Civic Union, as well as more radical opponents of reform as they dominated the Russian Congress ("Red Square" Ostankino television program November 21, 1992, in *FBIS-SOV-92-226*, November 23, 1992:27).

Second, Russia did not hold new elections after the collapse of the Soviet Union in 1991. Without elections to confirm the real balance of power in society, the Civic Union could pursue a political and economic agenda in the name of directors and workers, even with no electoral mandate from them. Moreover, the Civic Union could claim to act as intermediaries for these social forces in dealing with the state without any accountability toward the social units or threat of punishment from them, such as losing support in the next election.

In regimes without elections, lobby organizations representing special interests like the Civic Union have greater access to and influence over the state than do other kinds of intermediaries. Interests of mass-based groups (i.e., consumers' organizations or women's associations) and individuals are best represented in electoral, parliamentary systems.

Without elections, the voice of individuals and mass-based groups cannot compete next to associations representing sectoral interests of powerful economic actors. Under these conditions, political organizations representing special interests like the Civic Union have a unique opportunity to enter into corporatist arrangements with the state, especially one as weak as the Russian state (Cawson 1989). Moreover, because class associations have not organized nationally, competitors to sectorally organized associations typically found in Western corporatist systems had not yet emerged in Russia.

The perceived power shift away from liberal political groups to centrist and opposition groups, coupled with the institutional ambiguity of the early post-Soviet period, combined to undermine neoliberal ideas about reform and social policy. Gaidar's strategy for reorganizing Soviet-era welfare practices failed quickly, allowing old conventions, rules, and policies to continue.

The Gaidar-Chubais plan to separate ownership from management at the enterprise unraveled first. In compromising with the Russian Congress during negotiations over the privatization program in 1992, the Russian government allowed for Option Two to be added to their program (*Izvestiya* June 6, 1992:1; *Ekonomika i Zhizn'* No. 24, June 1992:1).[9] In contrast to Option One, which allocated the majority of all shares of an enterprise to outsiders, this second option allowed the "worker's collective" to obtain 51 percent ownership of their enterprise. Not surprisingly, three-quarters of all enterprises selected this option.

The liberals in Yeltsin's government, led most vocally by privatization czar Anatoly Chubais, strongly opposed insider ownership. Chubais argued that privatization must serve the interest of all Russian citizens and not just those who work at large, potentially profitable enterprises (*Izvestiya* February 26, 1993:2).

Comparing the experience with worker management schemes in the former Yugoslavia, Chubais feared that too much worker control of privatized enterprises would threaten the objective of privatization—efficient, profit-seeking, companies. In his view, such privatized enterprises would devote all profits to wages and salaries, leaving nothing for investment in production. (Chubais, as cited in *INTERFAX* June 10, 1992, in *FBIS-SOV-92-113*, June 11, 1992:51; and *Rossiiskie Vesti* January 28, 1993:3).

More generally, Chubais and his allies criticized the "political approach" of the parliament regarding privatization, warning that the achievement of "political goals of various (interest) groups" could sap the government's privatization program (Chubais's remarks, quoted in *ITAR-TASS* February 9, 1993 in *FBIS-SOV-93-025*, February 9, 1993:22). Given the balance of political power in Russia at the time, Russian liberals both in the government and the parliament could do little to block insider privatization.

Parallel to losing the battle for privatization, the neoliberals lost control of stabilization policies. Gaidar's price liberalization frightened everyone. In response, political forces and economic lobbies quickly mobilized against the Gaidar strategy.

Yeltsin also reacted to the anti-Gaidar coalition, losing confidence in his young reformers. As Yeltsin recalls, "Because of my initial respect for parliament as an institution, I took very hard the sharp criticism by the government that dogged the first three months of our reforms" (Yeltsin 1994b:165).

In particular, Yeltsin began to question whether a "social base" existed for Gaidar's reforms (Gaidar 1996:173). There was none (Mau 1995:46; Yavlinsky 1995). Yeltsin later reflected, "Soon it became evident that the Gaidar government, which was rapidly making one decisions after another, was in complete isolation" (Yeltsin 1994b:158).

Gaidar's team also did little to explain their policies to the Russian population. Significantly, the Gaidar team never published a "plan" as a communication device for the larger public. With so little public understanding of general market principles, the absence of government explanation created opportunities for other political actors to fill the information vacuum.

The industrial lobbies stepped in to fill the void, convincing both Yeltsin and the Congress that the government needed experienced industrial managers to run the government, not young economists. Yeltsin agreed. In the spring, he appointed three industrialists as deputy prime ministers in his government—Vladimir Shumeiko, Giorgy Khizha, and Viktor Chernomyrdin.

Shumeiko and Khizha represented the interests of the military-industrial complex in the government, while Chernomyrdin, the former director of Gazprom, represented the oil and gas lobby. For Gaidar, Khizha's appointment in particular was a blow to his reform course because "he absolutely was not able to understand fundamental principles of [state] management in market conditions. . . . From May 1992, Khizha became the chief fighter for increasing the budget deficit" (Gaidar 1996:206).

In June 1992, Yeltsin countered these "industrial" appointments by naming Gaidar as acting prime minister. Nonetheless, Gaidar and his associates claimed to have lost control of economic policymaking; instead of "shock therapy," the government was pursuing a "mixed" plan (Shokhin 1992). This mixed plan and coalition government resulted in freezing the liberalization of oil and gas prices and renewed state spending for enterprise subsidies. The expansion of state subsidies quickly undermined stabilization and increased monthly inflationary rates back to double digits (World Bank 1993).

Gaidar's appointment of Viktor Gerashchenko to head the Central Bank in July 1992 further exacerbated inflationary pressures as Gerashchenko quickly approved the printing of new money and the transfer of government credits to ailing enterprises. Within weeks after his appointment, inflation skyrocketed (Ulyukaev 1996:34). When Gaidar attempted to rein in Gerashchenko and the Central Bank, the new chairman hid behind the veil of institutional ambiguity of the time and claimed that he answered to the Congress and not the government.

The Russian Congress, however, was not content with this coalition government. Meeting in December 1992, Congress deputies pushed hard for and succeeded in removing Gaidar as acting prime minister. Lacking a new constitution, the rules governing executive and legislative power in forming a government were still ambiguous. Informally, Yeltsin sensed that compromise with the Congress of People's Deputies was necessary and a change in economic policy had to occur. The "coalition" government, or what Gaidar advisor Vladimir Mau labeled the "parliamentization of the government" (Mau 1995:55), that resulted from the Seventh Congress appeared to reflect more accurately the interests of important economic groups. By making these concessions and in effect forgoing policy coherence, Yeltsin believed he was constructing a political coalition supported by Russia's most important political forces and a majority of Russia's citizens (Press conference with Yeltsin, Ostankino Television, April 14, 1993, quoted here from *FBIS-SOV-93-071* April 15, 1993:17).

Viktor Chernomyrdin's appointment as prime minister did not end the struggle between the president and the Supreme Soviet over control of economic policy. Although initially supportive, Khasbulatov began to express reservations about Chernomyrdin. For the chairman of the Supreme Soviet, the issue was not necessarily the policies pursued by the new government, but the exclusive way in which these policies were adopted. For Khasbulatov, the superficial debates about economic reforms were proxies for real debates about political power. Khasbulatov and his allies in the parliament wanted more direct control over economic policymaking, and they took advantage of poorly defined political institutions and an uncertain balance of power to obtain this greater control.

In a protracted battle, the Supreme Soviet and Congress gradually wrestled several aspects of economic policymaking away from the president and his government. The Supreme Soviet acquired control over the Central Bank, reassigned the Fund for Privatization to its jurisdiction, obtained command of the pension fund, and subordinated the Antimonopoly Committee to the Congress. Yeltsin and his government eventually resisted Congress's encroachments on executive authority about control over the budget and privatization, as these two spheres of economic policymaking were deemed to be most critical to continuing economic reform.

To deal with the budget, the Supreme Soviet expanded government expenditures radically in 1993, approving in August a new budget with a deficit of nearly 25 percent of GDP (Sinel'nikov 1995). The Supreme Soviet handled privatization by seeking to increase the rights of enterprise directors beyond the already director-friendly privatization law of 1992. Coined "Option Four," a set of amendments to the privatization law sought to give insiders 90 percent control of their enterprise (Diskin 1993).

The Supreme Soviet's budget proposal of 1993 was unacceptable to Yeltsin and his government because a 25 percent budget deficit would have thrust Russia into hyperinflation. At the time, Finance Minister Boris Fyodorov called the Parliament's budget "catastrophic," saying that it had no economic purpose and, instead, it aimed to "destabilize the executive branch" (Fyodorov 1993).

Yeltsin's government also flatly rejected the Supreme Soviet's privatization proposal for even greater insider ownership, arguing that such an amendment would impede the creation of effective property rights for enterprises. These fundamental debates about economic policy ended only when the ambiguous political rules of the game that defined the division of power between the president and the Parliament were clarified.

Tragically, this resolution occurred only after these two branches of government fought in a military conflict in October 1993.

As a result of their political weakness, Gaidar's ideas for social policy reform were never tested. As Russian industrial lobbies gained control of the Russian government, they succeeded in implementing a privatization program and a set of fiscal and monetary policies that preserved the old Soviet practices of social welfare policy.

The government established an unemployment agency for workers, but this organization served more as assessor of the number of unemployed rather than a provider of unemployment benefits or retraining programs. Instead, the enterprise continued to serve as the main provider of social welfare, providing the same bundle of goods and services to the factory employees, regardless of the financial health of the enterprise. In 1993, Russian enterprises spent an estimated 14 percent of their total wage bill on social benefits and services; at industrial enterprises, social spending was 20 percent of the wage bill (Commander, Lee, and Tolstopiatenko 1996:53).

This situation impeded structural reform at the enterprise. In fact, given the tax system, the low cost of labor, and the extreme dependence of these workers on the enterprise, factory directors had real incentives to maintain Soviet-era employment levels and higher (Commander, Dhar, and Yemtsov 1996; Layard and Richter 1995). Threatening social chaos if workers had to be fired, enterprise directors also could blackmail the state to transfer subsidies to cover their wage bill, housing costs, retirement benefits, etc. In nonproductive enterprises, state transfers for wage bills serve effectively as unemployment compensation from the state.

In post-Soviet Russia, workers still had little independence from their enterprise directors. Insider privatization created the veneer of shared interests between directors and workers, even though directors continued to enjoy their now unlimited control over their enterprises. The bundle of social benefits provided by the factory also tied the worker to the enterprise, even if workers' salaries did not increase and were delivered late.

Moreover, without such a social safety net, the Russian labor market had little fluidity. Soviet practices that continued in post-Soviet Russia, such as the *propiska* system for controlling internal migration and *trudovaya knizhka* (workers' book) for registering workers' records, added additional impediments to worker mobility (Gaddy 1996).

Finally, the economic policies by the Yeltsin government in the first two years of independence did not produce growth, meaning that there were few new jobs available to workers, especially those who resided in one-company towns.

Social transfers provided directly by the state also did not change. Subsidies for housing, energy, phones, and vacations continued, with little effort devoted to targeting state assistance to those who needed it most (Aslund 1997:126). However, the actual welfare of the average Russian citizen receiving these "benefits" declined. Above all else, double-digit monthly inflation wiped out the value of pension checks and workers' salaries. State-provided incomes did not keep up with inflation. In claiming to protect working people and pensioners from the harmful effects of the market, those who succeeded in blocking market reforms impoverished these constituencies even further.

The Second Russian Republic: Ideas, Institutions, and Power

The October 1993 armed conflict between the president and the Parliament dramatically altered the ideas, institutions, and balance of power between political forces that shaped the definition and implementation of economic and social policy. Though each of these three factors changed greatly between the first Russian Republic (1991–1993) and the second Russian Republic (1993–present), the new mix of factors combined to produce little social policy reform.[10]

The Mixed Message of the 1993 Elections

Immediately after the October 1993 military clash, Yeltsin and his allies appeared to be in the driver's seat once again. Yeltsin ordered the arrest of his main political opponents, banned several opposition parties and newspapers, and called on his aides to rewrite the constitutional draft to give the presidency even more powers. Yeltsin and his allies hoped that the elections and constitutional referendum to be held in December 1993 would ratify both this new balance of power, by giving the reformers an electoral mandate in the parliamentary election, and the new constitution, which reflected the interests of this new balance of power.

Only one of these two ratifications occurred. Russia's Choice, the liberal reformist electoral bloc headed by Yegor Gaidar, anticipated that they would win between 30–40 percent of the popular vote (VTsIOM 1993). Even in the worst case scenario, reformist electoral blocs were certain they would constitute a solid majority in the new lower house. They were wrong. To everyone's surprise, Vladimir Zhirinovsky's ultranationalist Liberal Democratic Party won 23 percent of the popular vote, compared to only 15.5 percent for Russia's Choice. When counted together, antireformist blocs constituted 43 percent of the vote compared with only 34 percent for pro-reformist forces (McFaul 1994).

While supporting Zhirinovsky and other antireformist blocs such as the Agrarian and Communist Parties in the parliamentary elections, Russian voters ratified Yeltsin's constitution. When compared to Western constitutions, Russia's new basic law granted inordinate power to the executive branch of government. Yeltsin's political allies may have lost the parliamentary election, but the Parliament also had become much less important in governing Russia.

The 1993 elections directly affected the course of economic policy and policymaking. The results of the parliamentary election influenced the composition of the government. The two leading liberals in the government before the vote—Yegor Gaidar and Boris Fyodorov—resigned after their party's electoral defeat.[11] Chernomyrdin retained his position as prime minister (unlike Gaidar or Fyodorov, he personally did not participate in the parliamentary elections), but promised "an end to market romanticism." Chernomyrdin ordered his aides to draft plans for price controls and the indexing of wages and pensions.

Chernomyrdin's new government did not represent the balance of forces within the Parliament. On the contrary, Chernomyrdin assembled a coalition government dominated by industrial centrists—a team very similar to the government in place before the 1993 election. Civic Union, the bloc claiming to represent Chernomyrdin's "centrist" and "industrialist" orientation, won only 1.8 percent of the popular vote, yet Chernomyrdin's government was dominated by such people. In contrast, Zhirinovsky's Liberal Democratic Party, which captured 23 percent of the vote, received no government posts, while Russia's Choice (with 15 percent) and the communists and agrarians (with 20 percent) landed only one representative each in Chernomyrdin's new government.

Yeltsin and Chernomyrdin could ignore the balance of power in the Duma because the new constitution empowered them to do so. The new basic law made it very costly for the parliament to try to remove the prime minister. If the Parliament passed a vote of no confidence in the government three times, then the Parliament would be dissolved and new elections held. Only after new elections was the Parliament in a position to vote again on the prime minister, without the threat of being dissolved by the president. In addition, the new constitution gave the president the power to rule by decree. In sum, the new constitution shifted the onus of power and responsibility for governing to the executive branch and insulated the government from the influence of Parliament.

In shaping economic policy, Chernomyrdin used this new institutional configuration to pursue a perverse combination of macroeconomic stabilization without microeconomic reform. He and his government tackled inflation most vigorously (Ulyukaev 1996). Chernomyrdin made progress in closing the budget deficit by establishing real interest rates for government credits emanating from the Russian Central Bank and curtailing the amount of government subsidies to state enterprises. Rather than responding to expenditure requests from the Duma, Chernomyrdin's government submitted austere federal budgets to the Russian legislature, which, on paper, drastically reduced government expenditures. Chernomyrdin financed the remaining budget deficit by borrowing money through a domestic treasury bill market, foreign bond market, and securing IMF loans.

The Chernomyrdin government also privatized several important oil and mineral companies through the so-called loans for shares program, a scheme in which leading financial groups acquired controlling positions in these companies for a fraction of the market price (Johnson 1997). The executive branch and the Russian government executed this program without legislative approval.

Just as Yeltsin and Chernomyrdin took advantage of their new post-1993 power to unilaterally pursue stabilization and privatization, they could have used their newly institutionalized autonomy from the Duma to also pursue radical reforms regarding social policy. Ideas were in the air.

For instance, Mikhail Dmitriyev—a former Gaidar aide and eventual deputy minister of labor under Chernomyrdin—floated an ambitious proposal for privatizing pension funds (Dmitriyev 1996). Others pushed for more stringent bankruptcy procedures as a way to wrestle control away from directors practicing asset stripping and begin the long and arduous process of restructuring Russian enterprises. Still others, including Nizhny Novgorod Governor Boris Nemtsov, called upon Chernomyrdin to begin targeting welfare transfers so that the neediest received more assistance.

The Chernomyrdin government, however, did not devote serious attention to these social policy reforms for several years. On the contrary, the government actually achieved stabilization by delaying or not paying wage bills and pensions (Delyagin 1997). Instead of forcing financial industrial groups to pay taxes, the Russian government reduced its budget deficits by defaulting on money owed to workers and pensioners, forcing the costs of stabilization on society's poorest (Earle and Sabirianova 1998).

More generally, Russia's government leaders have done little to restructure welfare transfers, meaning that overall expenditures are still too high by West European standards, but that the neediest in society are still not targeted. (Aslund and Dmitriyev 1996; Aslund 1997; World Bank 1996; Alfandari, Fan, and Freinkman 1996). Heat, transport, and vacations to the Crimea are still subsidized, while pensioners scrape out a living below the poverty line. As Russian economist Oleg Vitte explained,

> In Western countries it is considered more or less acceptable if 50–60 percent of the aid to the needy reaches those for whom it is intended. In our country, according to expert evaluations, social assistance is distributed in the

proportions: 19 percent goes to those who need it and 81 percent goes to others. This means that in order to give a ruble to the poor, we must give 4 rubles to the rich. (Interview with Vitte in *Literaturnaya Gazeta*, July 16, 1997.)

In cross-national comparison of social assistance targeting, World Bank economist Branko Milanovic reports that only 6 percent of Russia's social assistance reaches the bottom quintile of the population, compared to 29 percent in Poland, 36 percent in Estonia, and 78 percent in the United States (Milanovic 1998:113).

Enabling Social Policy Neglect

Postcommunist Russia may be one of the only countries in the world that has pursued the control of inflation by simply not paying wages for months at a time.[12] How has the Russian government been able to achieve this record of neglect?

Again, the relationship between labor and management at the enterprise left over from the Soviet era provides part of the explanation. Workers who are not paid have few options. Exit is not a credible threat as the state still controls internal migration, welfare benefits (including especially nonmonetary benefits) are not transferable but rather tied to the enterprise, and new jobs are scarce (Earle and Sabirianova 1998). Except in strategic sectors, strikes also offer most workers little leverage against their factory directors.

As most enterprises are net subtractors of value, workers' demands for a greater share in the profits of the company are meaningless because there are not profits to share. The ambiguous demarcation of ownership at the enterprise further complicates the worker-management bargaining process as the veneer of "collective ownership" clouds the divide between employer and employee. If workers are also on paper owners, on which side of the table do they sit? The arrears crisis also gives the director a scapegoat to point to when workers demand wages.[13]

Beyond the factory walls, the interests of workers, pensioners, and the real poor in Russia can be ignored due to the structure and effectiveness of their representative organizations and institutions. After the demise of the Civic Union, which received only 1.8 percent of the popular vote in the parliamentary election in 1993, the Communist Party of the Russian Federation (the CPRF) has monopolized representative responsibilities for workers and pensioners at the national level of government.

The Communist Party looks like a real, national party with a well articulated social base and ideological niche. Strikingly, the party has not demonstrated an ability to legislate effectively on behalf of its constituents as the Duma's largest faction. Though it has blocked some governmental efforts to rationalize social policy and target social spending, significantly, the party has never succeeded in blocking the approval of any of Yeltsin's austere budgets. Even after the financial crisis of the summer of 1998, the Communist Party did not succeed in gaining control over the government because only one new member of prime minister's government, Yuri Maslyukov, was a member of the party.

Mass-based groups such as trade unions or pension organizations have not filled the representation void.[14] The Federation of Independent Trade Unions (FNPR) has claimed to retain 50 million members, but has never demonstrated this numerical muscle (Cook 1997; Connor 1996). In parliamentary elections in 1993 and 1995, the federation joined electoral blocs than garnered less than 2 percent of the vote (McFaul 1996b). In the 1996 presidential elections, the FNPR did not endorse a candidate. Likewise, their organization of street demonstrations or strikes has never garnered a policy response from the federal government.

Nor have truly independent trade unions filled the void (Cook 1997; Gordon 1995). The Independent Union of Miners, the coalition of strike committees that brought the Soviet government to its knees in 1991, lost its independence and credibility by consistently siding with the Yeltsin government over the last five years. Wildcat strikes, particularly in coal regions and in the Far East, have increased during the last year, raising some speculation that Russian labor finally has started to remobilize, but the lack of national organization suggests that these strikes will remain isolated instances. Independent pension organizations simply do not exist, relegating the work of representation of this sector of society to the Communist Party (Klyamkin 1996).

Business groups always constitute the most organized sector of society in capitalist democracies (Moe 1980:191–192). Presidential systems especially privilege small, well-organized interest groups and disadvantage mass-based groups. The same has been true in Russia. In particular, those powerful economic lobbies with an interest in partial reform have managed to sustain Yeltsin and his governments in power, while at the same time blocking genuine liberal market reforms (McFaul 1998; Hellman 1996).

Even in presidential systems, however, democracies provide deprived mass-based groups with an opportune moment to strike back on election day. As the 1996 presidential election approached, expectations grew that those most hurt by the lack of attention devoted to social policy would finally be able to oust Yeltsin and vote into office a president more disposed to their needs (Hough, Davidheiser, and Lehman 1996). The long-anticipated backlash to market reform finally seemed ready to occur. Throughout Eastern Europe, anticommunist leaders who won electoral victories in first elections lost to former communist leaders in second elections (Gati 1995; Osiatynski 1995). Russia seemed poised to follow a similar trajectory, especially as Russia's economic "reform" had produced more hardship than that of any of these East European countries (*Transition Report 1995* 1996).

This analysis failed to take into account the institutions that mediated between societal preferences and electoral outcomes in Russia during the 1996 presidential elections. Given Russia's two-ballot runoff system for the presidential election, those opposed to Yeltsin's "reforms" (or lack thereof) had to control a majority of votes to alter his policy course.[15] People adversely affected by the absence of social policy reform constituted a solid minority but not a firm majority of Russian voters. To dethrone Yeltsin, they had to ally with other social groups in backing an opposition candidate. This did not occur as no candidate emerged that could bring together such a wider coalition.

In the 1996 election, Communist Party presidential candidate, Gennady Zyuganov, succeeded in winning support from pensioners, unskilled labor, and the poorest people in Russian society, but he failed to appeal to any group beyond this core constituency (McFaul 1997). Given the structure of the electorate, Yeltsin could ignore the interests of those most adversely hurt by his policies and still win reelection.

Conclusion

The first objective of most political leaders is to stay in power. Political leaders use their power in office to assist those societal groups that can help them stay in office. Rarely do politicians do the right thing simply because it is the right thing to do. Only when their power is threatened do political leaders change policy. The threat must be credible because the costs and risks of policy change generally are much higher than the costs of policy continuity.

Yet social groups can never expect the state to act in their interests unless they can influence the fate of state leaders. Although some leaders act benevolently on behalf of the poor, dispossessed, or unfortunate, they usually act only in response to the most powerful. State leaders running weak states are especially vulnerable to strong societal actors.

Social policy in Russia has not been revamped over the last decade because Russia's political leadership has calculated that they can stay in power without initiating these kinds of policy changes. They made this calculation based on the assumption that those most in need of social policy reform were not strong enough politically to threaten their political futures. This weakness was in part a function of the ineffective and corrupt directors, parties, and trade unions that claimed to represent those in need of social welfare. After 1993, the institutional configuration of the Russian polity and the presidential system in particular also served to insulate Russian state leaders from the influence of pensioners, workers, and the poor.

The current situation is not stable. First, the number of people in need of social support is growing. Second, the Communist Party's lock on these voters is weakening. Third, the super-presidential institutions of the Russian state are also weakening. Eventually, the dispossessed in Russia will enjoy greater influence over state policy. The real question for the future is whether this influence will come through institutionalized democratic procedures, or through more revolutionary means.

References

Alesina, Alberto, and Nouriel Roubini, with Gerald Cohen. 1997. *Political Cycles and the Macroeconomy.* Cambridge, Mass.: Massachusetts Institute of Technology Press.

Alfandari, Gilles, Qimiao Fan, and Lev Freinkman. 1996. "Government Financial Transfers to Industrial Enterprises and Restructuring." In Simon Commander, Qimiao Fan, and Mark Schaffer, *Enterprise Restructuring and Economic Policy in Russia.* Washington, D.C.: World Bank, 166–198.

Aslund, Anders. 1995. *How Russia Became a Market Economy.* Washington, D.C.: Brookings Institution Press.

———. 1997. "Social Problems and Policy in Postcommunist Russia." In Ethan Kapstein and Michael Mandelbaum, eds., *Sustaining the Transition: The Social Safety Net in Postcommunist Europe.* New York: Council on Foreign Relations, 124–146.

Aslund, Anders, and Mikhail Dmitriyev. 1996. *Sotsial'naya Politika V Period Perekhoda k Rynku.* Moscow: Moscow Carnegie Center.

Barzel, Yoram. 1989. *Economic Analysis of Property Rights.* Cambridge: Cambridge University Press.

Berle, Adolf, and Gardiner Means. 1991. *The Modern Corporation and Private Property.* New York: Transaction Publishers.

Berliner, Joseph. 1957. *Factory and Manager in the USSR.* Cambridge, Mass.: Harvard University Press.

Bin, Alexander. 1992. "Role of the States in Transitional Postcommunist Economies." In Anders Aslund, ed., *The Post-Soviet Economy: Soviet and Western Perspectives.* London: Pinter Publishers.

Boycko, Maxim, Andrei Shleifer, and Robert Vishny. 1995. *Privatizing Russia.* Cambridge, Mass.: Massachusetts Institute of Technology Press.

Brzeski, Andrzej. 1992. "Post-Communism from a Neo-Institutionalist Perspective." *Journal of Institutional and Theoretical Economics.* 195–200.

Bush, Keith. 1991, "Yelsin's Economic Reform Program." *Report on the USSR.* (November 15): 1–6.

Callaghy, Thomas, and John Ravenhill, eds., 1996. *Hemmed In: Responses to Africa's Economic Decline.* New York: Columbia University Press.

Cawson, Alan. 1989. "Is there a corporatist theory of the state? in Graeme Ducan, ed., *Democracy and the Capitalist State*. Cambridge: Cambridge University Press: 233–252.

Commander, Simon, Une Lee, and Andrei Tolstopiatenko. 1996. "Social Benefits and the Russian Industrial Firm." In Simon Commander, Qimiao Fan, and Mark Schaffer, eds., *Enterprise Restructuring and Economic Policy in Russia*. Washington, D.C.: World Bank. 52–83.

Commander, Simon, Sumana Dhar, and Ruslan Yemtsov. 1996. "How Russian Firms Make Their Wage and Employment Decisions." In Simon Commander, Qimiao Fan, and Mark Schaffer, eds., *Enterprise Restructuring and Economic Policy in Russia*. Washington, D.C.: World Bank.

Connor, Walter. 1996. *Tattered Banners: Labor Conflict and Corporatism in Postcommunist Russia*. Boulder, Colo.: Westview Press.

Cook, Linda. 1997. *Labor and Liberalization: Trade Unions in the New Russia*. New York: Twentieth Century Fund Press.

Cooter, Robert. 1992. "Organization as Property: Economic Analysis of Property Law Applied to Privatization." In Christopher Clague and Gordon Rausser, eds., *The Emergence of Market Economies in Eastern Europe*. Oxford: Basic Blackwell. 77–98.

Delyagin, Mikhail. 1997. *Ekonomika Neplatezhei: Kak ì Pochemu My Budem Zhit' Zavtra*. Moscow: Derzhava. (February).

Diskin, Josif. 1993. "Mne simpatichen chetvertyi variant." *Nezavisimaya Gazeta*. (July 25: 3).

Dmitriyev, Mikhail. 1996. *Pension System in Russia: Alternative Scenarios*. Moscow: Moscow Carnegie Center, (September).

Earle, John, and Richard Rose. 1996. "Ownership Transformation, Economic Behavior, and Political Attitudes in Russia." Working paper, Stanford, Calif.: Center for International Security and Arms Control, (August).

Earle, John, and Klara Sabirianova. 1998. "Understanding Wage Arrears in Russia." Ms. (September).

Eggertson, Thrainin. 1990. *Economic Behavior and Institutions*. Cambridge, U.K.: Cambridge University Press.

Fama, Eugene. 1980. "Agency Problems and the Theory of the Firm," *Journal of Political Economy* 88 (April): 288–307.

Fiorina, Morris. 1981. *Retrospective Voting in American National Elections*. New Haven: Yale University Press.

Fyodorov, Boris. 1993. Quoted in *Segodnya*. (August 31). (Quoted here from *The Current Digest of the Post-Soviet Press* XLV:34 [September 22]: 8.)

Gaddy, Cliff. 1996. *The Price of the Past: Russia's Struggle with the Legacy of a Militarized State*. Washington, D.C.: Brookings Institution Press.

Gaidar, Yegor. 1996. *Dni porazhenii i pobed*. Moscow: Vagrius.

———. 1997. Interview by author, Moscow. (October 8).

Gates, Susan, Paul Milgrom, and John Roberts. 1993. "Complementarities in the Transition from Socialism: A Firm-Level Analysis." Ms. Stanford University.

Gati, Charles. 1995. "If Not Democracy, What?" In Michael Mandelbaum, ed., *Post-Communism: Four Perspectives*. New York: Council on Foreign Relations, 168–198.

Geddes, Barbara. 1994. "Challenging the Conventional Wisdom." *Journal of Democracy* 5:4 (October): 17–31 and 104–118.

Gordon, Leonid. 1995. *Oblast' Vozmozhnogo*. Moscow: Mirt.

Grazhdansky Soyuz. 1992. "Programma Antikrizisnogo Uregulirovaniya." Mimeo, Moscow.

Grigoriev, Leonid. 1992. "Ulterior Property Rights and Privatization: Even God Cannot Change the Past." In Anders Aslund, ed., *The Post-Soviet Economy: Soviet and Western Perspectives*. London: Pinter Publishers.

Grossman, Gregory. 1985. "The Second Economy in the USSR and Eastern Europe: A Bibliography." *Berkeley-Duke Occasional Papers on the Second Economy in the USSR* no. 1.

Haggard, Stephan, and Robert Kaufman. 1996. *The Political Economy of Democratic Transitions*. Princeton: Princeton University Press.

Hall, Peter. 1992. "The Movement from Keynesianism to Monetarism: Institution Analysis and British Economic Policy in the 1970s." In Sven Steinmo, Kathleen Thelen, and Frank Longstreth, *Structuring Politics: Historical Institutionalism in Comparative Perspective*. Cambridge: Cambridge University Press, 90–113.

Hayek, Friedrich A. 1967. "Notes on the Evolution of Systems of Rules of Conduct." In *Studies in Philosophy, Politics, end Economics*. Chicago: University of Chicago Press.

Hellman, Joel. 1996. "Constitutions and Economic Reform in Postcommunist Transitions." *East European Constitutional Review* 5:1 (Winter):46–56.

Hellman, Joel. 1998. "Winners Take All: The Politics of Partial Reform in Postcommunist Transitions." *World Politics* 50:2 (January): 204–205.

Hough, Jerry, Evelyn Davidheiser, and Susan Goodrich Lehman. 1996. *The 1996 Russian Presidential Election*. Brookings Occasional Papers, Washington, D.C.: Brookings Institution.

Huntington, Samuel. 1968. *Political Order in Changing Societies*. New Haven, Conn.: Yale University Press.

Huntington, Samuel and Joan Nelson. 1976. *No Easy Choice: Political Participation in Developing Countries*. Cambridge, Mass.: Harvard University Press.

Jensen, Michael, and William Meckling. 1976. "Theory of the Firm: Managerial Behavior, Agency Costs, and Ownership Structure." *Journal of Financial Economics* 3:3 (October): 305–360.

Johnson, Juliet. 1997. "Russia's Emerging Financial-Industrial Groups." *Post-Soviet Affairs*. 13:4 (October-December): 333–365.

Jowitt, Ken. 1992. *New World Disorder: The Leninist Extinction*. Berkeley: University of California Press.

Khasbulatov, Ruslan. 1991. Interview in *Narodnii Deputat*, no. 15, pp. 7–8. (Reprinted in *Yeltsin-Khasbulatov: Edinstvo, Kompromiss, Bor'ba*. Moscow: Terra, 1994).

Kiewet, Roderick. 1983. *Macreconomics and Micropolitics*. Chicago: Chicago University Press.

Klyamkin, Igor. 1996. "Politicheskie predpochteniya razlichnykh sotsial'no-professional'nikh grupp rossiiskogo obshchestva na parlamenskikh vyborakh 1995 goda." Ms., Moscow: Moscow Carnegie Center. (February).

Kornai, Janos. 1992. *The Socialist System: The Political Economy of Communism*. Princeton, N.J.: Princeton University Press.

Layard, Richer, and Andrea Richter. 1995. "How Much Employment Is Needed for Restructuring: The Russian Experience." *Economics of Transition* 3:1 (March): 35–58.

Levinthal, Daniel. 1988. "A Survey of Agency Models of Organizations," *Journal of Economic Behavior and Organizations* 9:2 (March).

Lipton, David and Jeffrey Sachs. 1990. "Privatization in Eastern Europe: The Case of Poland." *Brookings Papers on Economic Activity.* Washington, D.C.: Brookings Institution Press.

Litwack, John. 1990. "Ratcheting and Economic Reform in the USSR." *Journal of Comparative Economics* 14:254–268.

MacKuen, Michael, Robert Erikson, and James Stimson. 1992. "Peasants or Bankers? The American Electorate and the U.S. Economy." *American Political Science Review* 86:3 (September): 597–611.

Maravell, Jose Maria. 1994. "The Myth of Authoritarian Advantage." *Journal of Democracy* 5:4 (October): 17–31.

Mau, Vladimir. 1995. *Ekonomika i Vlast': Politicheskaya istoriya ekonomicheskoi reformy v Rossii 1985–1994.* Moscow: Delo.

McFaul, Michael. 1998. "Russia's "Privatized' State as an Impediment to Democratic Consolidation." Part I, *Security Dialogue* 29:2 (Spring): 25–33.

McFaul, Michael. 1993. "Russian Centrism and Revolutionary Transitions." *Post-Soviet Affairs* 9:4 (July-September): 196–222.

———. 1994. *Understanding Russia's 1993 Parliamentary Elections: Implications for American Foreign Policy.* Palo Alto, Calif.: Hoover Institution Press.

———. 1995. "State Power, Institutional Change, and the Politics of Privatization in Russia." *World Politics* 47:2 (January): 210–243.

———. 1996a. "Revolutionary Transformations in Comparative Perspective: Defining a Post-Communist Research Agenda." In David Holloway and Norman Naimark, eds., *Reexamining the Soviet Experience: Essays in Honor of Alexander Dallin.* Boulder, Colo.: Westview Press, 167–196.

———. 1996b. *Russia's Between Elections: What the 1995 Parliamentary Elections Really Mean.* Washington, D.C.: Carnegie Endowment for International Peace.

———. 1997. *Russia 1996 Presidential Election: The End of Polarized Politics.* Stanford, Calif.: Hoover Institution Press.

Migranyan, Adranik and Igor Klyamkin. 1990. In *Sotsializm i Demokratiya: Diskussionaya Tribuna.* Moscow: Institut Ekonomiki Mirovoi Sotsialisticheskoi Sistemy.

Milanovic, Branko. 1998. *Income, Inequality, and Poverty during the Transition from Planned to Market Economy.* Washington, D.C.: Word Bank.

Moe, Terry. 1980. *The Organization of Interests.* Chicago: University of Chicago Press.

Moe, Terry. 1984. "The New Economics of Organization." *American Journal of Political Science* 28:4 (November).

Moe, Terry, and Michael Caldwell. 1994. "The Institutional Foundations of Democratic Government: A Comparison of Presidential and Parliamentary Systems." *Journal of Institutional and Theoretical Economics* 150:1, 171–195.

Murrell, Peter. 1991. "Can Neoclassical Economics Underpin the Reform of Centrally Planned Economies? *Journal of Economic Perspectives* 5:4 (Fall): 59–76.

Naishul, Vitali. 1992. "Institutional Development in the USSR." *Cato Journal* 11:3 (Winter).

Nellis, John. 1991a. *Improving the Performance of Soviet Enterprises.* World Bank Discussion Papers, no. 118, Washington, D.C.: World Bank.

Nellis, John. 1991b. "Privatization in Reforming Socialist Economies." In Andreja Bohm and Vladimir Kreacic, eds., *Privatization in Eastern Europe: Current Implementation Issues.* Ljublana, Yugoslavia, International Center for Public Enterprises in Developing Countries.

North, Douglass. 1991. *Institutions, Institutional Change and Economic Performance.* Cambridge: Cambridge University Press.

Osiatynski, Wiktor. 1995. "After Walesa: The Causes and Consequences of Walesa's Defeat." *East European Constitutional Review* 4:4 (Fall): 35–44.

Pereira, Luiz Carlos Bresser, Jose Maria Maravall, and Adam Przeworski. 1993. *Economic Reforms in New Democracies: A Social Democratic Approach.* Cambridge: Cambridge University Press.

Pringle, Peter. 1992. "Gaidar & Co.: The Best and the Brightest." *Moscow Magazine.* (June-July).

Przeworski, Adam. 1991. *Democracy and the Market.* Cambridge: Cambridge University Press.

Puffer, Sheila, ed., 1992. *The Russian Management Revolution.* Armonk, N.Y.: M.E. Sharpe.

Roland, Gerald. 1995. "Political Economy Issues of Ownership Transformation in Eastern Europe." in Masahiko Aoki and Hyunk-ki Kim, eds., *Corporate Governance in Transitional Economies: Insider Control and the Role of Banks.* Washington, D.C.: EDI-World Bank, 31–57.

Rutland, Peter. 1990. "Labor Unrest and Movements in 1989 and 1990." *Soviet Economy* 6:3:345–384.

Sartori, Giovanni. 1994. *Comparative Constitutional Engineering.* New York: New York University Press.

Schmitter, Philippe. 1997. "Intermediaries in the Consolidation of Neo-Democracies: The Role of Parties, Associations, and Movements." Ms. (September).

Shokhin at a press conference on October 12, 1992. Reprinted in Aleksandr Shokhin. 1995. *Moi Golos Budet Vse-taki Uslyshan: Stenogramma Epokhi Peremen.* Moscow. "Nash Dom—L'Age d'Homme": 30–42

Shokhin in *Rossiskaya Gazeta.* (November 1, 1991). (Reprinted in Aleksandr Shokhin. 1995. *Moi Golos Budet Vse-taki Uslyshan: Stenogramma Epokhi Peremen.* Moscow: "Nash Dom—L'Age d'Homme).

Shugart, Matthew, and John Carey. 1992. *Presidents and Assemblies.* Cambridge: Cambridge University Press.

Sinel'nikov, Sergei. 1995. *Byudzhetnyi krizis v Rossii: 1985–1995 gody,* Moscow: Evraziya.

Solnick, Steven. 1998. *Stealing the State: Control and Collapse in Soviet Institutions.* Cambridge, Mass.: Harvard University Press.

Stark, David, and Laszlo Bruszt. 1998. "Path Dependence and Privatization: Strategies in East Central Europe." In *Postsocialist Pathways.* Cambridge University Press.

Steinmo, Sven, Kathleen Thelen, and Frank Longstreth. 1992. *Structuring Politics: Historical Institutionalism in Comparative Perspective.* Cambridge: Cambridge University Press.

Transition Report 1995: Investment and Enterprise Development. 1996. London: European Bank for Reconstruction and Development.

Ulyukaev, Aleksei. 1996. *Rossiya na puti reform.* Moscow: Evraziya.

Volsky, Arkady. 1992. In press conference on June 26 at founding congress of *Grazhdanskii Soyuz.* The author was in attendance.

von Brabant, Jozef. 1992. *Privatizing Eastern Europe: The Role of Markets and Ownership in the Transition.* Dordrecht: Kluwer Academic Publishers.

VTsIOM. 1993. "Rossiya i Vybory. Situatsiya do i posle sobitii 3–4 Oktyabrya." Moscow.

"Vystuplenie B. N. Yeltsina." 1991. *Sovetskaya Rossiya.* (October 29): 1.

Wallich, Christine, ed., 1994. *Russia and the Challenge of Fiscal Federalism.* Washington, D.C.: World Bank.

Weingast, Barry. 1994. "The Political Impediments to Economic Reform: Political Risk and Enduring Gridlock." Ms.

Willerton, John. 1992. *Patronage and Politics in the USSR.* New York: Cambridge University Press.

Williamson, Oliver. 1967. "Hierarchical Control and Optimum Firm Size." *Journal of Political Economy* 75:2 (April): 123–138.

Winiecki, Jan. 1991. *Resistance to Change in the Soviet Economic System.* London: Routledge.

World Bank. 1993. "Subsidies and Directed Credits to Enterprises in Russia: A Strategy for Reform," Report No. 11782-RU, Washington, D.C.: World Bank, (April 8).

———. 1996. *From Plan to Market: World Development Report 1996.* Oxford: Oxford University Press.

Yavlinsky, Grigory. 1995. "V raskole demokratov tragedii net." *Izvestiya* (July 12): 2.

Yeltsin, Boris. 1991. Address to the Fifth Congress. (October 28). Reprinted in *Yeltsin-Khasbulatov: Edinstvo, Kompromiss, Bor'ba.*

———. 1994a. *Zapiski Prezidenta.* Moscow: Ogonek.

———. 1994b. *The Struggle for Russia.* New York: Random House.

Primary Sources
Ekonomika i Zhizn
Financial Times
Foreign Broadcast Information Service: SCV (FBIS)
Izvestiya
Literaturnaya Gazeta
Rossiiskaya Gazeta

Notes

1. The topic of social policy is a large one. This chapter focuses on two particular groups in need of state support—pensioners and workers. Other groups and other social policies are given less attention.

2. Hall (1992) draws upon a similar constellation of independent variables to explain policy innovation in British economic policy in the 1970s. This chapter shows how these variables interact to block innovation.

3. This way of thinking about the relationship between economic performance and electoral outcomes has a long lineage in the American electoral literature. See MacKuen, Erikson, and Stimson (1992); Kiewet (1983); and Alesina, Roubina, and Cohen (1997).

4. The empirical record has not supported this hypothesis. See Maravell (1994) and Geddes (1994).

5. The empirical record throughout the postcommunist region suggests that this strategy has been more successful than the insulation approach. See Hellman (1996).

6. This division is in stark contrast to the level of consensus that emerged in most successful economic postcommunist reforms such as Poland. See Pereira, Maravall, and Przeworski (1993: 141).

7. In a sense, the Soviet system resembled a giant corporation in that all hierarchy—not markets—governed all economic transactions. On agency problems, see Moe (1984); Berle and Means (1991); Eggertson (1990); Jenson and Meckling (1976); Williamson (1967). As applied to the Soviet experience, see Solnick (1998) and Winiecki (1991).

8. The term, "aristocratic workers," was coined by Russia's new independent trade unions to describe these Soviet bureaucrats.

9. The Russian Congress also pressed for the addition of a third option that only a few companies adopted. Therefore, it will not be discussed here.

10. This phenomenon is called "equifinality"—i.e., when a different set of independent variables produces the same outcome but for very different reasons.

11. Gaidar had rejoined the government after October 1993 to become minister of the economy. Fyodorov was finance minister.

12. It must be noted that the wage arrears crisis is not simply a state problem but an economy-wide problem. Of the 50 trillion rubles in wage arrears reported by the Russian State Statistical Committee on January 1, 1998, only 10 percent were owed by the state while the rest were owed by "private" entities. However, the Russian state—still the largest employer in the country—established a poor precedent by sequestering budgetary transfers and delaying the payments of wages, a precedent that made it easier for enterprise directors to withhold wages. See Earle and Sabirianova (1998).

13. Directors also have an interest to collude on delaying wage payments. If all directors in a region delay wages in the same proportion, then laborers cannot improve their condition by seeking employment in another factory.

14. This substitution appears to be happening in many established democracies as well as many other new democracies. See Schmitter (1997).

15. In a parliamentary system with proportional representation, those opposed to Yeltsin's policies would not necessarily need a majority to alter policy, but could do so with a pivotal minority.

8

Conclusions

LINDA J. COOK, MITCHELL A. ORENSTEIN,
AND MARILYN RUESCHEMEYER

Method and Purpose of Study

In the early 1990s, communism, socialism, and left ideas generally seemed so discredited in Eastern Europe that one would have thought the return of former communists and other left groups to government inconceivable. Yet by the mid-1990s they had returned—the Communist Party in Russia, the Democratic Left Alliance in Poland, the Hungarian Socialist Party, and Social Democratic Parties in eastern Germany and the Czech Republic.

This book attempts to explain why, and to evaluate what the return of the left has meant for the social policy of the states they have helped govern. Two core chapters, by Cook and Orenstein, and Rueschemeyer and Wolchik, present parallel, in-depth case studies of the three major left party types in postcommunist Europe: the largely unreformed communist successor party in Russia; the reformed, social democratic successor parties of Poland and Hungary; and the historically based, revived social democratic parties in Germany and the Czech Republic.

In investigating five left parties, we ask how they evolved in the postcommunist years, who supported them, what their social policy programs promised, what they delivered once in government, and what constraints they faced. In short, we have chosen a comparative case study method, across a range of countries and party types. The carefully structured comparisons in this book reveal important similarities and contrasts among the cases, and some conclusions that can be generalized across the postcommunist states.

For instance, we show that different types of left parties present sharply differing policy platforms, and also that they thrive in different contexts. In the Czech Republic, social democrats govern while an unreformed communist successor party languishes on the electoral margins; in Russia the unreformed Communist Party of the Russian Federation dominates the Duma while social democrats remain marginal. The types of left parties that succeed change as we move from the historical democracies of Central Europe to the historically authoritarian and hegemonic Russian state.

Despite finding significant differences among the three left party types, the study also reveals that these parties share key features. All postcommunist left parties include socially weak groups as a major part of their constituency. All make prominent social policy and the social costs of transition in their party and electoral programs. Whereas most left parties are committed to the development of market economies, all recognize that the state has a significant role to play in social provision. Most made a good-faith effort to address the problems of the socially weak once in government. For this reason, we consider it valid to label them "left" within their particular national contexts.

The five case studies presented in this book are framed by cutting-edge analyses of the most important current trends and developments in postcommunist social policy. A data-rich second chapter by Dena Ringold specifies what impacts economic reform has had on well-being and on social services provision throughout Eastern Europe. Three additional chapters examine different aspects of social policy reform in specific countries: Michael J. G. Cains and Aleksander Surdej's chapter analyzes increased spending and delays in pension reform in Poland; Robert Jenkins' chapter examines the role of the nonprofit sector in Hungarian social policy; and Michael McFaul's chapter explains why Russian governments neglected social policy from 1991–1997.

Partisan Policy Preferences

The three left party types examined in this book have exhibited different partisan preferences in the area of social policy, which can be explained by their diverse organizational "genealogies" and constituency interests (Orenstein 1998). Successor parties that still use the communist label and are led by former hard-line communists, for instance the Communist Party of the Russian Federation and the Communist Party of the Czech Republic and Moravia, have advocated a restorationist social policy that aims to restore the guarantees of state socialism.

By contrast, social democratic successor parties in Central Europe advocate a social-market approach that aims to further the market transformation. They seek to reform welfare state institutions in order to serve important social goals, yet without impeding market-led growth or European integration. Historic social democratic parties, in particular the Czech and German social democratic parties, also advocate a social-market approach. But neither of these parties was in power for most of the period covered in this book. It is quite possible that the historical social democracies will be more vigorously leftist once in power than the communist successor social democracies.

Social democratic successor parties in Poland and Hungary have been split between liberal and leftist camps, with the liberals often winning the upper hand in government. This has raised important questions about their "leftness," which this book addresses. It will be interesting to see if the historic social democracies avoid these same battles. In the Czech Republic and eastern Germany, it may be easier to be left due to the existence of well-organized, ideologically coherent, and liberal center-right parties. This could enable the historic social democratic parties to position themselves more firmly to the left and leave liberal policies to the reliably liberal liberals.

Conversely in Hungary, center-right parties have avoided liberal economic policies and fueled enormous budget deficits with high levels of social spending. In Poland, the right is divided into a liberal and a populist camp, with disparate policy positions. In these countries, where large segments of the right are economically populist, the left may be under greater pressure to pursue liberal economic policies to stay on the road to Europe. Historic parties may also be less influenced by liberal managerial concerns that are prominent in the Polish and Hungarian successor parties. However, it is too early to tell whether the historical social democracies will behave much differently than the communist successor social democracies. We have found that two types of left policy preferences are evident in postcommunist Europe: restorationist and social market.

Government Behavior and Constraints

Garrett and Lange (1991) point out that governments may not be guided by their partisan policy preferences alone, but also importantly by a range of pressures and constraints that become evident once they attain office. We found that after left parties achieve electoral success, the realization of their policy preferences was limited by a variety of domestic and international constraints that varied across the cases. We will consider herein the following types of constraints: limits of state capacity; domestic political, institutional, and economic constraints; international constraints: and legacies of the past.

The primary constraint faced by left parties in implementing partisan social policy programs has been simply the limits of the postcommunist states' capacity to implement policies or to administer programs, once accepted politically. Yet the importance of this constraint varies considerably across our cases. The problems were most serious in Russia, where the state lacked an ability either to collect mandated taxes or to make mandated social payments. This, along with administrative corruption and the executive's arbitrary treatment of duly approved state budgets and allocations, often prevented the opposition Communist Party from exercising even that limited authority that the constitutional system gave it. In tandem with state weakness, the absence of the "rule of law" made social rights unenforceable, so that policies in place frequently had no practical effect. Central European postcommunist states also faced significant problems of state capacity, for instance, in implementing means-testing of benefits in several countries.

The European Union recently has made building administrative capacity a key component of its assistance to Poland, Hungary, and the Czech Republic in the run-up to enlargement. However, the problems of Central Europe in taxing and spending are much less severe than those of Russia. This can be seen in the ability of the Central European states to maintain relatively high shares of government spending relative to GDP. Eastern Germany is obviously exceptional in relying on a well-developed Western state apparatus to confront the problems of transition, although that brings other issues to the fore.

Second, left parties face numerous political-institutional and constitutional constraints, most importantly the constraints of coalition politics. With one exception, the left parties in our study did not gain absolute electoral majorities and had to govern in coalition with other parties that differed in their social policy agendas and priorities.

In perhaps the most extreme case, the Czech Social Democratic minority government has ruled not on the basis of a coalition agreement, but on an "oppositon agreement" between it and the leading right-wing party, the Civic Democratic Party, meaning that the Social Democrats must gain the agreement of the more fiscally conservative party for any major policy changes. This is likely to limit enactment of social policies promised in the Social Democrats' campaign, as will the German Social Democrats' need to mesh their priorities with their Green coalition partners and in eastern Germany with the reformed communists.

Similarly, the Polish Democratic Left Alliance was swayed toward higher spending by its coalition with the Polish Peasant Party, while an alliance with the Free Democrats enabled the Hungarian Socialist Party to carry out a more liberal policy agenda than planned. Constraints of coalition politics are particularly pronounced in the Central European parliamentary systems.

In Russia constitutional constraints proved more important. The Communist Party and its close left allies could not override the presidential vetoes that jettisoned most of their policy initiatives, even with a modest program that drew much support from outside the left. Yet here also arises one of the paradoxes revealed by our study: superpresidentialism, often considered the most effective institutional arrangement for pushing through reform, proved ineffective here, leading to conflict and stalemate over the presidential administration's own social policy reform package. Instead, East European parliamentary systems that facilitate compromise and consensus-building proved more effective at giving voice to the left, encouraging its moderation, and allowing for more progress on a compromise social policy agenda.

Domestic and international economic constraints were also important. All postcommunist left parties must find ways of fostering economic development, while at the same time providing and redesigning a safety net. Often, this means that left parties allow domestic or international economic considerations to reign in social spending. In Russia, for instance, the communists wanted to press for additional budget spending but feared triggering inflation. In Hungary in early 1995, the left government enacted a complete policy reversal, moving from talk of a broad social pact to the surprise launch of a radical liberal austerity program.

In addition to international financial pressures, there are also crucial international organizational constraints on social policymaking and policy dialogue in postcommunist states, though as Deacon (1997) shows, these are more diverse than commonly assumed. International organizations such as the World Bank and the European Union proffer different blueprints for reform of the social sector and come with economic incentives for implementation of their proposed models.

In the Russian case, models inspired by the World Bank for spending cuts and rationalization, strongly supported by key members of the presidential administration, set the terms for the policy struggle between government and Duma. Although, it must be pointed out that in the policy cycle under consideration here, the Bank saw little of its advice implemented, despite a substantial investment of funds. The problem was not only political opposition but also real dilemmas of trying to import policy blueprints. Concepts such as means-testing and targeting, for example, which are central to the World Bank's prescriptions, run into problems of weak state capacity and the large illegal economy in Russia.

Meanwhile, other international organizations, most notably the European Union, have pushed for the associated countries of Central and Eastern Europe to maintain "European" levels, styles, and norms of welfare state spending. In fact, the international community has spoken with a variety of voices on welfare state reform, constituting a running battle between different perspectives, and carried on through different ground-level welfare consultants who advocate different welfare state models. The Council of Europe's Economic and Social Charter has had nearly as

great an influence on East-Central European welfare state policy as the
World Bank. Even within the World Bank, different policy orientations
coexist (Deacon 1997).

Legacies of the previous communist regime have also had a lasting impact on the structure of postcommunist welfare states as well as on the
mentality and expectations of the people. The experience of communism
has taught most citizens to expect and desire a relatively high degree of
state social provision, and this demand has not been impeded by the development of market societies. Structural and psychological legacies shape
the policy environment for left governments and others seeking reform.

Left parties are further constrained by the expressed desires of their
own constituencies, and here trade unions play a particularly important
role as the most organized left constituency group. Trade unions are the
mass organizations that have best survived the transition from communism, with some degree of social support and organizational network intact. Though they have been drastically reduced in membership, and
often split into competing organizations, trade unions remain among the
largest and most institutionalized civil society organizations. They have
played an important role in voicing working-class concerns within left
parties in Poland, Hungary, the Czech Republic, and eastern Germany.
Left party social policies have often been constrained by whether trade
unions and other left constituencies would support specific measures.
Over the long term, left parties will continue to rely on trade unions to
bolster their left credentials and, therefore, must remain broadly responsive to their concerns.

Policy Outcomes

With all of these constraints, what differences have left parties really been
able to make? We have attempted to gauge the impact of left parties on
social policy by raising and answering three questions: Have left parties
maintained or increased social spending in postcommunist Europe?
Have left parties articulated and legitimized welfare state values, in the
face of a liberal-individualist onslaught? And have left parties developed
a realistic set of policy goals for restructuring welfare state institutions in
the postcommunist era?

In two of the three cases in which left parties held a majority in Parliament, left parties either increased social spending in real terms, as in
Poland, or fought hard for spending increases that were ultimately
blocked by presidential vetoes, as in Russia. In the case of Hungary, a
major policy reversal occurred when the left party, which was elected on
a platform of increased social cohesion, launched a major austerity program that included drastic cuts in social benefits. Why did the Hungarian

Socialist Party seemingly abandon leftist goals when it implemented the liberal Bokros package?

There are several explanations. First, Hungary did not have a radical liberal economic reform from 1989 to 1991, as did many of its neighbors in East-Central Europe, particularly Poland and the Czech Republic. Since the right in Hungary had pursued the same careful social policies as previous governments under "goulash communism," the left leadership felt it had to launch a radical liberal stabilization in 1995 to adequately confront an emerging fiscal and foreign exchange crisis. Liberals within the Socialist Party were prepared for such a policy shift, as the party contained many of the most forward-looking technocrats in the country—people like Bokros, who had been a prominent reform communist—and easily switched over to the private sector after 1989. A combination of the political ascent of a strong and experienced liberal leadership, the inaction of previous right governments, and the pressure of an emerging economic crisis produced the dramatic change of course in March 1995.

However, as Cook and Orenstein show in their chapter, social spending is not the only relevant measure of leftness in postcommunist Europe. In some countries, social spending had already increased to unsustainable levels when the left took over, while in others, spending had collapsed in real terms. Left government spending decisions were bound to be influenced heavily by the existing state of affairs and state of flux.

Another criterion of leftness is the extent the parties engaged in a discourse that sought to defend or reestablish welfare state values in a new political context. Again, in four out of five cases, we found that left parties played an important role in legitimizing welfare state institutions by defending the ideas of social cohesion and social rights against a liberal-individualist discourse that attacked the welfare state and other forms of state intervention in the economy.

Poland is perhaps the signal case in this regard, with the Democratic Left Alliance fighting for the inclusion of social rights in the new Polish constitution of 1997, against a liberal party that wanted instead to enshrine fiscal conservative principles and right-wing parties that wanted to dedicate the state to the preservation of Catholic conservative values, including a ban on abortion. In Russia, Germany, and the Czech Republic, left parties have also articulated pro-welfare state positions, and these continue to be central to political discourse in the postcommunist countries.

Hungary, again, is an exception, at least during the Bokros period (1995–1996), when the Socialist government articulated a liberal welfare state philosophy that envisioned smaller budgets, targeted rather than universal assistance, self-reliance, and subordination of social policy to fiscal goals. After Bokros's resignation in early 1996, the Socialist Party returned to more social market rhetoric, although leftists within the party remained weak.

More than spending, and more than rhetoric, the question of restructuring is the fundamental metric for left and right parties in postcommunist Europe. Everyone recognizes that the postcommunist welfare states need to change. Simply put, they were designed to function in an economic environment that has ceased to exist. Change must occur. It will continue to occur either haphazardly, as at present in many countries, or as part of a broad program of reform. There is good reason to think that programs for restructuring and institutional innovation decided during the transition will have an enormous impact on the social shape of the new Europe far into the future. Have left parties tried to restructure the welfare state in ways that differ from the right?

We have presented evidence from three countries, Russia, Poland, and Hungary, where left parties were in government. Again, it appears that in two of three cases, left parties took a distinct approach to restructuring. In Russia, the Communist Party has effectively blocked restructuring efforts launched by liberal governments. Yet it has not offered a credible or realistic restructuring program of its own. For this reason, it will be interesting to watch its actions in the future. The Polish Democratic Left Alliance has taken a distinctive approach to welfare state restructuring that differs greatly from that of center-right parties in Poland. The left government of 1993–1997 introduced a range of institutional innovations and began to develop a centrist social policy discourse that produced a major restructuring of the Polish pension system in 1997–1998, with widespread popular support. Czech and German social democrats advocate a range of institutional innovations.

Yet the Hungarian Socialist Party, at least during the Bokros era, provides an important exception. Here, a left party has made more progress than the right ever did in pushing a liberal reorganization of welfare state institutions, particularly by implementing means-testing for family benefits. Pension reform, however as in Poland, went in a more social market direction, with significant input from liberal policymakers, but also tempered by important compromises with trade unions and center and left factions in the Socialist Party.

We began this study expecting left parties to follow broadly social democratic welfare state policies, as described by Esping-Andersen's *The Three Worlds of Welfare Capitalism*, but we found that they have not followed such policies. This is perhaps the most surprising finding of this study: left parties in postcommunist Europe are not advocating what Esping-Andersen describes as a social democratic policy. Instead, they have either defended the socialist welfare state against a neoliberal or ad hoc dismantling, or taken a more centrist position, apparently speaking more to the median voter than to a purely left constituency on social policy matters (for a discussion of the median voter model, see Cain and Surdej in this book).

While no organized political force has advocated a Scandinavian welfare state model, liberal ideas have also had an ambiguous impact in the postcommunist welfare state debate. On the one hand, there have been strong liberal attempts at reform. However, in most cases, they have had the perverse effect of increasing state spending and have not served purported liberal goals of helping only the very poor, concentrating on minimum benefit levels and creating a residual welfare state. This failure has been most evident in the increased importance of pension spending in the region, which is generally badly targeted to the poor. Liberal ideas have not led to liberal practices, and now liberal parties in most of the region are dependent on alliances with other parties that do not share their liberal welfare state values. Few liberal parties have won more than 10–15 percent of the vote in recent postcommunist elections. Therefore, it is unlikely that a liberal welfare state model will be implemented in the region.

These findings call into question the usefulness of Esping-Andersen's categorization for understanding developments in postcommunist social policy. Instead, we concur with Gedeon (1995:438) that perhaps greater insight can be had into the main policy directions of postcommunist welfare states by using an older typology that draws a distinction between the Beveridge and Bismarckian welfare state models. The social market approach of the postcommunist left adopts elements of both. It relies heavily on the social insurance concept popularized by Bismarck, where the state mandates individual contributions for insurance against particular social risks, like old age, sickness, and unemployment. To this is added the Beveridge welfare state concept, which aimed to guarantee certain universal, minimum standards of living, a type of social citizenship approach, yet at a far less generous level than the universal Scandinavian systems. Add Beveridge-style minimums to a fundamentally social insurance-based welfare system, and you have the social market model pushed by the left in contemporary postcommunist Europe. This deviance from previous European models suggests that postcommunist welfare states may indeed constitute a new model consistent with the most advanced global social policy trends (Deacon 1997).

Social Policy Context and Trends

Although falling short of predicting the future, the chapters in this book make a substantial contribution to our knowledge of the key trends in postcommunist social policy. Dena Ringold's chapter provides a provocative and accessible review of the best available data on postcommunist social policy, compiled by The World Bank, UNICEF, and other international organizations. It also provides an analytical introduction to the current problems of social policy in the region and a bird's-eye view of important policy trends.

Cain and Surdej complement this overview with a detailed, theoretical analysis of one particular social policy phenomenon—the dynamic growth of pension spending in Poland and the delay of systematic reform. Combining contemporary "transitology" and rational choice perspectives in a fruitful way, Cain and Surdej show that legacies of the past regime, transition policies, and normal democratic politics all played an important role in inflating pension spending. However, these competing analytical perspectives tend to explain different aspects of the problem. Cain and Surdej show convincingly that combining them can allow analysts to provide more comprehensive explanations of important political phenomena and bridge an unproductive division in current academic discourse.

Read together, the chapters by Ringold and Cain and Surdej develop the most compelling analysis to date of how legacies of the past and transition politics have combined to shape the current dilemmas of postcommunist social policy.

Robert Jenkins's analysis of the role of the nonprofit sector in Hungary highlights the emerging role of the "third sector" and focuses on decentralization and the participation of civil society in the social safety nets. These issues tend to be elided in most work on postcommunist social policy, but Jenkins shows that this bias in the literature will have to be reversed, as nonprofits are playing an increasing role in social service delivery and policy advocacy.

The penultimate chapter in this book, by Michael McFaul, returns to the critical case of Russia and analyzes social policy trends within the broader context of economic policy in a polarized political system. McFaul shows that Russia arrived at its current crisis through a policy discourse that had no middle ground, but was characterized by a series of standoffs between radical liberal reformers and socialist conservatives. Both sides revealed an apparent preference to do nothing and let the welfare system suffer the consequences, rather than accept the proposals of the other side. In part, this reflects deep divisions in Russian society and the polarization of its political leaders, but also reflects the presidential institutions of Yeltsin's Russia that have caused Russian democracy to degenerate into a blocking game and attests to the ineffectiveness of available representative institutions. This focus on Russia is critical since Russia seems to have become a symbol of the near-collapse of the postcommunist welfare state in some of the former Soviet republics and an icon of global concern about the future of democracy and capitalism in states that lack the capacity to provide some modicum of social security.

Democracy and Markets

What are the broader implications of the resurgence of the left in post-communist Eastern Europe? In the first place, the return of the left represents a strength of democratic impulses that many did not expect. This conclusion remains valid, even if the democratic left in Eastern Europe differs in important respects from the democracies of the West. It is true that popular participation in politics is fairly low in Eastern Europe, even in East-Central European countries, and that therefore the political agenda is set by more narrowly based groups and elites than would be the case if civil society were more densely organized (see Jenkins in this book; also Rueschemeyer, Rueschemeyer, and Wittrock 1998).

This realization raises critical questions about the relation between parties and constituencies. How responsive are the political elites—on the left as well as in the center and on the right—to the needs and views of their constituencies? What is the quality of representation of different interests in the political arena, and how accountable are parties to their constituencies?

Accountability in any strict sense is limited as long as political participation remains weakly developed. Despite this, the left parties of Eastern Europe represented broad societal interests when they offered alternatives to radical liberal transformations of economy and society and sought to maintain significant social welfare policies. In East-Central Europe, this political reaction was tempered by a continuing consensus about the broad goals of market-oriented economic reform. Put differently, the need to gain broad-based electoral support and to form coalitions with different political forces after elections gave the positions of the social democratic and reformed communist parties in East-Central Europe a fairly moderate character.

Other left parties have been more extreme or particularistic. The Russian Communist Party expressed the needs and views of its constituency more sharply than the East-Central European parties of the left. Yet this also points to the problematic side of the party's position. Finding itself with a more limited constituency in a polarized political situation, it was able to block liberal reforms but could not overcome persistent stalemate.

The East German PDS is an example of a roughly similar though less radical constellation; its appeal is confined to eastern Germany. The party can express the pains of transition more sharply because the constituencies of the other parties lie primarily in West Germany. Being excluded from governing responsibility also made this articulation of frustrations easier until very recently, when the party participated in the governance of two East German states.

Yet when all particular features of political participation and representation in the countries of Eastern Europe are taken into account, the resurgence of left parties still suggests a significant vitality of democratic impulses. In the East-Central European countries, these parties are engaging in policies that are distinctive as well as moderately effective within a context of complex constraints. They combine goals of economic growth with social welfare concerns in a "social market approach," a political alternative that appears likely to gain considerable public support in the region.

The return of left-oriented parties will probably have important implications for the more distant future. Speculative as any prognosis must be, we suggest two major long-term effects. Even if the prospects for social policies are in many important respects uncertain, a strong political left makes it unlikely that the long-term outcome of social policy reform will be a "liberal," minimalist welfare system that offers little protection to large parts of the weaker social groups, leaving them to fend for themselves.

A social welfare state that gives the population at large some sense of social security will entail other long-term consequences. In the Atlantic community, social welfare policies after the Great Depression and especially after World War II served to support, stabilize, and enhance democracy. Effective social policy may well have the same result in Eastern Europe. If rising inequality were joined with serious deprivation and an unabated sense of insecurity on the part of many, the democratic system and the market might not be seen by large segments of the population as an order that works for them. Containing adverse impacts of a free market economy and retaining significant social security policies may well be necessary conditions for the long-term viability of democracy in Eastern Europe. The ideas of a social market economy that have shaped policy in many Western European countries suggest that even the long-term viability of the market is contingent on social policies containing its adverse effects. Left parties may play a large role in establishing the postcommunist countries within a European consensus on social policy matters.

References

Deacon, Bob. 1997. *Global Social Policy: International Organizations and the Future of Welfare*. London: Sage Publications.

Esping-Andersen, Gosta. 1990. *The Three Worlds of Welfare Capitalism*. Princeton: Princeton University Press.

Garrett, Geoffrey, and Peter Lange. 1991. "Political Responses to Interdependence: What's 'Left' for the Left?" *International Organization* 45:4 (Autumn).

Gedeon, Péter. 1995. "Hungary: Social Policy in Transition." *Eastern European Politics and Societies* 9 (Fall): 433–458.

Orenstein, Mitchell. 1998. "A Genealogy of Communist Successor Parties in East Central Europe and the Determinants of their Success." *East European Politics and Society* 12:3 (Fall): 472–499.

Rueschemeyer, Dietrich, Marilyn Rueschemeyer, and Björn Wittrock, eds. 1998. *Participation and Democracy East and West: Comparisons and Interpretations.* Armonk, N.Y.: M.E.Sharpe.

About the Editors and Authors

Editors:

Linda J. Cook received her Ph.D. from Columbia University in 1985. She is currently an associate professor in the political science department at Brown University as well as a faculty associate of Brown's Watson Institute for International Studies and the Davis Center for Russian Studies at Harvard University. She previously authored *The Soviet Social Contract and Why It Failed* (Harvard, 1993) and *Labor and Liberalization: Trade Unions in the New Russia* (Twentieth Century Fund, 1997). She is currently at work on a manuscript titled "Restructuring the Welfare State: The Politics of Safety Net Reform in the Russian Federation," with support from a grant awarded by the National Council for Eurasian and East European Research.

Mitchell A. Orenstein is assistant professor of political science at The Maxwell School of Citizenship and Public Affairs, Syracuse University. Orenstein was a post-doctoral fellow at Brown University's Watson Institute from 1996–1998. His 1996 Yale Ph.D. dissertation, "Out of the Red: Building Capitalism and Democracy in Post-Communist Europe," won the 1997 Gabriel A. Almond Award of the American Political Science Association for the best doctoral dissertation in comparative politics and is a forthcoming book by University of Michigan Press. He is currently studying international and domestic political influences on the development of postcommunist welfare states.

Marilyn Rueschemeyer is professor at the Rhode Island School of Design and has an appointment in the Department of Sociology and the Watson Institute for International Studies, Brown University. She is an associate at Harvard University's Russian Research Center. Her publications include *Professional Work and Marriage: An East-West Comparison* (Oxford, Macmillan series, 1981); *Soviet Emigré Artists: Life and Work in the USSR and the United States* (with Igor Golomshtok and Janet Kennedy, 1985); *The Quality of Life in the German Democratic Republic: Changes and Developments in a State Socialist Society* (edited with C. Lemke, 1989); *Women in the Politics of Post-Communist Eastern Europe* (second edition, 1998); and *Participation and Democracy East and West* (edited with Dietrich

Rueschemeyer and Björn Wittrock, 1998), all with M.E. Sharpe Publishers. She is currently continuing her research on the Social Democratic Party in Eastern Germany and also is working on a comparative study of art institutions and the state.

Authors:

Michael Cain is assistant professor of political science at the University of Mississippi. He received his Ph.D. from the University of Maryland in 1993. In 1995–1996, he was chosen by the International Research and Exchange Board to serve as a visiting professor in public policy at the Institute of Sociology, University of Warsaw. His research interests in rational choice theory include experimental game theory, constitutional and institutional design, and collective action problems in civil rebellions. Other work by Michael Cain appears in *Public Choice, The Journal of Theoretical Politics,* and *EMERGO: The Journal of Transforming Economies.* His current work on social welfare reform focuses on the institutional determinants of successful reform in transition economies.

Robert M. Jenkins is a researcher and consultant in Chapel Hill, North Carolina. He received his Ph.D. in sociology from the University of Wisconsin at Madison in 1987 and was a professor at Yale University from 1987 to 1995. Jenkins has published on careers and labor markets in Hungary, social and political movements in Central Europe, and the development of the nonprofit sector in Hungary. As a consultant he has worked with international and domestic organizations in the development of the nonprofit sector and the reform of higher education in Central and Eastern Europe. He is currently working on an overview of labor market structure and change throughout the region and has ongoing research on political, economic policy, and macroeconomic trends in Hungary.

Michael McFaul received his Ph.D. from Oxford University in 1991. He is currently an assistant professor in the political science department and a Hoover fellow at Stanford University as well as a senior associate at the Carnegie Endowment for International Peace. He is the author and editor of several monographs, including *Russia's 1996 Presidential Election: The End of Bi-Polar Politics* (Hoover Institution Press, 1997); with Nikolai Petrov, *Previewing Russia's Parliamentary Elections* (Carnegie Endowment for International Peace, 1995); *Post-Communist Politics: Democratic Prospects in Russia and Eastern Europe* (CSIS, 1993); with Sergei Markov, *The Troubled Birth of Russian Democracy: Political Parties, Programs and Profiles* (Hoover Institution Press, 1993); and with Tova Perlmutter, Privatization, Conversion and Enterprise Reform in Russia (Westview Press, 1995). His articles have appeared in *Foreign Affairs, Foreign Policy, International Organization, International Security, Journal of Democracy, Post-Soviet Affairs,* and *World Politics.*

He is currently completing a book called "Institutional Change during Revolutionary Transformations: Soviet Collapse and Russian Reform, 1985–1996."

Dena Ringold is a Policy Analyst at the World Bank in Washington, D.C., where she works on social policy operations in Central and Eastern Europe. Most recently, she has worked on labor and social assistance projects in Bulgaria and Romania and education in Turkey. She has also been extensively involved in cross-country research on social policy trends in the postcommunist countries and has published studies on labor markets, education, and health. She is currently studying the impact of fiscal decentralization on social services and welfare in the transition economies. Ringold holds an M.Sc. with Distinction in Political Economy from the London School of Economics and Political Science and a B.A. from Swarthmore College.

Dietrich Rueschemeyer is the Charles C. Tillinghast Jr. Professor of International Studies and professor of sociology at Brown University. At Brown University's Watson Institute for International Studies, he directs the Research Program in Political Economy and Development. Among his book publications are *Bringing the State Back In* (co-edited with Peter B. Evans and Theda Skocpol) 1985, *Power and the Division of Labour*, 1986, *Capitalist Development and Democracy* (co-authored with Evelyne H. Stephens and John D. Stephens) 1992, *States, Social Knowledge, and the Origins of Modern Social Policy* (co-edited with Theda Skocpol) 1996, and *Participation and Democracy East and West, Comparisons and Interpretations* (co-edited with Marilyn Rueschemeyer and Björn Wittrock) 1998.

Aleksander Surdej received his Ph.D. from Jagiellonian University, Cracow, in 1994. His dissertation investigated the political dynamics of economic transformations in Poland. He also received advanced graduate training from the Johns Hopkins School of Advanced International Studies. Surdej publishes regularly on political, economic, and policy topics in East European countries. His articles have appeared in Polish, English, and Italian. He is currently an assistant professor in European Studies at the Cracow Academy of Economics.

Sharon L. Wolchik is professor of political science and international affairs at the School of International Affairs at George Washington University. She received her Ph.D. from the University of Michigan in 1978. She is the author of *Czechoslovakia in Transition: Politics, Economics, and Society* and co-editor of *Women and Democracy in Latin America and Central/Eastern Europe; The Social Legacy of Communism; Domestic and Foreign Policy in Eastern Europe in the 1980s*; and *Women, State and Party in Eastern Europe*. She is currently doing research on the role of women in transition to postcommunist rule in Central and Eastern Europe as well as on the development of party systems and other aspects of politics in the Czech and Slovak Republics.

Index

Adeyi, Olusoji, 26, 32–34, 156
AFD. *See* Alliance of Free Democrats
Agh, Attila, 71, 74, 108(n5)
Agrarian party (Russia), 56
Albania, 17, 34, 38(figure), 42(figure)
Alesina, Alberto, 146, 165
Alfandari, Gilles, 224
Alliance 90 / Greens party (Germany), 115, 116(table), 119–120, 120(table), 130. *See also* Green Party
Alliance of Free Democrats (AFD; Hungary)
  and the Bokros package, 95
  coalition government with HSP, 91–99, 102, 178–179, 238
  and nonprofit organizations, 194–195
  social policies, 92, 98
Alliance of Social Associations (Hungary), 182
Allison, Christine, 22
Andrews, Emily, 16
Anheier, Helmut K., 176
Aslund, Anders, 210–212, 221–222, 224
Azerbaijan, 32, 41(figure)

Baczkowski, Andrzej, 88
Balcerowicz, Leszek, 47, 80, 157, 159, 160
Bárányi, Zoltán, 178
Barr, Nicholas, 13
Bartlett, David L., 178
Barzel, Yoram, 214
Bates, Robert H., 169, 170
Bekesi, Laszlo, 93–94

Benio, Marek, 154
Bergmann, Christine, 128
Berle, Adolf, 211
Bezlepkina, Lyudmila, 57
Birth rate, 14(table), 135
Blazyca, George, 84
Boeri, Tito, 80
Boguszak, Marek, 114
Bokros, Lajos, 94, 97, 179
  Bokros package of reforms, 93–99
Boycko, Maxim, 211
Brandenburg, 115, 117, 128, 130
Brandt, Willy, 71
Bruszt, Laszlo, 92–94
Brzeski, Andrzej, 211
Bulgaria
  decentralization of social policy, 31
  economy, 17
  education, 24(figure), 28, 28(figure), 29, 38(figure), 39, 39(figure)
  energy prices, 39
  health care, 34, 35(figure), 36, 36(table)
  life expectancy, 26, 27(table)
  payroll taxes, 34
  pensions, 41, 41(figure), 42(figure)
  Romany minority, 29
  social spending, 35(figure), 38(figure), 41, 41(figure)
  unemployment rate, 22, 23(table), 24, 24(figure), 25(figure)
Burbulis, Gennady, 211
Bush, Keith, 211
Buzková, Petra, 125

Cain, Michael J. G., 16, 80, 85, 151
Cambell, J. L., 160
Carey, John, 209–210
Castle-Kanerová, Mita, 114, 131, 132
Catholic Church, 89–90, 162, 241
Cawson, Alan, 217
CDU. *See* Christian Democratic Union
Central and Eastern Europe
  divergent social conditions in,
    12–13, 14(table), 17–18, 99–100
  economic growth, 17–18
  foreign influence on politics, 7–8
  income inequality, 20–22,
    21(tables)
  international trade, 149(table)
  social welfare trends, 14(table)
  unemployment rates, 22–25,
    23(table), 24–25(figures)
  See also specific countries
Central Bank (Russia), 219
Čermák, Martin, 132
Chellaraj, Gnagaraj, 26, 32–34, 156
Chernomyrdin, Viktor, 219–220,
    223–224
Child care, 15, 27–28, 57, 129–132, 179.
    See also Family and child
    benefits
Children, abandonment/
    institutionalization of, 26
Christian Democratic parties, 17,
    123(table). *See also* Christian
    Democratic Union; Christian
    Democratic Union-People's
    Party
Christian Democratic Union (CDU;
    Germany)
  and associations/organizations,
    118, 119
  decline of, 118
  degree of transitional problems not
    anticipated by, 110
  elections/electoral support, 115,
    116(table), 117–118, 120(table),
    121
  membership/constituency, 115

relationship with left parties,
    119–120
  social policies, 126, 127, 129
Christian Democratic Union-People's
    Party (Czech Rep.), 123(table),
    126
Chubais, Anatoly, 213, 218
  Chubais/Gaidar privatization
    plan, 213–214, 217–218
Cichomski, Bogdan, 164
Civic Democratic Party (Czech Rep.),
    16, 122, 123(table), 124, 136, 139
Civic Forum (Czechoslovakia), 122,
    123(table)
Civic Union (Russia), 215–217, 223, 225
Civil Code (Hungary), 180, 181
Class
  and left-party voting, 71–74,
    84(table), 91(table), 121
  and politics, 5, 7
Clem, Ralph S., 55
COMECON. *See* Council of Mutual
    Economic Assistance
Commander, Simon, 221
Communist Party, Czech. *See* Czech
    Communist Party
Communist Party, Czechoslovak. *See*
    Czechoslovak Communist
    Party
Communist Party (Former Soviet
    Union), 214–215. *See also*
    Communist Party of the
    Russian Federation
Communist Party of Bohemia and
    Moravia (KSČM), 123(table),
    125. *See also* Czech Communist
    Party; Czechoslovak
    Communist Party
Communist Party of the Russian
    Federation (CPRF)
  background, 50, 53–54
  coalition formed, 56
  elections/electoral support, 2,
    54–56, 55(table), 70, 72(figure),
    73(figure), 227

legislative ineffectiveness, 49,
  225–226, 238–239, 245
membership/constituency, 54
and the 1997 budget, 60–62, 239
policy agenda, 3–4, 54–55, 59–60,
  68–70, 99–100, 225–226
and social welfare reform, 65–69,
  242
Communist successor parties, 50
and economic reform, 5–6
electoral support, 72(figure),
  73(figure)
reformed, 2, 5–6, 70–75, 99. *See also*
  Social democratic parties
and social policymaking, 16–17
unreformed, 236. *See also*
  Communist Party of Bohemia
  and Moravia; Communist
  Party of the Russian Federation
See also specific parties
Communist Youth Federation
  (Hungary), 181, 182
Congleton, Roger D., 161
Connor, Walter, 226
Cook, Linda J., 17, 54, 226
Council of Mutual Economic
  Assistance (COMECON), 148
CPRF. *See* Communist Party of the
  Russian Federation
Craumer, Peter R., 55
Croatia
education, 28, 39(figure)
health care, 35(figure), 36
payroll taxes, 34
pensions, 41(figure), 42(figure)
social spending, 35(figure),
  41(figure)
unemployment, 22, 23(table),
  25(figure)
Csehák, Judit, 189
Csikán, Csaba, 189, 190
ČSSD. *See* Czech Social Democratic
  Party
CYF. *See* Communist Youth Federation
Czech Communist Party, 50

and the ČSSD, 126
elections/electoral support, 2,
  109–110, 125, 134, 138
See also Communist Party of
  Bohemia and Moravia;
  Czechoslovak Communist
  Party
Czech Lands. *See* Czech Republic;
  Czechoslovakia
Czech-Moravian Chamber of Labor
  Unions, 133
Czechoslovak Communist Party,
  121–125. *See also* Communist
  Party of Bohemia and Moravia;
  Czech Communist Party
Czechoslovakia, 27, 113–114, 121–123,
  123(table)
See also Czech Republic;
  Slovakia
Czechoslovak Socialist Party, 122–123,
  123(table), 125
Czech Republic
budget, 138
child care, 131–132
communist legacy, 131
divided leadership, 114
economic growth, 20
education, 24(figure), 28(figure),
  32, 37, 38(figure), 39(figure),
  136
elections (1990–1993), 2, 123(table),
  123–124
employment policy, 137
energy prices, 131, 133
family and child benefits, 131–133,
  135–136
health care/insurance, 31, 33–34,
  35(figure), 36, 36(table), 132,
  135–136
housing, 132, 133, 135
Klaus government, 114, 124–125,
  132–133
life expectancy, 27(table)
living standards, 132
minorities in, 135, 137

"opposition agreement"
  government, 126, 136–139, 238
pensions, 41, 41(figure), 42(figure),
  132–133, 136–138
political parties, 16, 50, 123(table),
  237. *See also* Christian
  Democratic Union-People's
  Party; Civic Democratic Party;
  Civic Forum; Czech Social
  Democratic Party;
  Czech[oslovak] Communist
  Party; Czechoslovak Socialist
  Party; Pensioners' Party
privatization, 32, 131, 135
retirement age, 134, 135
return of property to original
  owners, 132
rise of left parties, 114–115,
  121–126
social assistance, 131, 135
social democratic tradition, 6
social policy reform, 132–134
social spending, 30(table), 30–31,
  33, 35(figure), 37, 38(figure), 41,
  41(figure), 133–134
trade unions, 133
unemployment policies, 135, 137
unemployment rate, 22–23,
  23(table), 24(figure), 25(figure)
unofficial economy, 42
voter (dis)satisfaction, 134, 137–138
wages, 20, 21(table), 131, 134
See also Czechoslovakia
Czech Social Democratic Party (ČSSD)
background, 6, 109, 121–122, 126
elections/electoral support
  (1990–1998), 2, 110, 114–115,
  122–125, 123(table), 134–136
leftist competition, 125–126
"opposition agreement"
  government, 126, 136–139, 238.
  See also Civic Democratic Party
organizational weakness, 124–125
political strategy, 110
reasons for success, 125

social policies, 134–137
voter satisfaction with, 137–138

Davidheiser, Evelyn, 55, 226
Deacon, Bob, 65, 177, 239
Decentralization, 31, 37, 43–44, 178.
  See also Privatization
de Crombrugghe, Alain, 159, 172(n1),
  174(n21)
de Figueiredo, Rui J., Jr., 169, 170
Delyagin, Mikhail, 224
Democracy, in Eastern Europe, 3–4,
  246
Democratic Left Alliance (Poland)
  background, 71
  coalition government, 83–91, 102,
    238
  constraints upon, 83–84, 100
  economic policies, 74–75, 84–86,
    164–165
  elections/electoral support, 1–2,
    71–72, 72(figure), 84(table),
    164
  and the 1997 constitution, 89–90,
    241
  social policies, 73–75, 83–91,
    164–165, 242
  and trade unions, 173–174(n19)
Democratic Union (Poland), 16
Dhar, Sumana, 221
Disabled persons
  organizations representing/caring
    for, 187–190, 199–200,
    205–206(n22)
  services for, 187–189. *See also*
    pension *subheads under specific
    countries*
Disease, communicable, 26
Diskin, Yusif, 220
Dmitriyeva, Oksana, 66
Dmitriyev, Mikhail, 62, 224
Duma
  and the CPRF, 56, 59, 73(figure),
    107(n2)
  and the federal budget, 60–62

Gaidar removed as acting prime
minister, 219
left's power in, 69
limited powers of, 2, 52, 61–62,
102, 223
parliamentary elections, 222–223.
See also Russia: elections
(1991–97)
and social policymaking, 58–59,
65–68, 217, 218
DVU. *See* German People's Union

Earle, John, 224, 225
Eastern Europe. *See* Central and
Eastern Europe
Eastern Germany
child care, 129–131
communist legacy, 110–111
education, 128
elections (1990–1998), 2, 115–118,
116(table), 120, 120(table)
employment, 111, 127
family and child benefits, 130–131
housing, 128–129, 143(n9)
political parties, 114–121, 237. *See
also* Alliance 90 / Greens party;
Christian Democratic Union;
Free Democratic Party;
German People's Union; Green
Party; Party of Democratic
Socialism; Social Democratic
Party
pre-unification. *See* German
Democratic Republic
privatization, 128–129
return of property to original
owners, 128–129
rise of left parties, 114–121
trade unions, 115
unemployment rate, 115, 127, 131
unification and transition, 6,
110–112, 238
West German administrators in,
128
women's issues in, 129–131

See also Federal Republic of
Germany
Economic and Social Charter (Council
of Europe), 137, 239–240
Education
under communism, 26–28, 37, 40
decentralization, 37
employment and education level,
23–24, 24(figure)
employment in, 38–39, 39(figure),
128
enrollments, 18, 28(figure), 29, 40
expenditures, 28, 30(figure), 37–39,
38(table), 60(table),
76–78(tables), 197(table)
financing, 19, 28–29, 37–39,
193–194
preschool, 27–28. *See also* Child
care
privatization, 31–32, 37. *See also
under* Nonprofit sector,
Hungarian
quality and access, 26–29
student-teacher ratios, 38–39,
39(figure), 205(n16)
tertiary (university), 24(figure),
40
vocational, 23, 26, 37
and wages, 20, 22
See also under specific countries
Electoral laws, 52
Electoral protest against reform,
47–49, 52–53. *See also under
specific countries*
Elster, Jon, 175
Employment
in education, 38–39
and education level, 23–24,
24(figure)
emergence of unemployment, 19,
22–25, 23(table)
guaranteed under communism, 15,
19, 46(n1), 111
in the informal sector, 42
of women, 27, 130

See also Unemployment; *and under*
  specific countries
Energy prices, 39, 63, 131, 133, 219, 221
Epsing-Anderson, Gosta, 16, 65, 242,
  243
EU. *See* European Union
European Union, 90, 128, 156, 238,
  239–240
Europe, Central and Eastern. *See*
  Central and Eastern Europe
Evans, Geoffrey, 74, 108(n5)
Exit poll data, 108(n5)

Family and child benefits
  in the Czech Republic, 131–133,
    135–136
  in Germany, 130–131
  in Hungary, 76(table), 82, 94–97,
    179
  in Poland, 77(table)
  in Russia, 59, 63–64, 66–67,
    69(table), 78(table)
  See also Child care
Family formation, 26
Fan, Qimiao, 224
FDP. *See* Free Democratic Party
Federal Republic of Germany (FRG)
  child care, 129–131
  education, 128
  elections (1990–1998), 2, 116(table),
    117–118, 120, 130
  employment, 120, 130
  family and child benefits, 130–
    131
  health care, 112
  housing, 128–129, 143(n9)
  insurance programs, 112, 142(nn
    2–3)
  nonprofit sector, 176
  pension system, 112
  political parties. *See* Alliance 90 /
    Greens party; Christian
    Democratic Union; Free
    Democratic Party; German
    People's Union; Green Party;

  Party of Democratic Socialism;
    Social Democratic Party
  privatization, 128–129
  return of property to original
    owners, 128–129
  social spending, 126
  Sozialhilfe (social assistance), 112
  states' role in policymaking,
    128–129
  taxes, 126–127
  trade unions, 115, 120–121
  unemployment rate/benefits,
    25(figure), 112, 127, 131
  unification and transition, 110, 126
  women's issues in, 129–131
  See also Eastern Germany
Federation of Independent Trade
    Unions of Russia (FNPR), 216,
    226
Federation of Young Democrats–
    Hungarian Civic Party (Fidesz-
    HCP), 179–180
Ferge, Zsuzsa, 98, 176, 178
Fish, Steven M., 54
FNPR. *See* Federation of Independent
    Trade Unions of Russia
Fodor, Eva, 6, 9(n5), 48, 103, 108(n5)
Foley, Marc C., 58
Free Democratic Party (FDP; Eastern
    Germany), 115, 116(table),
    117
Freedom Union (Poland), 83, 88–89,
    102
Freinkman, Lev, 224
FRG. *See* Federal Republic of Germany
Fundusz Ubezpieczen Spolecznych
    (FUS), 147
Fyodorov, Boris, 220, 223, 234(n11)

Gaddy, Cliff, 221
Gaidar, Yegor, 210–211
  economic reform program,
    210–219
  Gerashchenko appointed to head
    Central Bank, 219

government positions, 219, 223, 234(n11)

social policy reform ideas, 212, 221

Garrett, Geoffrey, 51, 237

Gates, Susan, 211

Gati, Charles, 226–227

Gedeon, Péter, 178, 243

Georgia, 32

Gerashchenko, Viktor, 219

Gere, Adam, 97–98

German Democratic Republic (GDR), 110–111, 129–130. *See also* Eastern Germany; Federal Republic of Germany

German People's Union (DVU), 120, 120(table)

Germany. *See* Eastern Germany; Federal Republic of Germany; German Democratic Republic

Gero, Barnabas, 96

Gidron, Benjamin, 176

Goldstein, Ellen, 26, 32–34, 156

Golinowska, Stanislawa, 148, 149, 155

Gora, Marek, 89

Gordon, Leonid, 226

Göthe, Heiko, 119

Green Party (Germany), 120(table), 130. *See also* Alliance 90 / Greens party

Grigoriev, Leonid, 211

Grootaert, Christiann, 155

Gypsies. *See* Romany people

Haggard, Stephan, 52, 69, 146, 158, 208

Hanley, Eric, 6, 9(n5), 48, 103, 108(n5)

Hartl, Jan, 124

Hausner, Jerzy, 84–85, 87–88, 148, 154–155, 162, 173(n17)

HDF. *See* Hungarian Democratic Forum

Health
adverse trends, 18, 25–26, 33, 156

Infant mortality, 14(table), 32

Life expectancy, 14(table), 26, 27(table), 32

See also Health care; *and under specific countries*

Health care
under communism, 15, 32–33

declining conditions, 26, 32–33

expenditures, 35(figure), 60(table), 76–78(tables), 95, 197(table)

financing reforms, 33–37

health insurance, 19, 34, 36

health services (comparison), 36(table)

overstaffing, 26, 36

privatization, 31

See also under Nonprofit sector, Hungarian; *and under specific countries*

Hejthý, Lajos, 91, 92, 93

Hellman, Joel, 210, 226

Hoeppner, Reinhard, 128

Hořák, Jiří, 122

Horn, Gábor, 194–195

Horn, György, 194–195

Horn, Gyula, 93–94

Horn, Miklós, 194–195

Hough, Jerry F., 55, 226

Housing
communist/socialist subsidization, 15, 57, 63, 221

in the Czech Republic, 132, 133, 135

in Germany, 128–129, 143(n9)

in Russia, 57, 63, 63(table), 221–222

HSP. *See* Hungarian Socialist Party

Hungarian Democratic Forum (HDF), 82, 177–178

Hungarian Socialist Party (HSP)
alliance with NFHTU, 178

and the Bokros package, 93–99, 241

coalition government with AFD, 91–99, 102, 178–179, 238

constituency, 74

and economic reform, 74–75

elections/electoral support (1990–1998), 2, 49, 71–72, 91, 91(table), 178

factionalism in, 93, 95, 98–99
and the Leftist Youth Alliance, 182
membership in Socialist
    International, 71
and nonprofit organizations,
    194–195
origins, 71
social policies, 74–75, 91–101, 178,
    241–242
Hungary
  Bokros social/economic reform
    package, 93–99, 241
  budget, 95–96, 176, 191–195,
    197–198, 205(n18)
  child care, 179
  church-state relationship, 178,
    193–195, 201, 205(n20)
  Civil Code, 180, 181
  communist legacy, 176–177, 181
  constitution, 96
  decentralization, 178
  deficits/debt, 82, 92, 94–95, 102,
    179, 241
  disabled persons, 187–189, 192.
    See also National Federation
    of Associations of Disabled
    Persons
  economic reforms, 92–99, 179,
    239–241
  education, 24(figure), 28(figure),
    38(figure), 39(figure), 76(table),
    95, 177, 188, 193–197,
    197(table), 200–201, 205(nn 16,
    20–22). *See also under* Nonprofit
    sector, Hungarian
  elections (1990–1998), 2, 47, 49, 53,
    70–72, 72(figure), 73(figure), 91,
    91(table), 178–179
  family and child benefits, 76(table),
    82, 94–97, 179
  Fidesz-HCP government, 179–180
  HDF government, 177–178, 192
  health care/insurance, 31, 34,
    35(figure), 36, 36(table),
    76(table), 95, 178, 196–197,

    197(table). *See also under*
    Nonprofit sector, Hungarian
  HSP-AFD government, 91–99,
    178–179, 194–195, 238
  interest group politics, 177,
    189–191, 200–201
  Interest Reconciliation Council,
    91–93, 94, 98
  life expectancy, 27(table)
  living standards, 18, 82
  nonprofit sector. *See* Nonprofit
    sector, Hungarian
  pension expenditures, 41,
    41(figure), 76(table), 172(n1)
  pension system, 16, 42(figure), 43,
    97–98, 178–179, 204(n4), 242
  political parties, 50, 70–75, 237.
    See also Alliance of Free
    Democrats; Federation of
    Young Democrats–Hungarian
    Civic Party; Hungarian
    Democratic Forum; Hungarian
    Socialist Party; Patriotic
    People's Front
  political system, 52, 176–177
  privatization, 179, 204(n4)
  Social Council, 189–190, 192
  social policy development,
    176–177, 189–191, 205(n17)
  social spending, 30–31, 35(figure),
    38(figure), 41, 41(figure), 75,
    76(table), 79(figures), 81–83,
    94–96, 102, 172(n1), 178,
    196–197, 197(table), 198,
    206(n26)
  social welfare system/reform, 81–
    82, 93–99, 177–179, 241–242. *See
    also* Nonprofit sector, Hungarian
  taxes, 34, 95, 191, 195–196
  trade unions, 92–93, 98, 178, 181,
    190
  unemployment benefits, 76(table),
    82, 172(n1)
  unemployment rate, 22, 23(table),
    24(figure), 25(figure)

unofficial economy, 42
    wages, 94
Huntington, Samuel, 146, 208

Illner, Michael, 132
IMF. *See* International Monetary Fund
Income inequality, 20–22, 21(tables)
Independent Union of Miners
    (Russia), 226
Inequality, economic, 19–22. *See also*
    Poverty; Unemployment
Infant mortality, 14(table), 32
Inglot, Tomasz, 160
Interest group politics
    in Hungary, 177, 189–191, 200–201
    in Poland, 162–164, 167–168,
        173(n17)
    and presidential vs. parliamentary
        systems, 209, 226
    in Russia, 215–222
Interest Reconciliation Council
    (Hungary), 91–93, 94, 98
International Monetary Fund (IMF),
    94, 101
Ishiyama, John T., 54

Johnson, Juliet, 224

Kabele, Jiří, 114, 132, 133
Kaminski, Marek, 52, 146
Kasa Rolniczego Ubezpieczen
    Spolecznych (KRUS), 147, 162
Kaufman, Robert, 52, 69, 146, 158, 208
Kemme, David, 157
Khasbulatov, Ruslan, 210, 220
Khizha, Giorgy, 219
Klaus, Václav, 114, 126, 139
Klugman, Jeni, 58, 64
Klyamkin, Igor, 208, 226
Kohl, Helmut, 110
Kolodko, Grzegorz, 84, 87–88
Kornai, Janos, 50, 75, 82, 92, 214
Kostelecký, Tomáš, 124
Kovacs, Pal, 93
Kramer, Mark, 31, 132, 175

Kramer, Ralph M., 176
KRUS. *See* Kasa Rolniczego
    Ubezpieczen Spolecznych
KSČM. *See* Communist Party of
    Bohemia and Moravia
Kuhnle, Stein, 176
Kulczycki, Andrzej, 17
Kunc, Jiří, 124
Kux, Ulla, 119
Kwasniewski, Aleksander, 75, 89

Lange, Peter, 51, 237
Laporte, Bruno, 24, 27
Layard, Richer, 221
LDP. *See* Liberal Democratic Party
Lee, Une, 221
Leff, Carol Skalnik, 113
Leftist Youth Alliance (Hungary),
    182
Left parties
    defined, 4–5, 48–51, 236
    distinctions between, 2–3, 17, 50,
        99, 236
    and economic reform, 102–103
    electoral support, 53
    goals, 4, 236
    implications of resurgence,
        245–246
    legislative competence, 50
    past of ignored by voters, 3–4
    programs. *See* Left party programs
    resurgence of, 3–4
    social and political contexts, 6–7,
        243–244
    and social policymaking, 7, 53,
        102–103
    See also Communist successor
        parties; Social democratic
        parties; *specific parties*
Left party programs
    and communist legacies, 102, 240,
        244
    constrained by economic and
        international pressures, 51–52,
        101–102, 239–240

electoral vs. coalition government
    programs, 49
failures of, 243
and party "genealogy," 49–50,
    236–237
and political institutions, 52–53,
    101–102, 238–239
social market model, 243
state's ability to carry out, 52, 61–
    62, 101, 237–238. *See also* Russia
and trade unions, 240
and welfare state values, 241–242
See also under specific parties
Lehmann, Susan Goodrich, 55, 226
Lepik, Ryszard, 88
Liberal Democratic Congress (Poland),
    16
Liberal Democratic Party (Russia), 56,
    67, 222–223
Liberalism, 4, 16–17, 80–82
Liberal Social Union (Czechoslovakia),
    123, 123(table)
Life expectancy, 14(table), 26,
    27(table), 32
Linz, Juan J., 52, 146
Lipton, David, 211
Lissowski, Grzegorz, 52, 146
Lithuania, 34
Living standards, 18–29, 82, 85, 90,
    132, 222

Macedonia, FYR
    communist legacy, 27
    education, 28, 28(figure), 37,
        38(figure), 39(figure)
    health care, 33, 35(figure)
    payroll taxes, 34
    pensions, 40–41, 41(figure),
        42(figure)
    social spending, 31, 33, 35(figure),
        37, 38(figure), 40–41, 41(figure)
    unemployment rate, 25, 25(figure)
Maleva, T., 58, 64
Maltese Charity Service (Knights of
    Malta), 192, 205(n19)

Mandelbaum, Michael, 175
Maravall, Jose Maria, 208
Mareš, Petr, 132
Market reforms
    approaches to, 208–209, 234(nn
        4–5)
    electoral backlashes against,
        226–227
    obstacles to, 208–210
    See also under specific countries
Marody, Mira, 50, 164
Maslyukov, Yuri, 61, 226
Matějůs, Petr, 124
Mau, Vladimir, 212, 218, 219
McFaul, Michael, 17, 213, 222, 226, 227
Means, Gardiner, 211
Mecklenburg-Vorpommern, 120
Medgyessy, Peter, 97–98
Migranyan, Adranik, 208
Milanovic, Branko, 31, 70, 75, 80, 207,
    225
Milgrom, Paul, 211
Miller, Leszek, 73–74, 87–88
Minorities, 29, 205–206(n22), 209–210.
    See also Romany people
Mlynarczyk-Misiuda, Jolanta, 154
Moe, Terry, 226
Moldova, 26, 27(table), 41(figure),
    172(n1)
Moravia, 125
Motivation (nonprofit organization),
    188, 189, 199
Murrell, Peter, 208
Musil, Libor, 131

Nagy, Sandor, 95
Naishul, Vitali, 214
National Association of Large Families
    (Hungary), 190, 192
National Federation of Associations of
    Disabled Persons (NFADP;
    Hungary), 189–190, 192, 200
National Federation of Hungarian
    Trade Unions (NFHTU), 178,
    190

NATO. *See* North Atlantic Treaty Organization
Navrátilová, Jana, 133
NDR. *See* Our Home is Russia party
Nellis, John, 215
Nelson, Joan, 47
Nelson, Joan M., 155, 175, 208
Nemtsov, Boris, 62, 63, 66, 224
Neugebauer, Gero, 119
NFADP. *See* National Federation of Associations of Disabled Persons
NFHTU. *See* National Federation of Hungarian Trade Unions
Nonprofit sector, Hungarian, 175–206
  associations, 180–183, 181(table), 186, 204(n6). *See also specific subheadings*
  church institutions, 187–188, 193–194, 200–201, 205(n20), 206(n26)
  continuity of organizations, 182–183, 204(n8)
  cultural foundations, 183, 184(table), 185(table), 197(table), 206(n25)
  distribution of organizations, 182–185, 184(table)
  educational organizations, 182–183, 184–186(tables), 185, 188, 193–198, 197(table), 200–201, 205(nn 10, 16, 20–22)
  fire brigades, 182–183, 184(table), 185(table), 204(n8)
  foundations, 180, 181(table), 183, 186. *See also specific subheadings*
  funding, 191–196, 200, 205(n18), 205–206(n22), 206(n23)
  growth of, 180, 181(table), 182, 187–188, 197(table), 198
  health foundations, 183, 184–186(tables), 185, 192, 196–198, 197(table), 205(nn 11–12, 22)
  income of organizations, 183–184, 185(table), 186(table), 186–187, 205(nn 13–14)
  leisure and hobby associations, 182–184, 184(table), 185(table), 204(n8)
  mutual insurance funds, 180, 204(n6)
  origins, 180–183, 198
  pension funds, 184(table), 185(table)
  pluralism offered by, 199
  politically-oriented organizations, 182–183, 184(table), 185(table)
  professional/economic interest organizations, 182–185, 184(table), 185(table), 198
  and social policymaking, 189–191, 199–201, 205(n17)
  social policy share, 185–187, 186(table), 198–199
  social service expenditures, 196–198, 197(table), 206(nn 25–26)
  social service provision organizations, 183, 184–186(tables), 185, 187–189, 192–193, 196–199, 197(table), 205(nn 11, 19), 205–206(n22)
  sports associations, 182–184, 184(table), 185(table), 197(table), 204(n8), 205–206(n22), 206(n25)
  tax benefits, 196, 201, 206(n24)
North Atlantic Treaty Organization (NATO), expansion of, 50
NSZZ. *See* Solidarity trade union

Okolicsányi, Károly, 177
Oleksy, Jozef, 75
Olson, Mancur, 146
Orenstein, Mitchell A., 3, 17, 49–50, 114, 132, 158
Orosz, Eva, 177
Osiatynski, Wiktor, 226–227

Our Home is Russia party (NDR), 56, 67

Palacios, Robert, 98
Palik, Ruth, 112
Pamfilova, Ella, 66
Parliamentary systems, 52, 209, 239
Party of Democratic Socialism (PDS; Germany)
   and associations/organizations, 118–119
   elections/electoral support, 2, 115, 116(table), 117–119, 120(table), 138
   membership/constituency, 117, 245–246
   party reform, 109, 138
   relationship with SPD, 119–120
   social policies, 127–128, 131
   and trade unions, 119
   and women's issues, 130, 131
Party of the Democratic Left (Slovakia), 123
Pataki, Judith, 178
Patriotic People's Front (PPF; Hungary), 181–182. *See also* Alliance of Social Associations
Pensioners' Party (Czech Rep.), 123(table), 124
Pensions
   communist legacies, 152–155, 169
   contributors-beneficiaries ratio, 42(figure)
   expenditures, 40–43, 41(figure), 76(table), 172(n1)
   insurance systems, 40, 147, 172(n2)
   See also Pension system, Polish; *and under specific countries*
Pension system, Polish, 145–174
   benefits, 81, 158, 163–165, 172(n4), 173(n14)
   communist legacy, 151–156
   contributors-beneficiaries ratio, 42(figure)

and democratic/public choice theory, 161–170
and disability benefits, 155–156
distribution of benefits, 81, 155
early retirement encouraged, 16, 81, 148–149, 158–159
and economic reforms, 157–159
and electoral politics, 164–165, 167
expenditures, 31, 41, 41(figure), 77(table), 86–87, 145, 148–150, 150(table), 156, 158–159, 173(n14)
and farmers, 156(table), 162
financing/taxation, 147–151, 150(table), 153–155, 173(nn 6, 8)
indexation, 158, 163–165, 173(n18)
and interest group politics, 162–164, 167–168, 173(n17)
and miners, 162
pensioner/retiree statistics, 149, 150(table), 151(figure), 156(table), 162
pension funds, 147, 162, 172(n3)
pension reform, 43, 87–90, 100, 108(n6), 242
and the poor, 155
public choice analysis, 152, 161–165
reforms, 85, 162–165, 168, 173(n11), 174(n22)
retirement eligibility/benefits, 147, 172(n4)
and transitional policies, 152, 156–161
Pereira, Luiz Carlos Bresser, 208
Pietrzak-Paciorek, Malgorzata, 87
Pistor, Katharina, 16
Poland
   black economy, 166
   budget and deficits, 160, 167
   church-state relationship, 89–90, 162, 241
   citizen opinions on social welfare, 164–165
   constitution, 85, 89–90, 241

disability benefits, 155–156
economic growth, 17, 20, 85–86,
    89–90
economic reforms, 80, 84–87, 148,
    157–159, 169
economy, 148–149, 149(table)
education, 23, 24(figure),
    28(figure), 37, 38(figure),
    39(figure), 77(table)
elections (1990–97), 1–2, 47, 49, 53,
    70–74, 72(figure), 73(figure),
    83–84, 84(table)
employment, 87, 150(table),
    151(figure)
family and child benefits, 77(table)
health, 156
health care, 34, 35(figure), 36,
    36(table), 77(table)
interest group politics, 162–164,
    167–168, 173–174(n19)
left government, 83–91
life expectancy, 27(table)
living standards, 18, 82, 85, 90
Mazowiecki government, 158,
    162
Pawlak government, 162
pension system. *See* Pension
    system, Polish
political parties, 16, 50, 70–75, 83,
    237. *See also* Democratic Left
    Alliance; Freedom Union;
    Polish Peasant Party; Social
    Democracy of the Republic of
    Poland; Union of Labor party
political system, 52
population, 150(table)
social assistance programs, 86–87,
    147
Social Insurance Office (ZUS). *See*
    Zaklad Ubezpieczen
    Spolecznych
social spending, 29–31, 30(table),
    35(figure), 37, 38(figure), 41,
    41(figure), 75, 77(table),
    79(figures), 81–83, 86–87, 102,

145, 156, 172(n1). *See also*
    Pension system, Polish
social welfare reform, 85–91,
    157–161, 173(nn 11–12), 242.
    See also Pension system, Polish
taxes, 147–148, 150, 153–154, 155,
    173(nn 6, 8)
trade unions, 164, 173–174(n19)
unemployment benefits/policies,
    77(table), 81, 86–87, 148, 158,
    172(n1), 173(n12)
unemployment rate, 22–23,
    23(table), 24(figure), 25(figure),
    46(n1), 85, 149(table)
wages, 20, 21(table), 154
and the World Bank, 81, 86, 88, 90
Polish Peasant Party (PSL)
    coalition with Democratic Left
    Alliance, 83–84, 86, 102, 238
    elections/electoral support, 164
    and the 1997 constitution, 89
Popular Power party (Russia), 56
Potůček, Martin, 114, 132, 133
Poverty, emergence of, 18–19. *See also*
    Living standards
PPF. *See* Patriotic People's Front
Preker, Alexander S., 26, 32–34, 156
Presidential systems, 52
    and interest group politics, 209,
    226
    and social policymaking, 101–102,
    238–239
Pringle, Peter, 211
Privatization, 31–32, 37, 43–44
    in the Czech Republic, 32, 131,
    135
    in Germany, 128–129
    in Russia, 211–214, 217–218,
    220–221, 224
Protestant church, German, 119
Przeworski, Adam, 49, 146, 158, 208
PSL. *See* Polish Peasant Party
Public Against Violence party
    (Slovakia), 122, 123(table)
Public choice analysis, 146

of Poland's pension reforms, 152,
161–165
and social welfare policies,
168–170
Puffer, Sheila, 214

Rabušic, Ladislav, 132
Rak, Vladimír, 114
Rapacki, Ryszard, 84
Rashid, Mansoora, 16
Red Cross, Hungarian, 192, 205(n19)
Reform
backlash against, 47–49, 52–56,
226–227
social welfare reform. *See under
specific countries*
Řeháková, Blanka, 124
Remington, Thomas F., 56
Rendlová, Eliška, 134
Republikaner party (Eastern
Germany), 115
Restructuring. *See* Transition
Richter, Andrea, 221
Ringold, Dena, 22, 24, 27, 57, 80
Roberts, John, 211
Rocha, Roberto, 98
Roland, Gerald, 208
Romania
economy, 17
education, 24(figure), 28(figure),
37, 38(figure), 39(figure)
health care, 34, 35(figure), 36,
36(table)
life expectancy, 27(table)
living standards, 18
pensions, 41, 41(figure), 42(figure),
172(n1)
social spending, 30, 30(table),
35(figure), 37, 38(figure), 41,
41(figure), 172(n1)
unemployment rate, 22, 23(table),
24(figure), 25(figure)
Romany people, 29, 135, 137
Rose, Richard, 60
Rostock, Germany, 129

Rueschemeyer, Dietrich, 48, 53
Rueschemeyer, Marilyn, 118, 121, 129,
130
Russia
antireform backlash, 54–56,
226–227
budget, 60(table), 60–62, 65, 68,
220, 223–224
Chernomyrdin government,
222–225
child care, 57
communist legacies, 56–57, 102,
213–222
constitution, 222–223, 238–239
deficits, 58(table), 220, 223–224
economic reform (Gaidar plan),
210–213, 215–219
economy at Soviet Union's
collapse, 210
education, 28(figure), 38(figure),
39(figure), 60(table), 64–65,
78(table)
elections (1991–97), 47, 49, 53–56,
55(table), 72(figure), 73(figure),
222–223
energy prices, 63, 219, 221
family and child benefits, 59,
63–64, 66–67, 69(table),
78(table)
financing of social programs, 57,
58(table), 63, 63(table), 65
health care, 35(figure), 60(table),
61–62, 64, 78(table)
health trends, 25–26
housing, 57, 63, 63(table), 221–222
and the IMF, 101
inability to carry out reforms, 212,
214, 238
income disparities, 207
inflation, 212–213, 219, 222–223,
225
interest group politics, 215–222
labor market, 221
life expectancy, 26, 27(table)
living standards, 222

pensions, 57, 59, 64, 67–68,
68(table), 78(table), 224–226
political parties, 56. *See also*
Communist Party of the
Russian Federation; Liberal
Democratic Party; Our Home
is Russia party; Yabloko party
political system, 3–4. *See also*
Duma
power shift from liberal to
centrist/opposition groups,
216–217
Primakov government, 70
privatization, 211–214, 217–218,
220–221, 224
representation, 225–227
social insurance, 63–64
social policy neglect, 58–59,
207–208, 225–228, 238, 244–245
social spending, 35(figure),
38(figure), 57, 60(table), 60–63,
68, 68(table), 69(table),
79(figures), 221
social welfare reform, 62–68, 242
social welfare system, 56–59,
68–69, 99, 213–214, 221–222,
224–225
suicide rate, 26, 46(n3)
taxes, 57–58, 224, 238
trade unions, 215–216, 226. *See also*
Civic Union
unemployment rate/benefits, 22,
23(table), 58, 78(table), 221
unofficial economy, 65
wage arrears, 224–225, 234(nn
12–13)
wages, 59, 68(table), 212, 222
workers, 214–215, 221, 224–225,
234(n8). *See also subhead* wage
arrears
and the World Bank, 65, 68, 239
Russia's Choice electoral bloc, 222
Rustow, Dankwart, 146
Rutkowski, Jan J., 22, 81
Rutkowski, Michal, 89

Rutland, Peter, 216
Rys, Vladimír, 131
Ryzhkov, Nikolai, 215

Sabirianova, Klara, 224, 225
Sachs, Jeffrey, 16, 80, 211
Salamon, Lester M., 176
Sawinski, Zbigniew, 164
Saxony-Anhalt, 117–118, 120, 128
Schroeder, Gerhard, 126–127
Sederlof, Hjalte, 65
Selle, Per, 176
Shleifer, Andre, 211
Shokhin, Aleksandr, 212–213
Shugart, Matthew, 209–210
Shughart, William F., 161
Shumeiko, Vladimir, 219
Šimoník, David, 133
Sinel'nikov, Sergei, 220
SLD. *See* Democratic Left Alliance
Slovakia
economic hardships of transition,
113
education, 24(figure), 28(figure),
32, 38(figure), 39(figure)
elections, 123(table)
health care/insurance, 31, 34, 36
life expectancy, 27(table)
pensions, 41, 42(figure)
privatization of social services,
32
social spending, 30, 30(table), 31,
38(figure), 41
unemployment rate, 22, 23(table),
24(figure), 25(figure), 113
Slovenia
education, 24(figure), 28(figure),
37, 38(figure), 39(figure)
life expectancy, 27(table)
social spending, 37, 38(figure)
unemployment rate, 22, 23(table),
24(figure), 25(figure)
wages, 20
Smith, Steven S., 56
Social Act (Hungary), 178

Social Council (Hungary), 189–190,
192, 205(n17)
Social Democracy of the Republic of
Poland, 71–72. *See also*
Democratic Left Alliance
Social democratic parties, 2, 50
constituencies, 71–74, 72(figure)
dedication to liberal reform, 101,
236–237
distinctions between, 99
electoral support, 70–74, 72(figure),
73(figure)
historic parties, 237
in Poland and Hungary, 70–75.
See also Democratic Left
Alliance; Hungarian Socialist
Party
revitalization of, 6
See also specific parties
Social Democratic Party (SPD;
Germany)
and associations/organizations,
118–119
background, 6, 109, 115, 117
coalition government with Greens,
118, 127, 238
elections/electoral support, 2, 110,
115, 116(table), 117–118,
120(table), 121
membership/constituency, 117
political strategy, 110
relationship with PDS, 119–120
social policies, 126–129, 131,
143(n5)
stance, 127
tax proposals, 126–127
and women's issues, 130, 131
Socialist International, 50, 71
Socialist Party, Hungarian. *See*
Hungarian Socialist Party
Social sector data (sources/quality),
12–13
Social spending
decreases in, 19, 77–78(tables),
79(figures), 240–241

disproportionality to resources, 15,
29–32, 30(table)
increases in, 75–80, 77–78(tables),
79(figures), 100, 240
as key issue, 145
and transitional policies, 75–80
See also under specific countries
Social welfare reform
and democratic/public choice
theory, 152, 161–165
and the international community,
239–240
necessity of restructuring, 242
and social change, 160
and state bureaucracies, 160–161
See also under specific countries
Social welfare systems
communist legacy, 5–6, 11, 15–16,
18, 29, 43–44, 110–111
economic difficulty of maintaining,
7, 18–19, 43
See also Child care; Family and
child benefits; Health care;
Pensions; Unemployment; *and
under specific countries*
Solidarity Electoral Alliance, 89
Solidarity trade union (NSZZ;
Poland), 88, 164, 173–174(n19)
Solovei, Valerii D., 54, 56, 60
Soviet Union, Former
economy at collapse, 210
enterprise organization, 213–215,
234(n7)
health care, 32
income inequality, 20, 21(tables)
social welfare system, 56–57, 214
unemployment rate, 22
wages, 22
SPD. *See* Social Democratic Party
Špidla, Vladimír, 136–137
Staines, Verdon, 32
Standing, Guy, 58
Stark, David, 92–94
Stepan, Alfred, 52, 146
Stevens, Evelyn Huber, 53

Stevens, John, 53
Suchocka, Hanna, 163
Surdej, Aleksander, 16, 80, 85, 151
Suryani, Gyorgi, 93–99
Swistak, Piotr, 52, 146
Sysuyev, Oleg, 62, 66, 67
Szacki, Jerzy, 162
Szalai, Julia, 177
Szelenyi, Ivan, 6, 9(n5), 48, 103, 108(n5)
Szilágyi, Zsófia, 179, 195
Szollosi, Ilona, 95

Three Worlds of Welfare Capitalism, The (Epsing-Anderson), 242
Tolstopiatenko, Andrei, 221
Topinski, Wojciech, 162
Tošovsky, Josef, 133–134
Trade, international, in Eastern Europe, 149(table)
Trade unions
  in the Czech Republic, 133
  in the Former Soviet Union, 214–215, 234(n8)
  in Germany, 115, 120–121
  in Hungary, 92–93, 98, 178, 181, 190
  and left party programs, 240
  in Poland, 88, 164, 173(n9)
  in postcommunist Europe, 72
  in Russia, 215–216. *See also* Civic Union
Transition
  backlash against reform, 47–49, 52–56, 226–227
  divergent social conditions during, 12–13, 17–18
  dual transition, 157, 159–160, 173(n10), 208–209
  and economic growth, 18–19
  economic hardships of, 19–25
  policy inertia, 210
  sequencing reforms, 208
  social policy development, 15–19, 43–44

social policy neglected during, 11
and social spending, 13, 15, 75–80
See also Market reforms; *specific countries*
Transitional politics
  analytical approaches, 146
  and social welfare policies, 158–161, 166–170
Twigg, Judyth L., 64
Two axes, theory of, 48, 74

Ukraine, 22, 26, 27(table), 172(n1)
Ulyukaev, Aleksei, 219, 223
Unemployment
  comparative rates of, 22–25, 23(table), 24–25(figures)
  failure of unemployment programs, 80
  illegality under communism, 46(n1)
  long-term, 24–25, 25(figure)
  rise of, 19, 22–25, 23(table)
  and social insurance programs, 42, 42(figure)
  unemployment insurance introduced, 16
  among women, 131
  youth unemployment, 22–23
  See also Employment; *and under specific countries*
Union of Labor party (Poland), 89
Unofficial economy, 42, 65, 166
Urban, Joan Barth, 54, 56, 60

Večerník, Jiří, 114, 132
Vidos, Tibor, 95
Vishny, Robert, 211
Vitte, Oleg, 224–225
Vlachová, Klára, 124
Vobruba, George, 114, 132
Volsky, Arkady, 215–216
von Brabant, Jozef, 211
Vujacic, Veljko, 54

Wages

in the Czech Republic, 20,
    21(table), 131, 134
declines in, 18, 19, 20
divergent trends, 14(table), 18
and education level, 20, 22
in Hungary, 94
in Poland, 20, 21(table), 154
in Russia, 59, 68(table), 212, 222,
    224–225, 234(nn 12–13)
teachers' wages, 38–39
Wallich, Christine, 213
Weingast, Barry R., 169, 170, 209
Welsh, Helga, 111
West Germany. *See* Federal Republic
    of Germany
Whitefield, Stephen, 74, 108(n5)
White, Stephen, 146
Wisniewski, Marion, 163
Wolchik, Sharon L., 113, 114, 132
Women
    employment/unemployment, 27,
        130–131
    women's issues in Eastern
        Germany, 129–131
Worgotter, Andreas, 80
Workers Party (Hungary), 71
Working Russia party, 56
World Bank, 239–240
    and Poland, 81, 86, 88, 90
    and Russia, 65, 68, 239
Wyman, Matthew, 55

Yabloko party (Russia), 56, 59, 66, 69

Yavlinsky, Grigory, 218
Yeltsin, Boris
    actions against opposition, 222
    and the Civic Union, 216
    confidence in reformers shaken,
        218–219
    and Gaidar, 210–211, 219. *See also*
        Gaidar, Yegor
    and the 1993 budget, 220
    and the 1996 elections, 68, 227
    post-1993 powers, 2, 222–223,
        224
    and the Russian parliament,
        219–220
    and social welfare reform, 59,
        67–68, 212
Yemtsov, Ruslan, 221
Yugoslavia, Former, 14(table), 34. *See
    also* Croatia; Macedonia, FYR;
    Slovenia

Zaklad Ubezpieczen Spolecznych
    (ZUS), 147–148, 153–155, 160,
    173(n8). *See also* Pension
    system, Polish:
    financing/taxation
Zeman, Miloš, 124–126, 136, 137
Zhirinovsky, Vladimir, 222. *See also*
    Liberal Democratic Party
ZUS. *See* Zaklad Ubezpieczen
    Spolecznych
Zyuganov, Gennady, 54, 61, 67–68, 70,
    227